Lawson's study of gristmills in West Virginia takes us back to a period when the state's swift-falling streams were vital. This book is a must-have for the collector of Mountain State history.

> David Sibray
> Historian/Preservationist

Historic Mills of West Virginia by Tracy Lawson is a delightful, well-organized trip into milling and the mills of this great state. It serves not only as an outstanding guide to the remaining mills of West Virginia, but also as a testament to creative ways for preserving these historic buildings. Tracy's style makes you feel right at home with each mill visit, and for serious researchers, the book is thoroughly footnoted.

History comes alive with each mill as Tracy tells stories, like the Potomac Mills, which used their stones for grinding limestone in the off season, to French's Mill in Augusta, now being saved by two local homeschooled teenagers with a unique recycling business. There are mills that supported the liquor industry, both legally and not, and a mill site that was the beginning of the Fitz Water Wheel Co.

At the end of her book's Introduction, Tracy asks, "Ready to head out to visit mills?" With your book in hand, Tracy, "You can bet I am!"

> Chuck Ketchie
> Editor, *Old Mill News*

HISTORIC MILLS
of
WEST VIRGINIA

Tracy Lawson with Elmer Napier

HISTORIC MILLS
of
WEST VIRGINIA

Tracy Lawson
with Elmer Napier

35th Star Publishing
Charleston, West Virginia
www.35thstar.com

Copyright. © 2022 by Tracy Lawson.
All Rights Reserved.
First edition, 2022.
Printed in the United States of America.

No part of this publication may be reproduced, distributed or transmitted in any form or by any means, including photocopying, recording, or other electronic or mechanical methods, without the prior written permission of the publisher, except in the case of brief quotations embodied in critical reviews and certain other noncommercial uses permitted by copyright law.

ISBN-13: 978-1-7378575-8-7
Library of Congress Control Number: 2022942196

35th Star Publishing
Charleston, West Virginia
www.35thstar.com

On the cover:
Shepherd's Mill, photo by Shannon Purvis Thomas
Yellow Spring Mill, photo by Tracy Lawson
Mitchell Mill, photo by Tracy Lawson
Homan Mill, millstones and crane, photo by Tracy Lawson
Blaker's Mill, interior millstone on crane, photo by Tracy Lawson

Cover design by Studio 6 Sense
Interior design by 35th Star Publishing

*To Keri and Alex
who started out together on Country Roads*

Back of the loaf is the snowy flour

And back of the flour the mill

And back of the mill is the wind and rain and sun

And the Father's will.

[From the hymn by Maltbie D. Babcock]

Table of Contents

Acknowledgments xiii
Introduction 1

Section One
  I. A History of Milling 9
  II. Milling in Colonial Virginia 17
  III. Innovations in Milling Make Flour Cheaper,
      More Portable, and Less Nutritious 61
  IV. Historic Preservation 65

Section Two
1 – Eastern Panhandle 73
      Counties: Berkeley, Jefferson, Morgan
2 – Potomac Highlands 155
      Counties: Grant, Hampshire, Hardy, Mineral, Pendleton,
      Pocahontas, Randolph
3 – Over the Mountains 303
      Counties: Highland County, Virginia
4 – New River / Greenbrier Valley 321
      Counties: Fayette, Monroe, Raleigh, Summers
5 – Mountain Lakes 377
      Counties: Lewis, Nicholas, Upshur, Webster
6 – Mountaineer Country 411
      Counties: Monongalia, Preston
7 – Northern Panhandle 429
      Counties: Ohio, Wetzel

Conclusion 445
Appendix: Recipes 447
Notes 453
Index 511
About the Author 525

Acknowledgments

Elmer Napier, whose knowledge of West Virginia's mills shaved at least a year off the research for this book. I had a super time on our road trip.

Steve Cunningham of 35th Star Publishing for his enthusiasm for this project. I appreciated our collaboration on this project and am so pleased with the results.

Alex and Keri Rubenstein, who aided with logistics and travel, and plotted all the mill locations on the state, regional, and county maps.

Susan Hughes of My Independent Editor, who has now worked with me on six of my books, and is not just a trusted editor, but also a friend.

Lisa Peterson of Studio 6th Sense for the beautiful cover design.

Others who gave assistance include:

Walter Ailes, Karen Giles Angus, David Ball, Larry and Kandise Berkel, Keith Bishop, Roy Bowers, Tom and Teresa Calhoon, Eric Clarke, Carola Croucher, Guy Davis, Kyle Dugger, Amy Homan DuPoy, Hannah Bird DuPoy, Betty Dzubba, Charlotte Cook-Fuller, Joe Germino, Dean Harden, Pat Hartman, Cathi Hartsook, Julie Hattier, Kenneth Linden Hawse, Robert Hiller, Greg Hoover, Olin Hoover, Dan Howell, Benny and Aleatha Howell, Barbara Ingersoll, Bob Johnson,

Ken Johnson, Wilmer Kerns, Chuck Ketchie, Dr. James Kiser, Rhonda Layton, Danny Lutz, Henry Manson, Jerry McDonald, Bill and Denise McNeel, Butch McNeill, Mitch McNeill, Dr. Brandon and Cara Homan Mitchell, Brenna Mitchell, Tom and Paula Mitchell, Beth Mollohan, Larry Mustain, Adam Northcraft, Dan Oates, Max Oates, George Padgett, Tyler Parker, Mary Pitts, Jana Reichelderfer, Becky Crouse Reina, Karen Rice, Moe and Janie Rubenstein, David Sibray, Nelson Simmons, Vicky Skavenski, the Southern Upshur Business Association, Joe and Teresa Strohmeyer, Sarah Stover, Daniel Taylor, Julie Taylor, Adam and Shannon Purvis Thomas, John and Karen Bryarly Trenary, Daniel Walker of West Virginia Public Radio, Brittany Walsh, Richard Walters, Dr. Greg Ware, Donna Simmons White, Kelly Williams, owner of the South Branch Inn, Jack Wills, Rob Wolford, and Fred and Barbara Ziegler.

Introduction

A picturesque, water-driven mill tucked away on a country road recalls an earlier time, when farmers transported their grain over dirt roads and mountain passes on horseback and brought home sacks of wholesome, stone-ground flour. Contemporary culture references recall skaters on frozen millponds, barefoot children with fishing poles, and young lovers' first kisses down by the old millstream.

Mills were one of the first structures planned and built in a community[1] and in many cases also served as the local post office and gathering place. Farmers went to mill several times a year and often brought their families along to renew acquaintances with distant neighbors and exchange news while waiting for their grain to be processed.

Traveling miles to the mill and lingering for hours might seem like an inefficient use of time, but grinding one bushel of corn between handheld stones took a person a full day's work. Water-powered mills, which could grind barrelfuls in a day, saved a great deal of time and labor.[2]

Because milling was seasonal work, some millers were also barbers; others had small manufactories for brooms, barrels, coffins, and furniture. Several mills profiled in this book served as electric power plants and water pumping stations. One even produced hydraulic cement.

Hundreds, if not thousands, of water-powered mills once dotted the hills and glades in West Virginia. In 1900, there were 428 mills in the state, and by 1918, fifty-nine remained active.[3] Though the vast majority are gone, towns all over the state bear the names of the mills that put them on the map.

Just dozens remain standing today, found in fewer than half the state's counties, with marked concentrations in the southern and eastern regions. Some remain in their original state, while others have taken on roles as private residences and museums.

The idea for this book came about after my daughter, Keri, then a grad student at West Virginia University, suggested we enjoy a girls' weekend at the Greenbrier Hotel and Spa to celebrate her birthday. She knew of several mills we could stop and see on the drive from Morgantown.

Keri knew mentioning the mills would pique my interest, but I don't think she expected the proposed trip to result in this book. In 2003, she and I made a cross-country road trip to retrace our ancestors' 1838 route from Cincinnati to New York City. My great-great-great-grandfather had chronicled the trip in his journal, which formed the basis for my book *Fips, Bots, Doggeries, and More*. I was excited at the prospect of taking another journey of discovery with my daughter.

It was a short leap from planning a visit to West Virginia to conceiving the idea for this book. Were there enough mills to make the project worthwhile? An internet search for extant water mills in West Virginia led me to WVU grad Elmer Napier, a retired teacher who spends his summers traversing the state photographing mills, churches, train stations, barns, and landscapes. I got in touch with Elmer and immediately found a kindred spirit. I invited him to join me on the project. His extensive knowledge of West Virginia's remaining mills and his prior contact with many of the mill owners gave me a huge head start on the research. Elmer spent hours compiling photos, helped me identify the mills and plot their locations, and then joined me on my second research trip to West Virginia.

This book is meant to celebrate West Virginia's cultural heritage, offer insights into eighteenth- and nineteenth-century industrial development in the United States, and highlight efforts to preserve these historic structures.

Section One gives an overview of the history of grain processing, from ancient evidence of breadcrumbs discovered in archaeological sites to the advent of modern technology that ultimately spelled the demise of the small, independent mill.

Section Two identifies, describes, and gives directions to publicly accessible mills in the Mountain State, with supplemental information about the histories of the structures and owners.

The fifty-three mills, constructed between 1735 and 1976, are examples of building techniques and technology in use during the upbuilding, the pinnacle, and the twilight of waterpower's role in heavy industry.

I hope this guide will help you gain a deeper appreciation for mills and their part in West Virginia's history and development. Whether operational or abandoned to decay, they stand in testament to the ingenuity and independent spirit of frontier entrepreneurs.

Spelling and grammatical errors in direct quotes have been left as-is.

Table 1 lists the mills chronologically by what is present at each site. Many were built to replace mills which had been destroyed by fire, flood, or invading armies.

Earlier histories, when known, are included in the narrative associated with each mill.

Ready to head out to visit mills? You may have a bit of a drive ahead of you, so buckle up, hand this book to whoever's riding shotgun, and have them read the introductory chapters aloud for a rundown on the history of milling. By the time you arrive at your destination, you'll be up to speed.

HISTORIC MILLS OF WEST VIRGINIA

Name	County	Year Built	Page
1. Bunker Hill Mill	Berkeley	1735	83
2. Shepherd's Mill	Jefferson	1738	143
3. Patterson Mill	Berkeley	1765	95
4. Mitchell Mill	Pendleton	1784	251
5. Gromer-Nickell's Upper-Rodgers Mill	Monroe	1785	345
6. Antioch Mill	Mineral	1787	205
7. Stephen-Hammond-Old Spring Mill	Berkeley	1790	105
8. Reed's Mill	Monroe	1791	357
9. Blaker's Mill	Lewis	1794	381
10. Bloomery Mill	Hampshire	1800	169
11. Bedinger Mill	Berkeley	1816	77
12. Rexrode Mill	Highland	1816	311
13. Boggs Mill	Pendleton	1820	217
14. Fidler's Mill	Upshur	1821	399
15. Homan Mill	Pendleton	1824	227
16. Potomac Mills, Shepherdstown Cement Mill Ruins	Jefferson	1826	137
17. Trumbo Mill	Pendleton	1831	273
18. Reed's Mill	Ohio	1834	433
19. Union Bryarly Mill	Berkeley	1835	117
20. Jackson's Mill	Lewis	1837	385
21. Beckley Mill Ruins	Raleigh	1838	367
22. Tuscarora Iron Works	Berkeley	b. 1840	109
23. McCoy Mill	Pendleton	1845	245
24. Hoover Mill	Pendleton	b. 1850	235
25. Beaver Mill	Nicholas	1852	393
26. Cotton Hill Mill	Fayette	b. 1854	325
27. Spaid-Eaton Mill	Fayette	b. 1856	181

Name	County	Year Built	Page
28. Cook's Old Mill	Monroe	1857	339
29. Botkin-Simmons Mill	Highland	b. 1860	305
30. Janney Mill	Berkeley	c. 1860	91
31. Easton Roller Mill	Monongalia	1867	415
32. Laurel Dale Mill	Mineral	1867	209
33. McNeel Mill	Pocahontas	1868	283
34. Circleville Mill	Pendleton	b. 1869	223
35. Cooper's Mill	Summers	1869	373
36. Day-Vandevender Mill	Randolph	1877	297
37. Beeler's Mill	Jefferson	1878	125
38. Onego Mill	Pendleton	b. 1880	261
39. Lyon's Mill	Grant	1882	159
40. Old Fields Mill	Hardy	1890	195
41. Mollohan Mill	Webster	1894	405
42. Yellow Spring Mill	Hampshire	1896	187
43. French's Mill	Hampshire	1897	177
44. Priest Mill	Pendleton	1900	265
45. A. M. Snider Mill	Hardy	c. 1900?	201
46. Darden-Elkins Mill	Randolph	1902	291
47. Patterson's New Mill	Berkeley	1910	99
48. Hazelton Mill	Preston	1914	423
49. Waggy-Mitchell Mill	Pendleton	1917	277
50. McClung Mill	Monroe	c. 1926	353
51. Howell's Mill	Wetzel	1930	439
52. Feagans Mill	Jefferson	1940	129
53. Glade Creek Grist Mill	Fayette	1976	331

SECTION ONE

I. A History of Milling

All primitive peoples employed some form of milling for food production.[4] About 32,000 years ago, our ancient ancestors first pulverized oats and other grains into flour.[5] The results of paleo peoples' early efforts likely produced a flat cake, porridge, or gruel. The oldest known charred remains of bread, found at an archaeological dig in Jordan, were left behind 14,000 years ago by the Natufians, a hunter-gatherer tribe.[6] The analyzed crumbs were a mixture of wild wheat, oats, barley, and starchy club rush tubers.

While we'll never know which of the Natufians left a mess in the communal toaster, the discovery of bread crumbs contradicted what scholars previously believed about ancient peoples' transition from hunter-gatherers to farmers. Those discarded crumbs are evidence that our ancestors learned to bake bread over 4,000 years before they abandoned their nomadic way of life. Archaeologists suggest that bread may once have been considered a treat. Over time, people's desire to eat it more regularly led them to begin cultivating cereals.[7]

Wheat has been a staple crop of civilizations for over 9,000 years, and bread was destined to become part of humans' diets. It was only natural that people would develop increasingly efficient ways to process it in

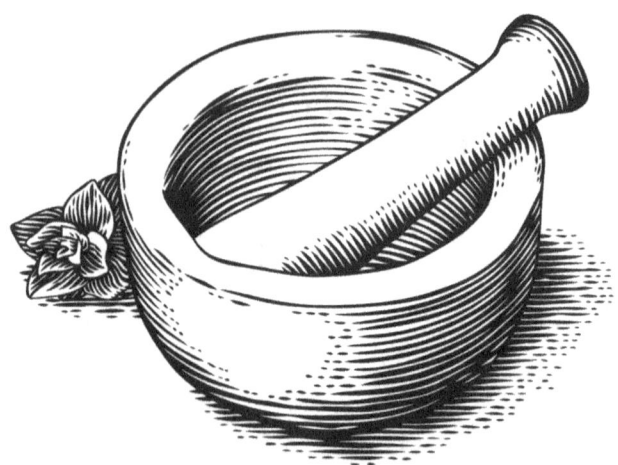

Mortar and pestle

Quern

quantity, though some technological advances came with unexpected consequences.

The mortar and pestle, described in the Ebers papyrus from ancient Egypt, dates to at least 1550 BCE[8] and is one of the earliest examples of a hand-operated grinding mill. You may have one in your kitchen, just as I do.

Saddle mills, in which a stone is rolled back and forth over grain in a curved basin, predated the quern. Querns came into use about 9,000 years ago, during the early part of the Neolithic Era, or the New Stone Age.[9]

A quern's upper stone, or muller, had a protruding wooden handle set in it. The user poured grain between the stones via a hole, or hopper, cut in the center of the muller, and then turned it by hand over the stationary lower stone. A concave rock or a wooden frame provided stabilization and caught the ground meal as it worked its way out from between the stones.

After about four thousand years of processing grain by these methods, mechanized mills came into use. The innovations that followed catapulted milling into its new role as one of the world's first industrial enterprises.

The earliest known example of a milling machine was used in Greece in the late fifth century BCE. Known as the Olythnus Mill, it had two rectangular stones. The top stone crushed the grain as workers pushed back and forth across the lower stone. This type of mill did not come into common use in places where rotary hand mills were common, like France and Spain.[10]

Around the same time, the Egyptians first made leavened bread,[11] which is thought to have occurred spontaneously when airborne yeast spores settled into someone's unattended dough.[12] Though millennia would pass before anyone learned to control the leavening process, bread consumption in the ancient world was, shall we say, on the rise.

Animal-powered rotary mills, more efficient than those driven by human effort, were first used in Italy in the third century BCE. The increased availability of flour led enterprising Romans to establish the first known bakers' guilds and open commercial bakeries.[13]

Waterwheel technology was available for nearly 500 years before its use in milling became widespread. In Greco-Roman societies in the last few centuries BCE, the monied classes viewed manual labor with

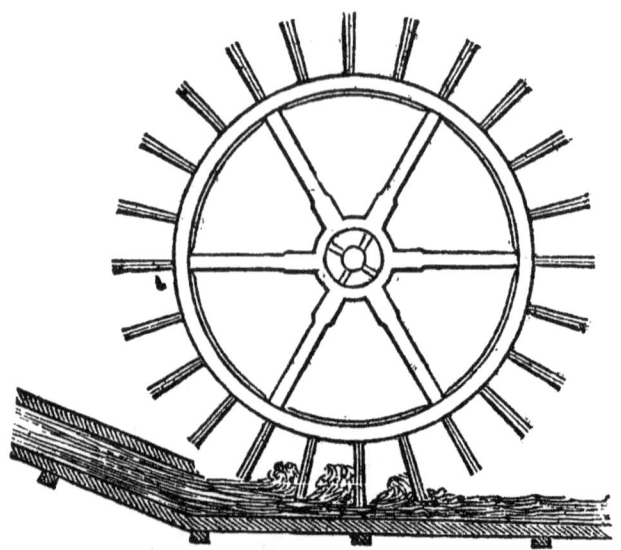

Undershot wheel

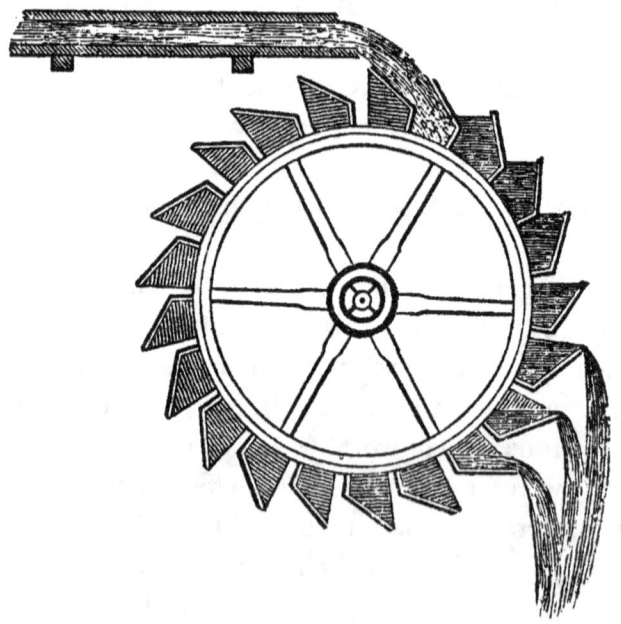

Overshot wheel

contempt, and those with the means to invest in mill construction were often reluctant to do so. Archimedes is said to have regarded the work "of every art that ministers to the needs of life as vulgar and ignoble."[14] So much for progress!

Furthermore, people believed money not spent was money well invested. Roman landowners contented themselves with horse-powered or hand mills rather than building more efficient water-powered mills.[15] The mills that did come into use in the first century BCE were simplistic, little more than a set of gears that drove the grinding stone.

Though wealthy Romans were disinterested in technological advancement, they did appreciate white bread.[16] Throughout most of human history, a person's social status could be discerned by the color of the bread they consumed.[17]

Simple Machines

The first water mills utilized horizontal wheels submerged in a stream or canal, turned by the water's current. Later people realized water could generate more power by striking a vertical wheel, and undershot wheels came into use around 100 BCE.[18] About 30 percent efficient, undershot wheels have a right-angle gear and two cogwheels to increase the velocity of the runner stone.[19]

A painting in the Roman catacombs that dates to the third century CE offers the earliest evidence of a wheel turned by gravity and the weight of the water as it flowed over the top of the wheel.[20]

These overshot wheels, about 75 percent efficient, required sluices and dams to concentrate the waterpower and direct it over the wheel.[21] Mechanically driven mills decreased the Romans' reliance on human labor and improved productivity.[22]

When the Germanic leader Odoacer overthrew Romulus, the last of the Roman emperors, in 476 CE, he became the first Barbarian to rule in Rome. The order and organization with which the Roman Empire had ruled western Europe for a thousand years was gone.[23]

The economic, intellectual, and cultural decline of the resulting Dark Ages slowed technological progress, but as people's interest and inclination rebounded in the later Middle Ages, the use of waterpower for processing grain spread across Europe. The Domesday Book, the census of the year 1080, recorded 5,624 mills in England operated by animal or waterpower.[24]

Big Business

We may assume the typical medieval miller was eager to innovate and improve the available technology. To increase his profits, we would expect him to position his business within a supply chain that ran from farmer to miller, from miller to baker, and finally, to the consumer.

This was far from the norm. Most medieval millers were serfs, the lowest class of peasants. Serfs were essentially slaves who lived on lands owned by a feudal lord where, in exchange for a place to live, they raised crops on shares and sometimes worked in skilled trades. Serfs paid rent over and above the share of their crops they paid to their landlords—and the landlords were quick to levy additional fees if tenants married or had a baby. Because money was scarce, serfs usually paid their rents and fees with crops.[25]

When it was time to have their remaining grain processed into flour for household use, a serf's only choice was to use the mill owned by the lord, who claimed yet another share for the privilege.

Of course, a nobleman would not have run the mill himself, and this placed the serfs who did the actual milling work in a difficult position. As agents of the ruling class, they were often looked upon as oppressors by their peers. Moreover, serfs who worked as millers had no incentive to be honest in their dealings, since they did not profit directly from their labors. Mills were local monopolies under no threat from competing businesses.

In Scotland, thirlage agreements restricted tenants from grinding their own grain. The baron who owned the mill had the right to compel tenants to bring all their grain to that mill.[26] If they defied him and used their own querns, the baron had the right to destroy the stones.[27]

It's easy to see how mill owners and their employees gained a reputation for taking advantage of their position. The milling industry was still centuries away from changes spurred by the ideals that led to the birth of America.

Quern at Blaker's Mill, Lewis County
Photo by Tracy Lawson

II. Milling in Colonial Virginia

"Millers were the first bankers, economists, and mechanical engineers."
– James P. Joyce, past president, The International Molinological Society of America

As we have seen, a dishonest miller could literally take food out of his customers' mouths. Believing, perhaps justly, that millers were unlikely to treat customers fairly without the proper incentive, authorities in Europe passed laws regulating the industry.[28]

In the seventeenth and early eighteenth centuries, milling culture and practice in Virginia resembled the feudal system in Europe, in which the miller was "uniformly a man of low estate."[29] Virginia planters used indentured servants or enslaved workers to run their mills, and just like their European counterparts, those who did the actual work had little incentive to provide a better service or to treat customers honestly. Deserved or not, the system perpetuated the miller's reputation for dishonesty.

Many legal restrictions on milling that were common practice in Europe crossed the ocean to the Americas. Milling in the colonies was also regulated by laws meant to discourage abuses. Every revision of

Tools for dressing millstones and a toll box on display at Blaker's Mill
Photo by Tracy Lawson

Virginia law included penalties and fines for millers found guilty of taking excessive tolls. The 1705 law read:

"That all millers shall grind according to turn; and shall well and sufficiently grind the grain brought to their mills; and shall take no more for toll or grinding, than one eighth part of wheat, and one sixth part of Indian corn."[30] Officials did regular quality checks to assure the flour was free of impurities and tested the scoops and measures used for accuracy.[31]

There are tricks to every trade, and a canny miller could outfit his wooden toll box with a false bottom that would decrease the area within and make it seem as though he followed the rules. Once the inspector was on his way, the miller would remove the false bottom and collect a bit larger toll.

Continued abuses within the system, whether real or imagined, spurred more legislation to regulate the milling industry as though it was a public utility. But as mills were typically owned by the Virginia gentry, other protective restrictions benefited them.[32] Local governments often gave millers eminent domain to access favorable water mill sites, and municipalities were responsible for maintaining roads leading to mills.[33]

Millers could also claim privileges denied to others, which didn't help their reputations. They were excused from militia service until 1780, when the need for able-bodied men became too pressing.[34] They were also exempt from jury duty—not, as some claimed, because they were so dishonest that they were unfit to render judgment on others, but because they could not take time away from the responsibility of their mills.[35] A West Virginia law that exempted millers from jury duty remained on the books until 1919.[36]

Despite the attention given to the regulation of the milling industry, it was tobacco, not wheat, that was the chief money crop in Virginia and Maryland until the last few decades of the American colonial era. In those two colonies, most planters grew only enough wheat and corn to feed their own households and animals. Mills were typically built on private land by individuals or syndicates of neighbors who shared construction and maintenance costs.[37]

Doing Business

In 1764, the English Parliament's Currency Act prohibited any entity in the American colonies from printing paper money. Imports from Britain far exceeded colonial exports, and without enough money in circulation, colonists were forced to buy on credit from the British merchants.[38] Transatlantic commerce left the planters in the colonies at the mercy of agents in England, who set prices for the crops and for the manufactured goods the planters ordered in trade.

Decades of this system left even the wealthiest planters in chronic debt to the English merchants. Convinced that the Crown viewed them as second-class citizens, they took umbrage when the Seven Years' War spawned a financial crisis, forcing merchants to call in their debts and bankrupt many colonial importers.[39] Planters seeking solvency and stability began to transact more domestic business.

William Byrd may have been the first to experiment with merchant milling in Virginia. Byrd owned two mills on the James River. In 1685, he ran a classified ad seeking two millers to run them. He also made inquiries about selling his flour in the West Indies.[40]

In smaller communities, custom milling, an example of the "domestic stage" of industrial evolution, prevailed. Under this system, the miller processed grain owned by others for a share, known as a toll, and did not have to worry about paying attention to changing market prices.[41]

Merchant milling became common later, when wheat, the best rotation crop for tobacco-exhausted soil, became the tobacco growers' second export crop. Plantation owners increased the grinding capacity of their personal mills and began shipping barrels of flour along with their hogsheads of tobacco. Some went so far as to bake the flour into bread for export—mostly in the form of ship's biscuit, which could keep for a long time without spoiling. In 1766, Virginia's Governor Fauquier noted in a report to the Board of Trade that Virginians "daily set up mills to grind their wheat into flour for exportation."

George Washington was among the planters who implemented crop rotation to increase his profits. In 1769, Washington rebuilt his mill on Dogue Run and purchased French buhrstones for his export flour as well as a pair of Cologne stones for doing the "country work" of grinding corn for his own use. Washington wrote in his later years that "as a farmer, wheat and flour constitute my principal concerns." There was no clear-cut transition between custom and merchant milling, with both types often existing in the same localities.[42]

The Crown did not shrink from passing more regulations to frustrate the colonists' ambitions, and the Stamp Act, the capstone of the Intolerable Acts of the 1760s, ultimately sparked the civil unrest that led to the American Revolution.[43]

Changing Attitudes Toward Trade

Just as attitudes had shifted away from Greco-Roman ideals centuries before, social perception shifted again in the mid-to-late 1700s. According to economist Deidre McCloskey, "People stopped sneering at market innovations and other bourgeois virtues. The new dignity of being in trade led to small businessmen reaping the rewards of their innovations."[44]

When the first shots ignited the American Revolution in 1775, the colonies' economy was largely agricultural. Artisans and craftsmen, not factories, dominated manufacturing. The fledgling nation's need for weapons and other war materials laid the groundwork for the transition to larger-scale manufacturing practices.

Small businessmen experimented with new ways of organizing manufacturing facilities, developing mass-production techniques, and integrating supply chains. The American Revolution helped usher in the American Industrial Revolution, and perhaps most important, it established a strong manufacturing economy in the new country. In the postwar years, the availability of land and labor, the absence of a landed aristocracy, and the growing prestige of entrepreneurship contributed to America's rapid industrialization.[45]

The first expansion in the years following the American Revolution afforded opportunities for veterans to obtain bounty lands in the western territories. Others bought portions of the 5.2-million-acre Fairfax Grant in western Virginia, which had once belonged to agents of the Crown.[46]

Counties set down rules and requirements for prospective mill owners, who were required to apply through the local court for permission to build. A committee would then be appointed by the court to conduct an environmental study to assure that the neighboring farms would not be depreciated because of flooding or other negative impact.[47]

Folks who moved to the less-developed regions of western Virginia did not have to compete with established plantations owned by the American gentry and were free to launch their own enterprises. Groups of families often migrated together, with each family responsible for a necessary skill or trade. Goods and services were used as barter on the frontier.[48] Until nearly the end of the nineteenth century, most West Virginians depended upon subsistence farming, and industries like milling and textile manufacturing were often farm-related.[49] In a 2009 article in *The Shepherdstown Chronicle* entitled "Group Wowed by Shepherd's Mill Tour," reporter Michael Theis wrote, "Unencumbered by European aristocrats' waterway privileges, which made it a nightmare for a non-aristocrat to build a mill, they built them as fast as they could. The abundance of water powered factories jump-started the American Industrial Revolution and established the nation as a powerful agricultural exporter."[50]

The earliest West Virginia mills were simply built, with a run of millstones, a measuring barrel for the incoming grain, and a bin for the ground meal.[51] On the frontier, where the laws governing mills were loosely enforced, a miller's reputation for honesty became more important. With competing mills cropping up all over, even a hint of unscrupulous business dealings would drive customers away.[52]

Aspiring millers sought convenient sites with an abundance of waterpower. Overshot wheels worked best when placed about ten feet below the elevation of the water supply, so mills were often constructed on small streams with steep gradients. Dams constructed on smaller streams were less likely to wash out during freshets than ones built near mighty rivers.[53]

Water remained the dominant source of gristmill power in Virginia for over a century. Long after millers in other states began installing steam engines, Virginia used a larger proportion of water for flour milling

II. MILLING IN COLONIAL VIRGINIA 23

than any other state.[54] Though data was not available for West Virginia, mountain streams continued to power many of the mills profiled in this book well into the twentieth century.

Milling 101

In a typical mid-eighteenth-century mill, only three adjustments could be made to the mechanism: the amount of water flowing over the wheel, the rate at which the grain was fed into the stones, and the distance between the stones.[55] Even so, a miller spent hours maintaining the dam, the headgate that shut off water flow, the millrace, the waterwheel, and other equipment, to protect against damage and deterioration.[56]

Example of a simple, mid-eighteenth-century grist mill

Outside, a canal or elevated trough called a millrace directed water from a river or stream downhill to the waterwheel, using the slope to increase velocity and pressure, sometimes over considerable distance. The miller controlled the water flow with a sluice gate close to the mill, and a head gate at the far end of the race, at the point of the dam that interrupts the water flow in the river or stream.

A series of dams was often required to operate a mill during both wet and dry seasons.[57] At the ruins of the Mount Healthy Mill in Ohio, built by my ancestors in the 1820s, the visible remains of the millrace enabled us to calculate its length at about 270 yards from the dam to the sluice gate at the drop above the waterwheel.[58]

When a farmer brought sacks of grain to be processed, the miller or his workers raised the sacks on a rope and pulley hoist to an upper floor and poured the grain into a hopper above the stones. A trough known as the shoe carried grain from the bottom of the hopper to the opening in the upper, or runner, stone. The vibration of the turning wheel jiggled the shoe and kept the grain flowing down between the stones.[59]

The grooves in the stones, cut as deep as a grain of wheat at the center, grew progressively shallower as they extended toward the outer edge. During the grinding process, centrifugal force from the spinning upper stone drew the crushed grain away from the center into the cuts.[60]

Stones were often mounted on a Hurst frame, a separate mortise and tenon timber frame that rests on a continuous stone foundation. Separating the grinding floor structure protects the rest of the building from vibration induced by the moving grindstones, gears, and other machinery.[61]

As the stones pulverized the wheat, the endosperm portion of the kernel reduced to a finer powder than the coarser germ and bran. The warm, moist meal fell off the edge of the lower stone into the wooden vat that encased the stones, and the draft from the rotating top stone blew it toward an opening in the floor. Here, another chute led to a wide, shallow bin where an apprentice called a hopper boy used a wide-toothed wooden rake to stir the flour, allowing it to dry and cool before it was conducted down another chute to the bolter.

During the bolting step, gravity sifted the flour through a series of mesh silk screens of graduated fineness ranging from eighteen to 170 threads per inch.[62] The finest flour particles passed through all the screens and collected at the bottom. Coarse pieces of bran with bits of flour clinging to them, known as middlings, were held back, mixed with molasses, and used for animal feed.

Grinding corn, which required no sifting or separation, was even simpler.

Gristmill technology reached a new height of complexity after the American Revolution, when a young inventor brought ideas to fruition that would radically change the milling industry.

Millstones at Bloomery Mill, Hampshire County
Photo by Tracy Lawson

Hopper and frame mounted over millstones
at Feagans Mill, Jefferson County
Photo by Tracy Lawson

II. MILLING IN COLONIAL VIRGINIA 27

Millstones on Hurst frame at Laurel Dale Mill, Mineral County
Photo by Tracy Lawson

Bags of unground wheat rest between the two millstones at Homan Mill, which ceased operation in the 1970s. Photo by Tracy Lawson

II. MILLING IN COLONIAL VIRGINIA 29

Two run of millstones and crane at Bloomery Mill, Hampshire County
Photo by Tracy Lawson

Bolter with flake auger at McNeel Mill, Pocahontas County
Photo by Tracy Lawson

II. MILLING IN COLONIAL VIRGINIA   31

Remnants of the striped silk fabric in the bolter
at Laurel Dale Mill, Mineral County
Photo by Tracy Lawson

Display of cooper's tools in Lyon's Mill, Grant County
Photo by Tracy Lawson

II. MILLING IN COLONIAL VIRGINIA

Oliver Evans Automates the Milling Process

Around 1785, inventor and businessman Oliver Evans (1755-1819) designed and built a conventional flour mill on Red Clay Creek near Newport, Delaware. Over the next five years, he developed it into an automated mill. His innovations changed the milling industry forever—though as often happens, the new technology took a while to become universally accepted.

Evans's system utilized bucket elevators to transport the grain to the top floor of the mill, where it was cleaned with fans and sieves prior to gravity transmission down to the hoppers. After it passed through the grinding stones, a second set of elevators brought the meal back to the upper floors to a mechanical hopper boy, a round enclosure with a rotating rake to cool and dry the newly ground meal before it descended again to be bolted and packed.

The innovations saved hours of manual labor and reduced the number of people required to operate a mill from three or four to one. Manpower was only needed to empty bags of wheat at one end of the machine, and to close and roll away the barrels of flour when the process was complete.

This was the first instance of an uninterrupted process of mechanical manufacturing from raw materials to finished product, in the history of industry.[63]

Evans's first attempts to sell his patented mill machinery disappointed him. Few millers were willing to pay for the right to use his innovations, and they were not interested in acting as agents to introduce other millers to the system, despite Evans's offer to improve their mills with his inventions in return. But they had no qualms about copying his ideas.

George Washington received one of the first licenses to use Evans's milling improvements and was one of the few who paid the fee.[64]

With poor prospects for making a living from his inventions, Evans contacted William Young, a printer and bookseller in Philadelphia, to make engravings for a pamphlet. Later, Evans developed his ideas into a book called *The Young Millwrights and Millers Guide*. Published in 1795, the book included engravings of Evans's mill equipment and explained theoretical principles of mechanics and hydraulics as applied to water mills. As time passed, more millers tried Evans's equipment, and when his innovations improved their profits, the license fee of forty dollars per pair of millstones did not seem so prohibitively costly.[65] In the last section of the book, "The Practical Mill-Wright," Evans gives detailed instructions for building mills, with proportions tables for all falls from three to thirty-six feet.[66]

In most wheel-driven mills, a large gear wheel called the pit wheel is mounted on the same axle as the waterwheel. It drives a smaller gear wheel, the wallower, which is mounted on the main vertical driveshaft that runs from the bottom of the building and supplies power to equipment on each level. This main drive shaft turns faster than the waterwheel. A medium-sized wheel may rotate at around 10 rpm, but a larger one, like the 24-foot wheel at Lyon's Mill in Williamsport, makes only 4.5 rpm.

The bottom millstone of the pair, called the bed stone, is stationary, while the top stone, or runner, is mounted on a separate spindle driven by the main drive shaft. The runner rotates faster than either the waterwheel or the drive shaft. The gear that connects the runner's spindle to the main shaft can be disengaged. This allows the main shaft to power other machinery, like fans and sieves, that refine the flour before grinding. The main drive shaft can also be used to hoist sacks of grain to the top floor of the mill house.[67]

By 1813, Evans's ideas had won acceptance and led to related innovations in other fields. *The Young Millwrights and Millers Guide* was the first technical manual published in any industry, and soon similar manuals dedicated to other trades began to appear.

Under Evans's system, mills could grind more grain using less power, and this increased the supply of grain to the market. Better plows, reapers, and threshers helped farmers keep up with the demand for more grain. Threshers and fanning mills reduced the average time required for culling and sacking an acre of wheat from twenty-six hours in 1830 to four hours in 1840.[68] The scythe and the flail faded from common use among all but the poorest subsistence farmers.

Technological improvements continued, and after 1840 the number of gristmills in Virginia declined for the first time, but the mills that remained increased in size.[69]

Pulleys and drive shaft in the lower level of
Shepherd's Mill, Jefferson County
Photo by Shannon Thomas

Wooden gears in the Botkin-Simmons Mill, Highland County, VA
Photo by Tracy Lawson

Gears, Mitchell Mill, Pendleton County
Photo by Tracy Lawson

Part of this gear's shaft was cut off and the metal sold for scrap during World War II. Mitchell Mill, Pendleton County
Photo by Tracy Lawson

II. MILLING IN COLONIAL VIRGINIA

View from below: the gears and drive shaft power the upper, runner stone, while the bed stone (visible) remains stationary.
Photo by Tracy Lawson

Gears at Union Bryarly Mill, Berkeley County
Photo by Tracy Lawson

Gears at Mitchell Mill, Pendleton County
Photo by Tracy Lawson

The equipment remains in the long-silent Hoover Mill, Pendleton County.
Photo courtesy of Jana Reichelderfer

II. MILLING IN COLONIAL VIRGINIA 43

Gears, Blaker's Mill, Lewis County
Photo by Tracy Lawson

Doing the Math

The Fitz Water Wheel Company, which began manufacturing all-metal wheels in the 1850s, designed their Overshoot Wheel system so the water would strike the top of the wheel at a point about ten inches behind vertical center. In this way, the buckets filled just as they passed the topmost point of the wheel[70] and retained the water for almost half the wheel's rotation before dumping it.

According to Fitz, when choosing the size of the waterwheel, the most important thing to determine is the "head," or how far the water falls. Fitz calculated fall as the vertical distance from the surface of the water in the forebay or tank above the top of the wheel, down to the surface of the water in the tail race below the bottom of the wheel. The diameter of an Overshoot waterwheel should be from two-and-a-half to three feet less than the total fall available.

Most waterwheels manufactured by the Fitz Company had a standard bucket design. For every foot of width, the bucket could handle 2.7 cubic feet of water per second (cfs),[71] with the buckets spaced about one foot apart on the wheel.

To get the wheel turning, the velocity of the water entering the wheel needed to flow at about twice the rate of the wheel's rotation speed, with the most efficient transfer of energy occurring when the wheel speed is 93% of the water speed.[72]

Stones of Life

Through the centuries and across the world, different types of stone have been quarried and shaped into monolithic or composite millstones. Types of stone found in the southeastern United States used for millstones are limestone, freshwater quartz, granite, flint, sandstone, conglomerate, which is a coarse-grained sedimentary rock, and gneiss, which is made up of feldspar, mica, and quartz transformed by heat or pressure.[73]

Some millers favored quartz conglomerate for its sharpness and the inequalities of its surface, while others chose to import top quality limestone from France. French buhrstone was in high demand throughout the American colonial period.[74] England also produced millstones.[75]

Between 1752 and 1778, the Virginia *Gazette* ran ads for Cullen millstones, dark bluish-gray lava from the Rhineland region, which was then part of France. These were considered best for grinding corn or buckwheat.[76] If a mill had two run (pairs) of stones, seldom would the miller use buhrs that had been grinding cornmeal for making flour. The oil in corn penetrates the stone and gives it a glaze which is difficult to remove and makes it unsatisfactory for grinding wheat.[77]

By the first half of the nineteenth century, Virginia millers outfitted their mills with fine buhrstones quarried in southwestern Pennsylvania and eastern Ohio. [78]

My great-great-great-grandfather, Henry Rogers, the miller from Cincinnati, noted in his journal that while traveling east on the National Road near Uniontown, Pennsylvania, he saw Laurel Hill, "the one from which a great number of millstones were taken and carried to the state of Ohio."[79]

The quarry on Laurel Hill may have been established by the Shacklett family in the late eighteenth century. Though long abandoned, millstones of varying sizes and in different stages of completion could be found on Chestnut Ridge, part of Laurel Hill, as late as 1983.[80]

Pottsville Conglomerate stone, found in the mountain ranges in the eastern part of Virginia, was called millstone grit. Millers who lived close enough to acquire it had their millstones cut from that material.

It is likely that some of the mills profiled in this book were outfitted with Brush Mountain Stones[81] from a quarry located on Brush Mountain near Blacksburg, in Montgomery County, Virginia. In operation by 1838, the quarry remained active through the early twentieth century. The area's sandstone conglomerate ranged in color from white to gray to bluish and at different grits. An 1853 ad in the Lynchburg *Daily Virginian* read, "The undersigned are now procuring from their celebrated quarry, at Brush Mountain, Montgomery County, Mill Stones and Burrs of the very best quality. The reputation of these stones is widely known, but the railroad giving us increased facilities in fulfilling orders, we have appointed McDaniel, Hurt & Preston and Lee & Johnson, Lynchburg, our agents for the sale who will receive orders and have them fulfilled at the shortest notice."

A pair of millstones weighs between 600 and 1,000 pounds.[82] French buhrstones, used as ballast on ships, arrived in pieces that were joined together with a mixture of sand and plaster of paris and encircled with an iron hoop.

Some quarries sold stones with furrows already cut, but if they needed to be "dressed" before use, the miller took up his chisel and hammer, cutting furrows in the upper stone and patterns on the lower.[83] The land, or uncut portions, did the actual shearing of the grain. The furrows directed the ground meal toward the edges of the stones and ventilated the heat generated by the grinding process.[84]

It was the task of dressing the millstones that gave the miller his "mark." Tiny bits of metal from the chisel, driven backward toward the miller's hand, embedded themselves in his skin and left a gray patch. It may be that this miller's mark led to the expression, "He's proved his mettle."[85] Conscientious millers dressed and balanced their stones regularly and cleaned and inspected the grain to make sure small stones or metal filings did not find their way between the buhrs. The better quality the stone, the less often it had to be dressed.[86] The miller, who judged the quality of the grind by the texture of the meal, was able to raise or lower the runner stone as little as a fraction of an inch until the resulting product was up to his standards.[87]

Millstone quarrying and production, both for flour milling and for other uses, continued even after the increasing popularity of roller mill systems in the 1880s caused a sharp decline in use of buhrstones to grind wheat flour.[88]

According to *Mineral Resources of the United States*, which reported information on millstone producers in key states, conglomerate millstones were made in Fayette County, West Virginia, and in Morgantown, in Monongalia County, as late as 1941.[89]

Millstone, Jefferson County - Photo by Tracy Lawson

Some millstones, particularly French buhr stones, came in pieces, and were held together with Plaster of Paris and an iron hoop around the perimeter.
Photo by Tracy Lawson

A crane lifts the runner stone for dressing and cleaning.
Blaker's Mill, Lewis County
Photo by Tracy Lawson

II. MILLING IN COLONIAL VIRGINIA   49

Some Rural Mills Lag Behind Changing Technology

Over the course of a century, the following innovations had the largest impact on the milling industry: Oliver Evans's inventions developed between 1785 and 1790; the widespread substitution of turbines for waterwheels in the 1860s; the introduction of roller mill technology in the 1880s; and the end to reliance on undependable water sources, made possible by using steam, gasoline, or diesel engines.

Leonardo DaVinci is credited with designing the turbine, a horizontal wheel with curved paddles that, when submerged, turned with a stream's current. An improved version of the concept was introduced in 1827 by Benoit Fourneyron.[90] Since the turbine used all the openings between its blades simultaneously, it could be built smaller and turn faster, and still generate power commensurate with larger wheels. Though the turbine became popular in the mid-nineteenth century,[91] many millers declined to change, either because of the cost or because they believed the waterwheel was a superior source of power.

Stout, Mills & Temple sold turbines in their 1870 catalog that ranged from $200 for a thirteen-inch model to $2,050 for one that measured eighty-four inches in diameter.[92] Installing a turbine was an expensive investment for any business, and for many small country mills, the greater risk lay in taking on debt or a mortgage that could potentially bankrupt the business.[93]

Millers who shouldered the financial burden to upgrade from waterwheels to turbines soon faced another technological change, in the form of "reduction" milling that threatened the relevance of their buhrstone mills.

Thomas Kemp Cartmell noted in *Shenandoah Valley Pioneers and Their Descendants: A History of Frederick County, Virginia from its Formation in 1738 to 1908*, that many mill owners grappled with the new style and were driven out of the lucrative businesses they previously enjoyed. "The milling business [became] confined to very few persons, who [were] men of means; and by concentrating capital with an intelligent handling of the new system, it prove[d] a good investment."[94]

In the new reduction style of grinding, invented in Philadelphia in 1876, grain passes through a series of steel or porcelain rollers, first grooved, then smooth in the final stages, which gradually crushed the grain into fine flour. Bolting then removed the bran particles before bagging.[95]

Roller mills processed flour with a more uniform and appealing appearance and extracted more flour from the same amount of wheat than millstones.[96]

In the 1890s, rock emery imported from Greek and Turkish mines and processed in Germany struck another blow toward the buhrstone's demise. Emery could be ground, mixed with crushed glass, and cemented into solid wheels that did not require dressing. It ran cool and surpassed other stones in hardness.[97]

In the final decade of the nineteenth century, the market for imported buhrstones declined again.[98] By 1900, sources say buhrs had "almost disappeared from mills in the United States."[99] While it looked like the turbine and the roller mill would render the waterwheel and the buhrstone extinct, the remaining mills in West Virginia prove this was not the case. The remote location of mills that served rural communities worked in their favor, as many continued in business well into the mid-twentieth century—often with few adaptations.

Concerns over the changes in the industry were not just financial. Many millers and doctors spoke out against the reduction method, claiming the process stripped flour of nutrients and fiber.

II. MILLING IN COLONIAL VIRGINIA 51

Roller mill and chutes, French's Mill, Hampshire County
Photo by Joe Strohmeyer

Scourer/Separator, Spaid-Eaton Mill, Hampshire County
Photo by Tracy Lawson

A conveyor belt with metal scoops straggles outside a chute at Homan Mill, Pendleton County.
Photo by Tracy Lawson

This chute once conducted grain into the roller mill at
Mitchell Mill, Pendleton County.
Photo by Tracy Lawson.

Pair of roller mills at Homan Mill, Pendleton County
Photo by Tracy Lawson

Conveyor belts with metal scoops stored in
McNeel Mill, Pocahontas County
Photo by Tracy Lawson

II. MILLING IN COLONIAL VIRGINIA 57

Bodney and Lane steam engine at Easton Roller Mills, Monongalia County
Photo by Tracy Lawson

Bits of wool cling to the carding machine in Priest Mill, Pendleton County. Photo by Tracy Lawson.

II. MILLING IN COLONIAL VIRGINIA   59

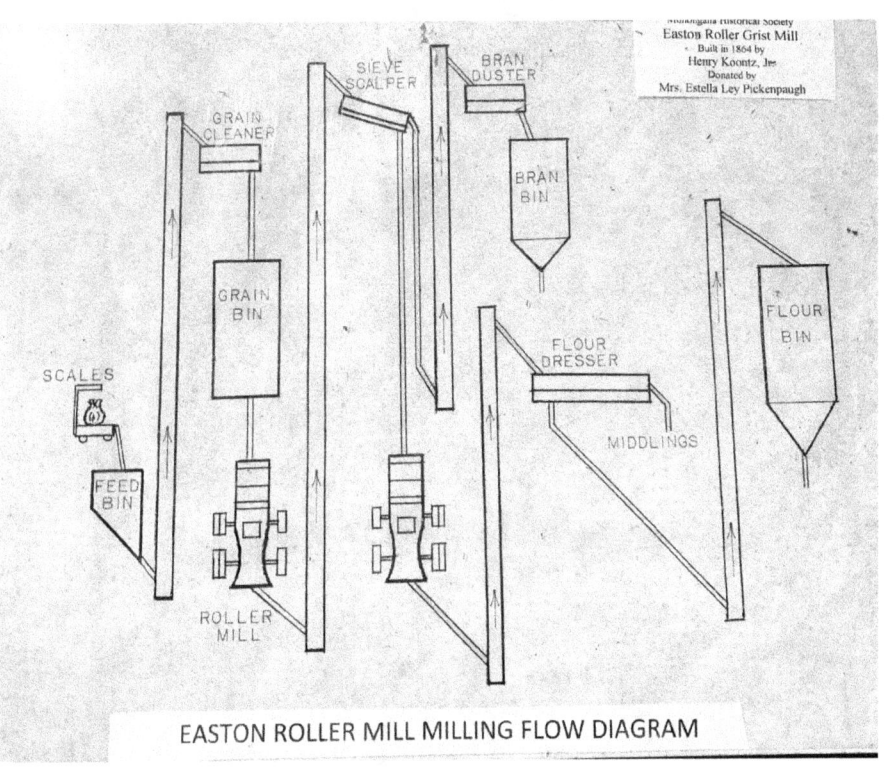

This flowchart from Easton Roller Mill maps out the path from unground grain to finished flour.
Photo by Tracy Lawson

III. Innovations in Milling Make Flour Cheaper, More Portable, and Less Nutritious

If stone-ground flour was more healthful, why didn't millers insist on using production methods that retained nutrients and fiber in the finished flour? One answer lies in America's mid-nineteenth-century westward expansion.

In the years leading up to the American Revolution, Pennsylvania was known as the colonies' breadbasket. Farmers in the eastern states had always cultivated spring wheat, which grows best in temperate climates. Buhrstone mills were well suited to grind the soft spring wheat.

In the nineteenth century, the center of American wheat production shifted west to the Midwestern plains. Summers there were too hot for spring wheat, so Midwestern farmers grew winter wheat, which adapts to a wide range of weather conditions. Planted in the fall, winter wheat sprouts and then lies dormant through the winter. It begins to grow again in spring and is ready for harvest in early summer.[100]

This hardier variety of wheat has a higher gluten content and more easily removed bran, which responds well to roller mill processing.

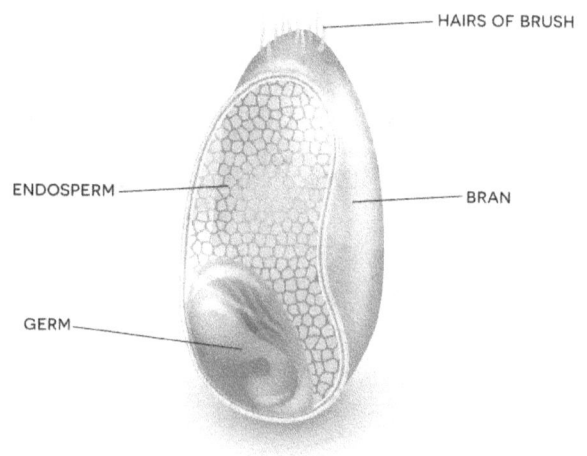

Anatomy of a Wheat Kernel

The germ is the root of the wheat kernel. The endosperm is the food for the seed, and the bran is the outer layer of the kernel. A typical wheat kernel is 83 percent endosperm, 14 percent bran, and 3 percent germ.[105]

The endosperm surrounds the germ. It contains most of the dry matter in the kernel of wheat. Though it is the only part of the grain needed to make flour, most of the nutritional value in wheat is found in the germ and the bran.

Overall, the roller system proved to be faster, more economical, and eliminated the labor-intensive process of hand-sifting out the bran.[101]

Whole, or unbolted, meal retains the nutrients and fiber in the grain, but wheat germ, crushed during the milling process, releases oils which quickly turn rancid when exposed to air. Whole-meal flour must be used, or frozen, soon after it is ground, but nineteenth-century pioneers needed flour that wouldn't spoil on long journeys to the western reaches of the continent.[102]

Whether they realized it or not, the tradeoff was less nutritious bread. Filtering out the germ and bran created flour that lasted for months without spoiling, but most of the vitamins, minerals, and fiber were lost in processing. The starchy powder left behind was but a pale substitute for the nutritious, whole-wheat flour our ancestors called the staff of life.[103]

When they lacked access to yeast, frontier families relied on sourdough to make bread and biscuits, and the term "sourdough" was used to refer to both the Yukon gold prospectors and their bread-making methods. A sourdough starter, or sponge, was a thick flour-and-water batter, often with milk, sugar, potato water, or yeast added to aid fermentation. The sponge was mixed with flour and water and allowed to rise. After each baking, the starter pot was replenished with a little of the dough and the process began anew. Nineteenth-century bread recipes often called for saleterus, which was sodium or potassium bicarbonate, and an old-fashioned term for baking powder.

Setting a bowl of starter in a pan of heated salt to keep it warm overnight yielded "salt-rising" bread. Adding salt to the sponge delayed the growth of bacteria that soured the milk.

Though many millers rejected the roller method of refining flour, consumers preferred it for its convenience and the texture of the bread it produced, either not knowing, or not caring, that wheat's natural nutrients and fiber were almost entirely lost in the roller-milling process. It was not until 1941 that a wartime measure required mills to add synthetic vitamins to their flour to replace thiamine, riboflavin, niacin, and iron. But the full amounts were not added back, and there is evidence that our bodies do not absorb synthetic vitamins as well as they do natural ones.[104]

Other Types of Flour

Graham flour, developed by Sylvester Graham as a health food in the 1830s, has finely ground endosperm mixed in with the bran and germ, and is sweetened with honey. Though it has a coarser grind than whole-wheat flour, the FDA makes no distinction today between the two.

Buckwheat, a seed which comes from a different botanical family than wheat, is most closely related to rhubarb and is naturally gluten-free. After buckwheat is dehulled, the seeds, called groats, can be ground into flour. Note: those with gluten sensitivity and celiac disease should always read labels before consuming buckwheat products, as buckwheat can be subject to cross-contamination and is often processed in facilities that also process wheat, barley, and rye.

IV. Historic Preservation

In the early stages of this project, I experienced the thrill of discovery and a growing desire to assist preservation efforts on the behalf of West Virginia's historic mills so that future generations can appreciate and learn from them.

Each mill profiled in this book, along with its builder and its string of owners, was a member of the communities it served, with their fortunes inexorably intertwined. Several of the mills predate our country's founding, and all have seen the societal changes and growth West Virginia has experienced in the ensuing years. They have a story to tell.

For every mill that has been repurposed or preserved, there are many others with just as much historical significance. It is my hope that this book will shed light on opportunities for historic preservation and bring together entrepreneurs, investors, and mill owners so that these structures can begin a new chapter and once again serve their communities as retail outlets, community gathering places, or living history centers.

The following organizations provide various forms of assistance for the redevelopment of historic properties in West Virginia:

West Virginia Department of Arts, Culture & History, State Historic Preservation Office
The mission of the Department of Arts, Culture & History's State Historic Preservation Office is to encourage, inform, support, and participate in the efforts of the people of West Virginia to identify, recognize, preserve, and protect West Virginia's prehistoric and historic structures, objects, and sites. SHPO offers historic preservation development grants for certified local governments, as well as state and local government agencies, not-for-profit organizations, for-profit firms and organizations, and education institutions.
https://wvculture.org/

Vibrant Communities Drive Change
VCDC connects developers, investors, and communities with the mission to build affordable housing and revitalize historic properties to create thriving neighborhoods that benefit all residents. With such partnerships in place, VCDC supports viable, healthy communities by bringing resources to small economies where traditional banks won't operate.
https://vibrantcommunities.us/about

WV Leap: From Liability to Viability
West Virginia University College of Law provides a legal toolkit to address neglected properties in West Virginia.
https://wvleap.wvu.edu

National Park Service
The National Park Service offers programs for preservation activities.
https://www.nps.gov/subjects/nationalhistoriclandmarks/preservation-programs.htm

IV. HISTORIC PRESERVATION

National Trust for Historic Preservation
: The National Trust for Historic Preservation leads the movement to save America's historic places. A privately funded nonprofit organization, NTHP works to save America's historic sites, tell the full American story, build stronger communities, and invest in preservation's future. Main Street America is a program of the nonprofit National Main Street Center, Inc., and a subsidiary of the National Trust for Historic Preservation.
Main Street America is a resource center dedicated to helping revitalization professionals foster innovative entrepreneurship and bolster small business communities.
https://savingplaces.org

Federal and State Historic Preservation Tax Incentive Program
: Federal and state rehabilitation tax credits are dollar-for-dollar reductions in income tax liability for taxpayers who rehabilitate historic buildings. The amount of the credit is based on total rehabilitation costs. The federal credit is 20 percent.
https://www.irs.gov/businesses/small-businesses-self-employed/rehabilitation-credit-historic-preservation-faqs

Preservation Alliance of West Virginia
: PAWV offers historic preservation loans for individuals, nonprofits, and for-profit business entities.
https://www.pawv.org/

As of April 26, 2021, West Virginia has made its historic tax rehabilitation credit program permanent. The bipartisan bill makes available a 25 percent tax credit for those who rehabilitate historic, income-producing properties.
https://www.pawv.org/historic-rehabilitation-tax-credits.html

Advisory Council on Historic Preservation: Preserve America

Administered by the ACHP, Preserve America encourages community efforts to preserve and enjoy the country's cultural and natural heritage.

ACHP believes preservation is key to stimulating West Virginia's economy while simultaneously maintaining the state's proud heritage for future generations. ACHP offers webinars and workshops for those interested in historic preservation. The organization partners with AmeriCorps to recruit crews of Preserve WV volunteers for one year of service. Visit their website to learn more about opportunities and ideas for funding your historic preservation project.
https://www.achp.gov/preserve-america/

National Register of Historic Places

Thirty-one of the fifty-three mills profiled in this book have been added to either the West Virginia State or the National Register of Historic Places. The National Register may include buildings, structures, districts, and sites that can provide documentation of historical significance.[106] The designation is an honorific and does not come with any restrictions as to what the property owners may do to the property, though local laws apply. It does not guarantee the property will be preserved in the future, but it does make technical assistance available for preservation projects. Property owners that receive federally and state-funded grants or other assistance may be subject to restrictions as to what may be done to the site.

IV. HISTORIC PRESERVATION

SECTION TWO

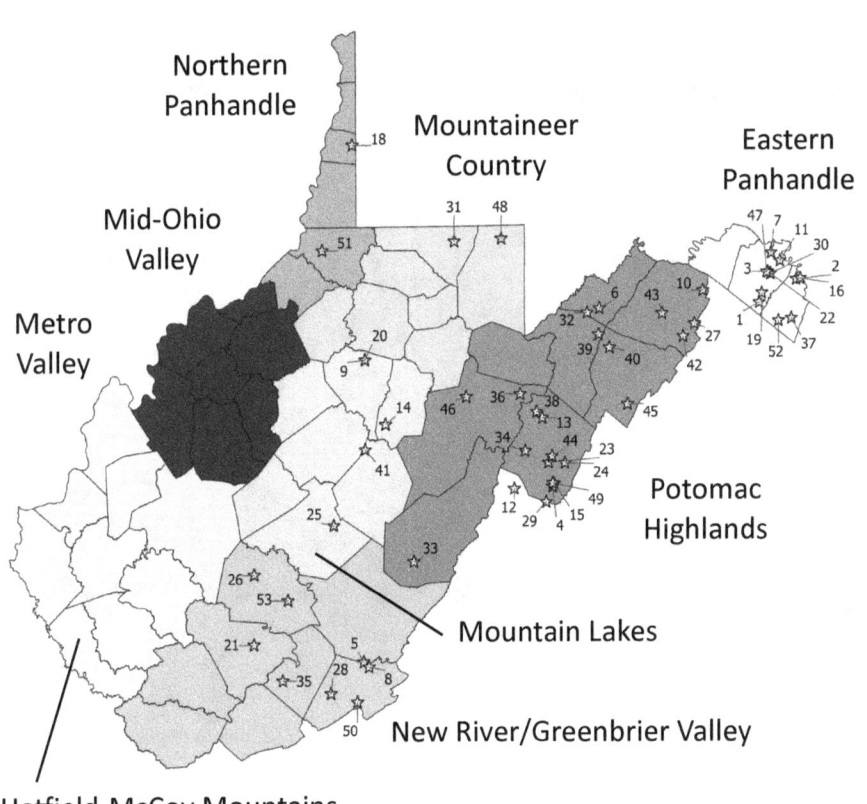

Chapter 1
Eastern Panhandle

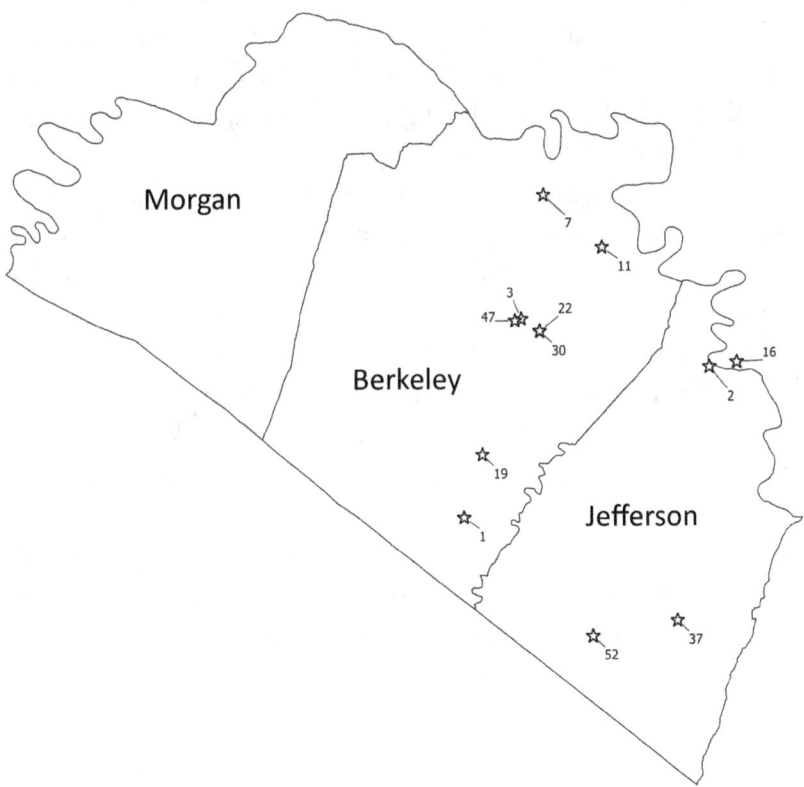

In 1730, brothers John and Isaac Van Meter acquired orders to settle 40,000 acres east of the Opequon Creek. They sold these orders in 1731 to Jost Hite, who brought a group of settlers to the area in 1732. Also in 1730, Alexander Ross and Morgan Bryan acquired orders to settle as many as 70,000 acres west of the Opequon Creek and east of North Mountain. Ross and Bryan brought a group of Quakers and Presbyterians to the area in 1733.[107]

Most of the Eastern Panhandle lies within the Ridge and Valley physiographic region. Harper's Ferry, in Jefferson County, is the state's low point, with an elevation of 247 feet. The region drains into the Potomac River by Patterson Creek, the South Branch of the Potomac, the Cacapon, and the Shenandoah.[108] Each is fed by lesser streams referred to as runs, branches, and creeks, along which many mills were located.

Two gristmills established in the Eastern Panhandle in the 1730s are still standing.[109] Once Virginia's westernmost outpost, the region developed into an important agricultural and industrial center by the mid-nineteenth century. Mill Creek in Berkeley County had as many as fifteen mills on its banks producing flour, lumber, plaster, wool, flax oil, and paper.[110]

When West Virginia was formed in 1863, Hardy, Hampshire, and Morgan counties were included in the new state—in large part to assure the Union retained control of the Baltimore & Ohio Railroad during the Civil War.[111] Berkeley and Jefferson counties also voted to join the Union, but their large slave-owning populations cast their loyalties into doubt, and their status remained unsettled until after the Civil War.[112]

The Eastern Panhandle is considered part of the Washington, DC, metropolitan area and is known for its historic sites, mineral springs, and charming small towns.

Today, nearly a dozen mills and the factory that pioneered the manufacture of steel waterwheels can be found in a range of urban and rural settings in Berkeley and Jefferson counties.

Berkeley County
Formed from Frederick County in 1772

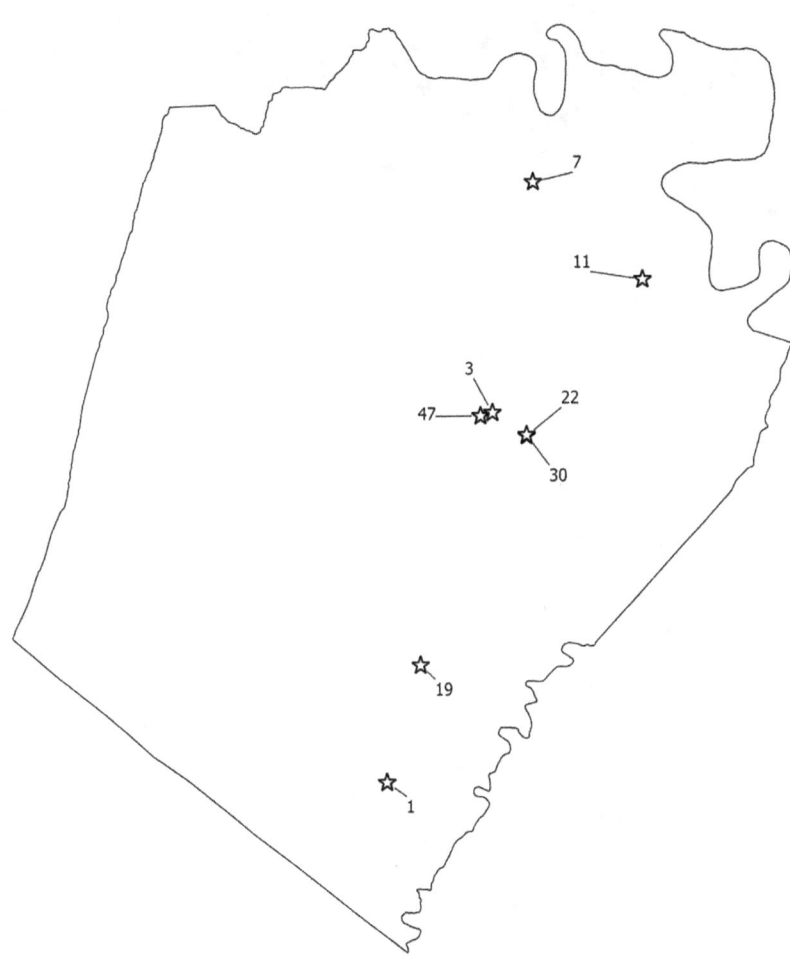

BERKELEY COUNTY 77

11. BEDINGER MILL

Berkeley County
Address: 1084 Bedington Road (CR 5), Martinsburg, WV 25404
Coordinates: 39.5200329, -77.9006743
Year Built: 1816
Period of Significance: b. 1783-1930s
Added to the National Register of Historic Places in 1984

© Google Maps

Aerial view of the Bedinger Mill - Photo by Alex Rubenstein

Bedinger Mill, bound up in the earliest history of the region, made a significant, long-term contribution to commercial development in the area. Now, it is ready for a new chapter—and a new owner.

In 1734, Morgan Bryan, an early settler, received a land grant of 1,250 acres that included the mill site.[113] Peter Light settled in Berkeley County around 1770 and purchased the original mill and a log miller's house from Bryan.[114] Light is recognized by the Daughters of the American Revolution as a patriot who supplied wheat and beef to the Continental Army during the war.[115] One source says Henry Myers (1756-1834) built the first mill,[116] but it seems more likely that the young man either refurbished the existing mill for Peter Light or built one of the others that stood on the property. Myers married Susannah Light, Peter's daughter, in 1783. Over time, Peter Light acquired around 1,500 acres and built the stone mansion known as Lick Run. In 1791, Light leased the merchant mill, a custom mill, a sawmill, and a hemp mill to John Maxwell.[117]

Thomas Shepherd, founder of Shepherdstown and builder of Shepherd's Mill, is credited with positioning Jefferson County as a breadbasket and establishing the grain export market that utilized shipping routes by canal, road, and later, rail. *(See Shepherd's Mill, page 143)*

Had Captain Henry Bedinger (1752-1843), an army comrade and brother-in-law of Shepherd's son, Abraham, not been involved in a public and protracted legal struggle over his election to clerk of the Jefferson County court in Jefferson County, he might have stayed in that county. Instead, he applied his business acumen in neighboring Berkeley.

When the twenty-three-year-old Bedinger enlisted in the Continental Army in June 1775, he was made a sergeant in Captain Hugh Stephenson's militia unit before he left the recruiting rendezvous. After Stephenson's promotion to colonel, Bedinger's friend, Abraham Shepherd, became the commanding officer. Bedinger kept a journal of the Virginia volunteers' 1775 "Beeline March" to join General Washington at Boston. In 1776, when his unit was re-organized, Henry was promoted to second lieutenant. After his entire unit was captured at Ft. Washington in November 1776, Henry spent nearly four years as a prisoner on Long Island. Upon his release, he and two other officers walked to Philadelphia, where they bought a horse and took turns walking and riding until they reached Richmond, Virginia. There, Henry raised another company, serving as its captain, and marched south to join the army at Yorktown, arriving after Cornwallis's surrender.[118]

Bedinger returned home and went into the mercantile business in Shepherdstown, dealing in grain and produce. His business flourished in the postwar boom, and he sent wagons to Alexandria with his goods several times a year. He was commissioned a major in the First Battalion of the 55th Regulars of the Virginia militia,[119] and was known by the townspeople as Major B.[120] He and Abraham Shepherd both married into the prominent Strode family.

Major Bedinger served in the Virginia Legislature in 1793, and in 1798 he was appointed postmaster in Shepherdstown and was elected clerk of the county court. His election was vigorously contested by his opponent, Colonel David Hunter, who brought a lawsuit that dragged on for eight years, during which time Bedinger held the office.[121] When the suit finally went against Bedinger in 1801, he left Shepherdstown and built a home, which he called Protumna, on property in nearby Martinsburg.

The name *Protumna*, which appears to have Latin roots, does not translate directly, but the first two syllables, when taken individually, mean *for then*. Perhaps Bedinger saw Protumna as a place to begin his life's next phase. After Peter Light's death, Bedinger bought Lick Run Plantation in 1816.[122] At that time, the property included a large mill, barn, plantation house, blacksmith shop, a school, and a Methodist church.[123]

Bedinger had the old mill torn down and the present mill, with two large waterwheels powered by dependable year-round springs on upper Hoke Creek, built in its place. Some sources say this mill was built by Henry Myers, Peter Light's son-in-law.[124] The mill is still the newest structure on the Lick Run Plantation property.

The early establishment of mills on the site encouraged other development in the area, and the town of Bedington, named for Henry Bedinger, became a commercial center. His mill shipped flour as far as Alexandria, VA, via the Potomac River and later the Chesapeake & Ohio Canal.

Upon his death in 1843, Henry left his "Bedington estate" to his daughters Sarah Bedinger and Elizabeth Davenport, to be divided equally.[125]

According to Walter Ailes, whose family owned the mill from 1941-2021, Henry Bedinger never ran the mill himself or even lived on the Lick Run property. Ailes came across depositions filed in 1821 in which the man Bedinger hired to build the mill didn't get it done fast enough, and Bedinger lost the profits of a growing season. A millwright deposed in the case was asked to comment on the quality of the millstones and replied that the stones would "last my lifetime and after that I don't give a damn."[126]

Over the next century, the Bedinger Mill passed through several owners. When the technology became available, the mill was converted

This postcard shows another view of Bedington Mill, before the tandem mills were removed. Image courtesy of West Virginia & Regional History Center. Used with permission

to a roller mill. This is not surprising, as the mill was always a major player in the area's industrial landscape. The tandem waterwheels were removed at an unknown time.

Information reported in the different editions of the *West Virginia Gazetteer and business directory* tracks Bedington's growth. In 1882, the village had about 60 residents, a store, and the flour mill, which was run by John Kennedy. Among the amenities listed were daily mail service and express shipping from the local railroad stop.[127]

The 1904 *Gazetteer* boasted of a local telephone connection for the town's 110 residents. Mr. Kennedy still held his position at the mill.[128]

No records have been located that indicate when John Kennedy ceased working at the mill. In 1941, Wendell S. Porterfield sold 320 acres of land, the plantation house, and the Bedinger Mill to Helen W. and Stephen Ailes. Stephen Ailes' maternal grandfather had been governor of West Virginia. The mill was no longer operating, and when the Aileses nominated the property for inclusion on the National Register of Historic Places in 1983, the mill was described as "somewhat dilapidated."

The Ailes family owned the property for eighty years, during which time the stunning mansion house was featured in the Berkeley County Tour of Homes. Ailes sold the property to Joe Germino in July 2021. Since taking possession, Germino had a structural engineer assess the mill, revealing several rotten and broken supports that need to be replaced. The engineer expressed surprise that the mill was still standing and was wary of walking in several spots.

He also discovered it was "a heck of a lot of work" clearing out brush and poison ivy from the side of the mill where the waterwheel once was. He says workers at the mill doing repairs saw a stone marked with the date 1834.

Germino plans to have the mill made structurally sound, and if funds are available, install a waterwheel to produce electricity, and have a workshop on the first floor. One of his neighbors is an expert in carpentry and restoration, so perhaps it will happen someday. His primary objective is to keep the mill around and preserve the area's history for the next generation of folks.[129]

1. BUNKER HILL MILL

Berkeley County
Address: 714 Giles Mill Road (CR 26), Bunker Hill, WV 25413
Coordinates: 39.330220, -78.040194
Year Built: 1735
Period of Significance: 1735-1964
Added to the National Register of Historic Places in 1980

© Google Maps

Bunker Hill Mill, nestled in a curve on Giles Mill Road, occasionally suffers damage from passing trucks. Photo by Tracy Lawson

The Bunker Hill Mill, which dates to 1735, is the last remaining mill in Berkeley County's Mill District.

Just a few years after its completion, its builder, Thomas Anderson, sold the mill and 271 acres to his son Colbert, who owned it from 1738 until his death in 1749 at the age of thirty-six. The mill remained in the Anderson family until 1804, when Colbert Anderson, Jr. traded the mill and thirty-two acres of land for over 2,000 acres of Kentucky farmland.[130] Colbert married Isabel Van Meter (1811-1885), a daughter of Abraham and Nancy Van Meter. The Van Meters were a large, pioneering family, and doubtless Colbert and Isabel decided to head west with family members who moved to Kentucky around the turn of the nineteenth century. *(See Lyon's Mill, page 159 and Old Fields Mill, page 195)* Federal Census records from 1850 show Colbert Anderson III, the grandson of Colbert, Jr., and his family residing in Bath County, Kentucky.[131]

Much of the land around the hamlet of Bunker Hill belonged to General Elisha Boyd (1769-1841), a veteran of the War of 1812 who established an industrial village along the Mill Creek in the latter part of the eighteenth century, not unlike Henry Bedinger, who built up the village of Bedington for the same purpose. *(See Bedinger Mill, page 77)* Boyd had two mills, a brick-making operation, a cooperage [barrel factory], and a store built on Edgewood Manor, his plantation. He also helped establish the Martinsburg Academy.[132]

After the Civil War, Elisha's son, John E. Boyd, sold lots and built a second store, hoping to develop a town, selling the southernmost lots to newly freed black people.[133] Mt. Tabor Baptist Church, one of the original buildings raised on Ebony Way, is representative of a segregated community in the post–Civil War era. Ebony Way is located less than a mile from the Bunker Hill Mill via Giles Mill Road. Turn left at the corner by Bunker Hill Market and Country Store to view the historic church building.

The mill passed through a series of owners in the first half of the nineteenth century. Alfred Ross owned it in the 1850s, when the area was humming with business and the number of mills along the creek had reached its peak. Ross built a large brick residence in 1851, but by 1856 he was deeply in debt and was forced to sell the mill and adjacent acreage.

Samuel Matthews and Henry Zollickoffer bought the mill and engaged George T. Legg to run it.[134] The mill's tandem overshot waterwheels, then made of wood, could produce thirty horsepower.

The Bunker Hill Mill was a hybrid operation, with three-quarters of the mill's output flour for the commercial market and the rest custom-grinding for local farmers.[135]

In a twelve-month period in 1879-1880, the mill ground 22,000 bushels of wheat, valued at $19,800, into approximately 4,000 barrels of flour. The mill also ground 1,000 bushels of rye and barley, produced 27 tons of cornmeal and 166 tons of livestock feed. The total value of the mill's output that year was $25,790. With raw materials valued at $20,200, the mill showed a gross profit of $5,590, out of which they paid wages, purchased supplies, and maintained the machinery.[136]

Though this may seem like sufficient profit to avoid financial difficulties, records show that the mill ran at only three-quarters capacity for nine months of the year, and at only 50 percent capacity the remaining three months. It was not unusual for mills to operate at less than capacity at certain times of the year, especially when there was little rainfall. Frequent changes in ownership attest to how difficult it was to keep the mill running at a profit. After nearly two decades of running the mill for a wage, Legg purchased it in June 1881, but sold it just three months later. On at least three occasions the mill was sold at Chancery Court to settle its owners' debts.[137]

By 1880, only four of the fifteen mills that had dotted the landscape along Mill Creek in 1850 remained. Bunker Hill Mill was one of two with tandem waterwheels[138] but now has the only remaining set of tandem wheels in the state.

The 1892 *West Virginia Gazetteer and business directory* lists just one miller in Bunker Hill, J. B. Cunningham.[139] In 1904, S. B. Cunningham was operating a flour mill.[140]

A devastating fire in March 1887 added to the mill's woes, destroying the interior and leaving only the outer stone walls standing. The Martinsburg *Statesman* reported, "The flames are said to be the largest ever seen in this place. The ruin is visited daily by large numbers."[141]

Bunker Hill Mill has the last tandem wheels in the state.
Photo by Tracy Lawson

Within months, the mill was almost completely rebuilt, and by the end of that year operations resumed under the supervision of George T. Legg, the mill's longtime operator and short-lived owner. The grain elevator system extant in the mill suggests its original, eighteenth-century mechanicals were upgraded to an Oliver Evans-style system, though it may have been installed before the fire. The roller mills may also have been installed in 1887. The existing buhrstones would have been retained for grinding corn and animal feed.

The Overshoot Wheels Set #7741, manufactured by the nearby Fitz Water Wheel Company in Martinsburg, was likely installed during the rebuild by technicians trained by the manufacturer. This was standard procedure, with Fitz guaranteeing perfect balance and placement for wheels installed by their employees. The wheel closer to the millpond measures 14 feet 8 inches in diameter and 5 feet wide. The outside wheel, nearest the road, is 16 feet 2 inches in diameter and 6 feet wide. Each of the current wheels connects to an external spur in the basement and turns on a separate line, but a pulley system on each line shaft permits the cross connection, so one wheel can power both line shafts when necessary.[142]

The mill changed hands three more times by the turn of the twentieth century, and when Samuel S. Cline purchased it in 1906, and the mill became known as the Cline and Chapman Roller Mill. The mill ran exclusively on waterpower until 1920, when a twenty-horsepower Fairbanks-Morse diesel engine was installed and connected to the line shaft. This engine freed the miller from worries presented by an unreliable and insufficient water flow. A direct-current electric generator illuminated both the mill and the miller's house and powered the two flour-bleaching machines.[143] The DeHaven family, the last millers, owned the property from 1936 to the late 1960s and kept it in operation until 1964.[144]

Late in its life, the mill experienced years of renewed usefulness and prosperity, due to the increased demand for flour during the two World Wars. In the end, though, it did not fare well against larger mills due to the lack of a railroad spur to facilitate shipping.

In 1971, Paul and Janita Giles purchased the mill and ran a retail feed business there until 1995. Eric Custer, their grandson, is the current owner. Most of the equipment from the mill's nineteenth- and twentieth-century operations remains in the building, making it "more like a museum."[145] Bunker Hill Mill is an excellent example of an evolved mill that utilized changing technology to stay relevant well into the twentieth century.

The Bunker Hill Mill's Historical Architecture and Engineering Record (HAER) form gives detailed information about the milling process and the uses of its machinery and equipment:
Wheat brought into the mill was unloaded at the dock and shoveled into one of three basement hoppers. Elevators carried the grain to the mezzanine level, where chutes fed the grain to a Monitor Receiving Separator manufactured by Huntley, Cranson and Hammond.
Using sieves and screens, the separator removed coarse impurities like sticks, straw, and stones. An air blower removed dust and chaff. The Huntley machine could clean about 500 bushels of wheat per day. A Eureka Dustless Receiving Separator also on site may have been used with, or replaced, the Monitor.
The cleaned wheat was sent down chutes to the first floor for weighing, then to a temporary bin. Before grinding, the wheat was fed through a Eureka Perfected Milling Separator and a Eureka Horizontal Scourer for further cleaning. Then the wheat was ready for the roller mills.
The bulk of the flour was ground by a single Midget Marvel rolling mill, located on the first floor. The Midget Marvel employed two passes through corrugated "break" cylinders and then two passes through reduction reels. The resulting fine bran was sifted into two or three grades. The Midget Marvel could produce twenty-five barrels of flour per day.
Sent by elevator to one of eight storage bins on the second floor, some of the flour would be bleached by passing it through an Alsop Flour Bleacher, which used a high-voltage, low amp DC current, mixed with air to create oxide of nitrogen, which

whitened the flour. Corn crackers, a sifting machine, animal feed mixer, and automatic packing machine were also located in the mill at the time of the HAER inventory.[146]

30. JANNEY MILL

Berkeley County
Address: 100 Exchange Place, Martinsburg, WV 25401
Coordinates: 39.4619449, -77.9626451
Year Built: c. 1860
Period of Significance: c. 1860-1885
Added to the National Register of Historic Places as part of the Baltimore and Ohio Railroad and Related Industries Historic District in 1980

© Google Maps

The G. Campbell Janney building has housed several businesses.
Photo by Robert T. Kinsey

The building known as the G. Campbell Janney Mill may have spent the bulk of its existence housing other industries. Its origins are unknown. The two-and-a-half-story frame structure has reportedly been a plaster mill, a fertilizer plant, and most recently used for coal storage.[147] It is part of a complex of buildings at Exchange Place and the Baltimore & Ohio Railroad right-of-way that also contained the Tuscarora Iron Works/Matthews Foundry and the Middlesex Hosiery Mills/Martinsburg Paper Box Company.[148]

Though Janney may not have been in business there for more than a few years, members of the Janney family have been involved in milling since the late eighteenth century. Over a century later, one of their descendants emerged as an innovator in grain processing.

Aquilla Janney, a Quaker who migrated from Pennsylvania to Virginia before the American Revolution, was a miller who established his home on the banks of the Potomac nine miles below Alexandria. He was acquainted with General George Washington and had once entertained Washington in his home.[149]

Janney was pressed into service in the colonial army, but, being a Quaker, he refused to carry a weapon. Washington noticed a man in the ranks without a gun, and when he rode up to question him, recognized his acquaintance. Knowing Janney's religious objection to fighting, Washington wrote out a note discharging him and sent him home "until he was needed."[150]

In 1805, Janney was struck by lightning and killed while transporting a boatload of wheat across the Potomac from Maryland to Virginia. His widow, Ruth, moved to Martinsburg with their nine children, where she remarried. Aquilla's son Israel, who was just five years old when his father died, was educated in Martinsburg and married Mary Tabb in 1831.

Israel's son John Tabb Janney (1832-1919) ran a woolen mill in Martinsburg. In 1860, his mill processed 7,000 pounds of wool, purchased for $1,500, into cloth valued at $9,500. It has not been determined whether that mill was in the building known as the Janney Mill. On the population schedule for the census that year, he listed his occupation as "manufacturer."[151]

The 1880 Census shows John running an agricultural store and his 22-year-old son George working as a clerk. In the 1882-1883 *West Virginia Gazetteer*, George C. Janney has a business selling agricultural implements.[152]

George's son G. Campbell Janney headed west about this time and married Mary Howell in Clark County, Ohio, in 1881.

The J. H. Miller & Sons company moved into the Janney building. The following advertisement appeared in the local newspaper in 1892: "J. WM. & C. A. MILLER, Successors of J. H. MILLER & SONS, ESTABLISHED 1886. Agricultural Implements, Fertilizers, Coal, Wood & c. & c. We carry the largest stock in the city. Buy all our goods in car load lots and can sell at lower prices than our competitors. All goods sold on their merits. WE GUARANTEE TO GIVE SATISFACTION. Wagons and Fine Buggies A SPECIALTY. Near the B&O Freight Depot, Martinsburg, W. Va."[153]

In 1893, the Muncie, Indiana, Directory listed G. Campbell Janney as the president and treasurer of the Common Sense Engine Company, manufacturers of corn planters, hay rakes, and corn grinding machines.

The Janney Manufacturing Company incorporated in Ottumwa, Iowa, on August 1, 1889, with G. Campbell Janney as president, M. H. Janney as vice president, and R. Janney as secretary.[154] M. H. Janney may have been Mary Howell Janney, Campbell's wife, and the full identity of R. Janney is uncertain. Mr. Janney was "born in Virginia, but for many years was in business in Indiana. His present business has been his life work, and he has met with great success."[155]

The company's Common Sense Corn Husker, Fodder Shredder, and Triple Gear Feed Mill were "especially designed and built for handling the corn crop in the greatest corn state in the Union."[156]

The triple-geared grinding mill, run with the power generated by two horses, could grind a bushel of dry corn in three and a half minutes.[157]

Janney's technological innovations made home corn grinding an option for farmers and reduced the need for the small custom mills that had once been an integral part of every community.

This pin advertises the Janney Common Sense Mill.
From the author's collection

3. PATTERSON MILL

Berkeley County
Address: 600 North Tennessee Avenue, Martinsburg, WV 25401
Coordinates: 39.470976, -77.979728
Year built: 1765
Period of Significance: 1765-c. 1930
Added to the National Register of Historic Places as part of Tuscarora Creek Historical District in 1980

© Google Maps

Patterson Mill
Photo by Tracy Lawson

The four-story, limestone Patterson Mill dominates the northern edge of War Memorial Park in Martinsburg. It is in very good condition for a building that has not been in use for nearly a century.

Richard Beeson, Sr., owner of the original patent, sold the land to William Patterson in 1758. Patterson built the mill in 1765. Before he died in 1782, Patterson began construction on a second mill nearby, known as Patterson's New Mill.[158] *(See Patterson's New Mill, page 99)* In his will, Patterson left:

> ...to my son, Hugh Vance Patterson, my old mill and the remainder of my land on Tuscarora that is all the land from my son William's line along the line of that land I bought of Samuel Strode and adjoining the lands of Jas. Mendenhall, Joseph McCay, Matthew Duncan, Edward Beeson and Adam Stephens and with his to the Division Line of my son David's and with his Line that is the new road cutting from my old mill to Martenburgh and from thence bounding on my son David's and my son Williams' site it intersects the aforesaid Line of the land I bought of Samuel Strode to him his heirs and assigns forever.[159]

Hugh Patterson operated a merchant mill in Berkeley County during the War of 1812.[160] He died sometime before 1850. The Federal Census for that year shows the couple's twin sons Samuel and William, unmarried and aged 35, living with their widowed mother, Elizabeth Christie Patterson.[161]

After Hugh Patterson's death, the mill's next owners are not known, but I did find some clues in census data.

In 1860, William T. Yontz, John G. Fisher, and John Cushwa, all millers, lived near the Patterson Mill in Martinsburg's District 9,[162] though none of their names appear as mill owners on the 1860 Federal Census Non-Population Industry Schedule.

In 1870 census records, William T. Yontz, Barnet and George Cushwa, David Daniels, and William Plowman, all found on the same page, report working as millers.[163]

It seems likely William T. Yontz (1817-1875) was the longtime miller at Patterson Mill after Hugh Patterson's death. Yontz was born in Shepherdstown, in neighboring Jefferson County, where a Yontz Mill was once in operation.

By 1882, Hedgesville was an incorporated village and was made a separate entry in the *West Virginia Gazetteer* for that year. There is no miller at work in the village's business directory that year,[164] nor in the 1891-1892[165] and 1900-1901 directories.[166] In the 1904-1905 edition, though, Thomas Ardinger was operating a mill.[167]

Census data from 1900 shows twenty-three-year-old Thomas operating a mill with his father, Joseph Thornton Van Lear Ardinger.[168] In the elder Ardinger's will, dated 1904, Joseph leaves his stock in the Independent Roller Mill Company to his wife.[169]

Thomas Ardinger does not appear to have worked in the milling business after his father's death, instead holding a variety of jobs from insurance agent to furniture store manager. No records pertaining to the Independent Roller Mill Company could be located.

Bill and Karen Rice, the mill's current owners, are the third generation of the Rice family to live at Elm Dale, the farmhouse adjacent to the mill. While they know little of the mill's history, a surviving ledger from the 1860s lists soldiers who purchased flour there during the Civil War.[170]

Bill's grandfather, Lacy I. Rice Sr. purchased the property from the Kilmer family in 1931. He gutted Elm Dale, built an addition on the rear of the house, and added side porches.

When Lacy, Jr.'s mother died about six weeks before his wedding, he and his new bride moved into Elm Dale with his father. Bill, the current owner, has lived in Elm Dale his entire life.

The Rice family has had about half the stones repointed and the tin roof put on the building. Some of the equipment, chutes, and buhrstones remain inside.[171]

The miller's house across the street is included in the Tuscarora Creek Historical District.

When you visit, be sure to park in the public lot at War Memorial Park rather than in the Rice's driveway.

Patterson Mill is not open to the public, but you're free to take a stroll around the outside. Take note of a long, narrow depression in the earth. That is the path of the millrace that once flowed to the mill's south side. Though cattails fill the stone-lined tailrace and the millpond, the opening on the south wall where the mill wheel was mounted on its shaft is visible. This is a great spot for taking photos.

Cattails line the mill race and mill pond.
Photo by Tracy Lawson

47. PATTERSON'S NEW MILL

Berkeley County
Address: 200 Old Mill Road, Martinsburg, WV 25401
Coordinates: 39.4699270, -77.9858390
Date Built: 1910
Period of Significance: c. 1782-1908
Added to the National Register of Historic Places as part of the Tuscarora Creek Historical District in 1980

© Google Maps

Patterson's New Mill, which once stood near this site, is one of at least three built by James Patterson in the late 1700s. Photo by Elmer Napier

The mill became a private residence in the 1990s.
Photo courtesy of Sarah Stover

Three mills stood on this site at different times, but it was always Grandma's house to the young wife and mom who now calls it home.

Sarah Stover has fond memories of growing up in the area. Her parents' property was connected to the mill property by a field that led to Tuscarora Creek. She and her brothers would follow the creek under the interstate bridge on the walk to visit their grandmother. They had a rope swing and had dammed up the creek to make a swimming hole. After playing in the creek, they would go spend the day at their grandmother's.

"The best thing about living in this house," she said, "is that I still have a piece of [my grandmother] with me. It doesn't feel like her home anymore since she's not here, sitting in her chair, but it's nice to know I get to continue what she started."

William Patterson, who purchased the land on which the mill stands in 1758,[172] built at least three mills in what is now Berkeley County, which was formed in 1772 from the northern part of Frederick County, Virginia.[173] His will, dated 1782, refers to the "saw mill now erected" and makes provision the completion of "the mills I am now erecting." Patterson willed that his executors could choose either to rent or sell the mills once completed, and the proceeds go toward supporting his daughters.[174]

William Patterson built a second mill in the area prior to his death in 1782, which burned down in the 1820s. Aaron Hibbard, a Quaker, built a fulling mill on the ruined mill's foundation. Woolen cloth created on a manual loom has a very loose weave and frays easily. Fulling mills were used to pound the fabric to tighten the fibers, while also eliminating excess fat and animal hair.[175]

The National Register of Historic Places (NRHP) Nomination Form for the Tuscarora Creek Historical District, filed in 1979, states that "remains of the fulling mill, in operation by 1810, survive, though in derelict condition. Some machinery remains inside, along with evidence of its later use as a grain mill, including a stencil 'Dixie Corn Mill' on the framing timbers."[176]

In 1797, Patterson's son, William, Jr., the last surviving executor, sold the sawmill and gristmill to Jacob Hess.[177] Three years later, Hess sold to James Mendenhall, who died intestate in 1816.[178] According to records in Sarah Stover's possession, the property was divided among Mendenhall's heirs, and one portion was sold to Aaron Hibberd around 1817.

Ten years later, Abel and Lydia Mendenhall Janney, heirs, also sold their portion to Aaron Hibberd: "a lot of land on which stood the grist mill or merchant mill and sawmill both of which were burned a few years since."[179] Abel Janney's father, John Jonas Janney (1749-1829), was a younger brother of Aquilla Janney.[180] *(See Janney Mill, page 91)*

Aaron Hibbard rebuilt the mills sometime in the 1830s, and in 1839, the remaining Mendenhall heirs sold their portions to him. His daughter, Mary Ann Hibbard, inherited the mill when he died around 1850. However, it appears Mary Ann sold the land to her sister, Lydia Dare, who paid taxes on the property until 1867.[181] Lydia's heirs sold the property, which included twelve acres of land with the gristmill, sawmill, and a dwelling house to Henry Bender for $4,500 in 1868.[182]

Bender, who reported his occupation as a lumber dealer,[183] set up a trust in 1869 for the use and benefit of his wife, Rebecca Doyle Bender, and transferred the mills, the house, and twelve acres of land to his brother Americus to manage.[184] Less than a year later, Americus conveyed the same property back to Henry.[185]

As I pored over the documents regarding the trust, questions came to mind. Did Henry have health problems that would make it prudent to plan for his wife's maintenance after his death? Did Henry have Southern sympathies, and thought putting the property in trust for his wife was a way to keep his assets from being seized?

Americus reported having "no profession" in the 1870 Census.[186] The same census data shows Americus was eligible to vote, so he was not disenfranchised after the Civil War. He had registered for the draft along with another brother, Peter.[187]

Americus was about twenty years younger than his brother Henry and was living with Henry and Rebecca in 1870 and 1880. He died relatively young, before the age of sixty.

Americus was likely disabled, perhaps due to a war wound, or had recurring health problems related to his military service that precluded him doing physical labor.

Rebecca Bender apparently did not share Henry's sense of over-preparedness. When she died in 1905, she had not prepared a will, and a special commissioner was appointed by the Berkeley County Circuit Court to settle her estate. In 1908, Charles Wolford purchased the Bender's Mill property, the same twelve acres and buildings conveyed to Rebecca Bender by Americus Bender.[188]

Sarah Stover's great-great-grandfather, Charles Wolford, who was the first in her family to own the mill, came into possession of it in 1908. After a fire destroyed the mill the following year, Charles tore down the burned section and built the present building on the foundation around 1910. The mill's turbine remains in the basement, and some lower-level beams show signs of fire damage.

An old photo of the mill and sawmill as they appeared prior to 1910 shows a squat, hipped-roof structure, clapboard over a stone foundation, with a gable-roofed building immediately to the rear. The house built on the foundation of the building which sat closest to Old Mill Road has the shape and character of its predecessor, except it has modern siding and a wraparound deck. A dam remains across Tuscarora Creek, which flows through an opening in the stone wall that abuts the mill's foundation.

The property has been passed down through members of the Wolford family, including Sarah's great-grandfather Frank Wolford, who sold it to his only daughter, Sarah's grandmother, Frances Ridgeway, in 1991 for three dollars. Frances took on the task of restoring the house and lived there until her death in 2018.

Sarah, her husband, RJ, and their three young children have lived in the house since 2019. Because the house has been in the family so long, some of Sarah's relatives don't want to see it changed at all, but the Stovers plan to renovate the house to better fit the needs of their young family.

Sarah says that even though the house requires constant attention and care, she would not trade living there for anything. "My husband loves having his own garage, tractor, and land to take care of. He always said when he grew up, he wanted to buy this house. I don't think he realized what he was getting into when he married me!"

7. STEPHEN-HAMMOND-OLD SPRING MILL

Berkeley County
Address: 2868 Hammonds Mill Road, Hedgesville, WV 25427
Coordinates: 39.5592122, -77.9546341
Year Built: c. 1790
Period of Significance: 1790- c. 1945
Added to the National Register of Historic Places as part of Spring Mills Historical District in 2004

© Google Maps

The Stephen/Hammond/Old Spring Mill was built by Robert Stephen, the brother of Martinsburg's founder, in 1789. Photo by Elmer Napier

Both Union and Confederate forces prowled the area near Hedgesville's Hammond Mill during the Civil War. Now, locals say the spirit of one soldier haunts a lonely stretch of Route 901 near the deserted mill. But its origins go back much farther, to the post-Revolutionary period, when settlers hastened to start businesses in the "west," on the far side of Virginia's Blue Ridge.

In 1789, Robert Stephen, brother of Martinsburg's founder, Major General Adam Stephen, paid 1,850 pounds Pennsylvania currency for 276 acres near the village of Hedgesville and built the three-story stone mill and the 1,800-square-foot stone miller's residence that stands across the road.[189] Adam Stephen established at least three mills in Martinsburg.[190]

Berkeley County land records from 1820 show the mill and 700 acres owned by Adam Stephen, who may have been Robert Stephen's son. By the late 1830s, Robert, in debt to his brother, Alexander, turned over the property to him and his brother-in-law Isaac Lauck. Alexander Stephen listed the mill and 400 acres for sale in 1839: "A mill, 45' by 65', three stories, of stone and a hip roof, giving the five floors all garnered off complete. There are in the mill three turn of stone, and all labor-saving machinery, metal gearing from pit to garret, and all nearly new. Within 30 yards of the mill is a large stone distillery with full patent stills, and now in operation."[191]

While there is no way to know what Alexander meant by "labor-saving machinery," it is possible the mill was outfitted with an Oliver Evans system, which would have been available around the time the original mill was built.

In October 1839, Dr. Allen C. Hammond bought the Spring Mill property for $18,000. It is likely that Dr. Hammond hired a miller to handle the day-to-day responsibility of the mill while he practiced medicine.[192]

The 1860 Federal Census Non-Population Schedule provides the following information about Hammond's milling enterprise:

- Water powered Grist Mill 1,000 bushels of wheat flour valued at $6,000

- Water powered Chopping Mill processed 8,000 bushels of (corn and rye) valued at $5,500
- Steam powered Distillery used 5,000 bushels of corn and rye to produce 30,000 gallons of whiskey valued at $6,000.[193]

During the Civil War, both armies frequented the area. Historians believe Stonewall Jackson's troops crossed the Potomac at Williamsport and camped at Hammond's Mill during the Chalmersburg campaign in 1862.[194] In the summer of 1864, Confederate troops were known to pass by the mill on at least three occasions.[195] A map illustrating the route of Stuart's Cavalry Division October 9-12, 1862 & June 25-July 2, 1863, shows an encampment on October 5, 1862, near Hammond's Mill.[196]

A Southern sympathizer whose son served in the Confederate forces, Dr. Hammond spent the war years as an army surgeon and suffered financial reversals as a result. Max Oates, a local businessman whose family has owned the property since the 1940s, stated that the Hammonds were among few Southern sympathizers in the area, and because of Dr. Hammond's political affiliation, county officials raised his taxes after the war, until he could no longer maintain the property.

Hammond asserted that both armies used his home as a hospital during the war. A report written by Lieutenant Richard G. Prendergast, First New York Cavalry, states Prendergast's troops attacked and pursued a detachment of the Seventy Virginia Cavalry, wounding and capturing thirteen of them:

Headquarters Cavalry Picket, Hammond's House, Va., December 11, 1862…I pursued them to the base of Bunker Hill when, seeing that they were supported by the rest of that regiment…I halted, and returned unpursued. My only casualty is the slight wounding of one horse. Two of the prisoners are wounded with the saber, one very seriously.[197]

Dr. Hammond sold the mill and 415 acres to Joseph Duvall in 1866.[198] By 1870, he was retired and living in neighboring Jefferson County.

It is not known if the Duvalls continued the milling enterprise.[199] After Joseph's death in October 1885, the property remained in the family until 1945, when it was sold to the Oates family, who repointed the stone and put in new trusses and a tin roof. The mill is empty inside, and the family has no plans to do anything with it in the future.

Max Oates, instrumental in the renovation and preservation of the Dr. Hammond House after it suffered extensive fire damage in the 1970s, recalled that as a boy, he ventured out to the spring house on the property, which was used for refrigeration until the 1950s.

While he acknowledged rumors of the ghostly history of the Hammond house and mill, he puts no stock in them, as paranormal investigators spent three weekends on the property and found no evidence of otherworldly activity.

Other paranormal investigators report that people have seen ghostly lights and heard sounds coming from the second and third stories of the mill, even though there's no way to access the upper levels where the floors have rotted away.[200] Theresa's Haunted History of the Tri-State website combines "the fact with the folklore," and posted the story of a couple driving Route 901 near the mill late one foggy night. As the story goes, a wounded, ragged Confederate soldier limped out of the fog. The startled driver slowed the car, and, seeming desperate for help, the soldier placed his hands on the hood of the couple's car with a thump. He looked pleadingly at them and then collapsed. When they got out of the car, he had vanished, but the bloody handprints on the car remained.[201]

Hedgeville's cluster of older homes gave way to rolling fields and farms and a sprinkling of new subdivisions. The mill is nestled in a blind curve, and there's no safe place to stop. After I passed it once, I turned around and made a somewhat risky turn into the short driveway at the mill.

Though a chain across the drive is meant to discourage trespassers, the mill had suffered some recent vandalism. The site is overgrown, and all the windows shuttered. I did not venture into the vegetation near the mill. Graffiti aside, the mill's attractive stone exterior is in very good condition.

22. TUSCARORA IRON WORKS

Berkeley County
Address: 420 Queen Street, Martinsburg, WV 25401
Coordinates: 39.4615051, -77.9626332
Year Built: before 1840
Period of Significance: 1840-1902
Added to the National Register of Historic Places as part of the Tuscarora Creek Historical District in 1979

© Google Maps

The Tuscarora Iron Works, an early industrial building, is expected to be adapted for reuse. Photo by Tracy Lawson

"A man with a valuable [source of] water power cannot afford to take an inefficient wheel as a gift." *The Fitz Water Wheel Company Bulletin No. 70*, 1928.

A section of the Opequon Creek forms part of the eastern boundary of Berkeley County. Three smaller creeks empty into the Opequon and increase its water flow before it empties into the Potomac. Tuscarora Creek is the largest of these three.[202]

The Tuscarora Creek Historical District contains the early industrial building built around 1840, which grew to national prominence as the home of the Fitz Water Wheel Company. The stone foundry building, built prior to 1840, has two stories with lofty twelve-foot ceilings and is 140 feet long and 45 feet wide. The factory drew waterpower from the Tuscarora Creek using the same dam as Equality Mills, which stood across the street.[203]

The building is rubble stone with corner quoining and was extended later, so there are several brick courses atop the stone sides with brick parapets on the gable ends.[204]

Wooden waterwheels were constructed with "elbow bucket" sections that had buckets, or pockets, set at about a forty-five-degree angle to receive the water that flowed over the top of the wheel.[205]

Wooden wheels swelled and dried, resulting in loose parts and leaky buckets that reduced efficiency. In winter, wooden wheels froze, so northern millers often placed them inside the mill. Bloomery Mill in Hampshire County is one such example. Even under optimal circumstances, Fitz claimed wood wheels and turbines "will often allow enough water to leak away at night through its defective gates, to run a Fitz Overshoot Wheel for several hours a day."[206]

The average life of a wooden wheel was ten to thirty years, depending on how diligently the miller attended to repairs and maintenance. All-metal wheels, in contrast, required less fuss. They didn't freeze, and unlike turbines, which lost efficiency with a small shift in water pressure, vertical waterwheels could continue to run in a low water-volume situation. This made metal wheels ideal for factories and farms where product production must continue even though water tables varied during the year.[207]

In 1840, Samuel Fitz was operating the Hanover Foundry in Hanover, Pennsylvania, a machine shop that fabricated spur gears and metal parts for horse-drawn wagons, as well as wooden waterwheels. Ten years later, Fitz took over the Tuscarora Iron Works in Martinsburg. At the time, some waterwheels were being made with metal hubs and axles, and all-metal wheels had been manufactured in England.[208]

Fitz's all-metal wheel, introduced in 1852, is believed to be the first of its kind manufactured in the United States.[209] Samuel's son John is credited with improving the design to produce the Fitz Overshoot Water Wheel in 1870. The Overshoot Wheel used a curvilinear bucket, rather than the elbow buckets that had been in use for a century which were not shaped to the optimum curve to retain water. The Fitz Company was the first to apply mass-production techniques to waterwheel construction.

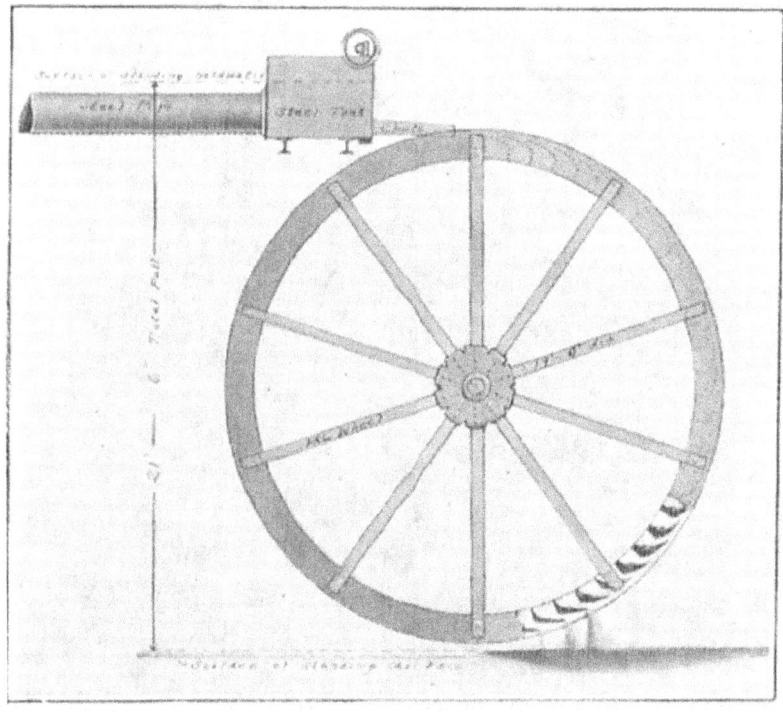

Fitz Wheel diagram

This Leffel turbine is on display at Indian Mill in Wyandot County, Ohio. Photo by Tracy Lawson.

The first all-metal wheel off the line was installed in Samuel Fitz's flour mill, Equality Mills, which was located across Queen Street from the foundry. The 1860 Federal Census Non-Population Schedule for Industry in Berkeley County shows Samuel Fitz operating a flour mill, a chopping mill, a foundry, and machine shop.[210] The wheel installed at Equality Mills was still in use there seventy years later.[211]

In Fitz's design, the water enters the buckets ten inches behind vertical center. The curved buckets reduce impact and spillage and retain the water longer in the wheel—almost to the bottom vertical position at the tailrace. The Fitz Overshoot Water Wheel claimed up to 90 percent efficiency.[212]

With Fitz's standard bucket design, for every foot of bucket width, the wheel could handle 2.7 cubic feet of water per second (cfs).[213]

Under John Fitz's management, the company merged the Hanover and Tuscarora factories in the 1870s and acquired a turbine company. Fitz continued to manufacture wooden wheels for clients who preferred them, and manufactured and repaired metal wheels.

In the 1880s, something of a propaganda war developed between The Fitz Water Wheel Company and its chief competitor, the James Leffel Turbine Company of Springfield, Ohio.

Leffel's *Illustrated Handbook to the Improved Turbine Water Wheel* warned, "To those about to select a water wheel: Do not purchase a common water wheel because from its *low* price it may *seem* to be *cheap*. The *best* is the cheapest because it *does more work*, lasts longer, and *costs no more to erect* than a common wheel. The Leffel Improved Double Turbine Water Wheel is the *best*, and consequently, the *cheapest*."[214]

Fitz Company literature claimed, "It is well known that when you buy a turbine from any builder you don't get near as good a wheel as one he builds especially to be tested,"[215] and "The capacity of a turbine is unchangeable. If you have more water than you need, it is wasted. If less, it will hardly turn the wheel. The Fitz Wheel is able to adapt to varying conditions."[216]

After the consolidation, by 1902, the workings of the Martinsburg plant were moved to Hanover. The company continued to grow and changed its name to the Fitz Water Wheel Company of Hanover, PA.[217]

Fitz produced waterwheels that ranged from four to forty-five feet in diameter and one to sixteen feet in width, built in sections for assembly on site. By the late 1920s, Fitz was the largest vertical waterwheel manufacturer in the world and offered a full line of turbines.

As steam, diesel, and gas engines rose in popularity in the 1930s, Fitz stayed in business by restoring existing wheels and fabricating other machine parts. The company reported record sales in 1932, in the depths of the Depression.[218] Fitz wheels were also used to power municipal hydroelectric plants and water systems and to run pumps for farms and greenhouses.

After the Fitz Company ceased business at the death of Samuel Fitz's grandson John Samuel Fitz in 1965,[219] Leffel purchased and then destroyed the Fitz templates and patterns so no other company could revive the manufacture of Fitz products.[220]

The foundry remained with Fitz heirs until 1894, when it was sold to H. T. Cushwa. In 1913, brothers Thomas Edward (1861-1934) and Josiah David Matthews (1863-1941), who were a machinist[221] and an iron moulder, respectively, in the foundry in 1910,[222] bought a half interest in the building and acquired the other half in 1921. The 1913 Martinsburg City Directory listing reads:

"Matthews, T. E. and Bro. (Thomas E and Josiah D) Founders and Machinists, 420 N. Queen."[223]

In 1930, Thomas was the manager at a foundry[224] and Josiah was a foundryman and the owner of the business.[225] Among their products are most of the ornate ironwork, coal chutes, and manhole, sewer, and water drain covers found in Martinsburg.[226]

After the Matthews Foundry ceased operations for good in 1994, redevelopment efforts were tinged with the worry that the site would need a great deal of remediation to make it safe for public use. But in 2013, a report from Boggs Environmental Consultants in Frederick, MD, concluded there was "no recognizable environmental concern" at the site and "the perceptions about the foundry's contamination are misplaced."[227] Residual levels of contaminants in the soil inside the foundry could easily be capped by a layer of concrete.

Several groups have taken an interest in bringing the foundry back to life. Main Street Martinsburg, an organization formed to assist in revitalizing the downtown commercial district through historic preservation and economic redevelopment, acts as a liaison with other state agencies. Its parent organization, the National Main Street Center, is affiliated with the National Trust for Historic Preservation.[228]

In 2014, Main Street Martinsburg received a $3,000 technical assistance grant from West Virginia Redevelopment Collaborative, a program of the Northern Brownfields Assistance Center at West Virginia University. The center exists to help community organizations develop funding and marketing strategies for successful redevelopment of "brownscape" sites, which are blighted properties with potential hazmat issues.

In 2018, Martinsburg-based D&W Property Management purchased the foundry building and two acres of land surrounding it on North Queen Street, which includes a now-closed concrete bridge over Tuscarora Creek.[229] The owners are researching the property's history and intend to install a waterwheel to generate some portion of the power for the structure.

Recently, the Martinsburg Mills & Rail Corridor Revitalization Initiative has made reuse recommendations for the building, and teams of West Virginia University and Johns Hopkins University students were asked to help spur redevelopment of Matthews Foundry by designing environmentally sensitive plans for the building's future use. A microbrewery and a restaurant are popular suggestions.[230]

The Berkeley County Historical Society reports that, as of April 2021, current owner, D&W Properties, is in the early processes of adapting the building for reuse.

19. UNION BRYARLY MILL

Berkeley County
Address: 88 Bryarly Mill Lane, Inwood, WV 25428
Coordinates: 39.3748381, -78.0210426
Year Built: 1835
Period of Significance: 1791-1900
Placed on National Register of Historic Places in 1980 as Union Bryarly's Mill and as part of the Darkesville Historical District

© Google Maps

Union Bryarly Mill - Photo by Elmer Napier

The second mill to stand on the site, Union Bryarly Mill has been owned by the same family since it was built in 1810.
Photo by Tracy Lawson

Union Bryarly Mill, the only remaining brick gristmill in Berkeley County,[231] is the second mill on the site, on land that has been owned by the Bryarly family for well over two centuries. The two-story, three-bay, gable-roofed structure has much of the milling equipment inside, but the waterwheel was removed and sent to another mill around 1890.[232] The mill and the nearby distillery, also owned by the Bryarly family, operated until around 1900.

The first mill on the site was built in 1791 by James Buckles, Edward Beeson, and Benjamin Shipman. Buckles laid out the town first known as Bucklestown on plantation land acquired from his father, Robert Buckles, a Revolutionary War soldier. He built the mill to establish industry in his new community and to draw trade from the people on neighboring farms and plantations. The town was later renamed Darkesville in honor of General William Darke.

The original mill had one pair of buhrstones and one pair of culling stones. Cologne stones from the Rhine region were used for the coarse or country grinding of cornmeal, buckwheat, and animal feed.[233] The Cologne stones may have been used as the "chopping mill" for their distillery.

Robert P. Bryarly (1783-1848), bought a 900-acre tract of the Buckles land in 1802 and later built the large brick mill that stands on the site. Bryarly built a manor house for his eldest son, Richard, and six other houses on parcels of land for his children to inherit when he died.

The mill property, which has passed from Richard Henry Bryarly (1812-1880) to Henry Payne Bryarly (1869-1947), and Robert P. Bryarly (1910-1993), is currently owned by Karen Bryarly Trenary. The manor house has also passed to each of the mill owners.

In 1882-1883, the *Gazetteer* lists Mrs. M. P. Bryarly as the owner of a grist and sawmill,[234] which would have been Henry Payne Bryarly's wife, Mary. In the 1891-1892 *Gazetteer* she was still the owner, but the listing was for a gristmill only, so it appears any sawmill business had ceased in the years between.[235] There is no way to know if Mrs. Bryarly took part in the day-to-day operations, but it speaks to women taking a role as a partner in running a rural enterprise, especially in the dawning of the modern age.

In the 1860 Federal Census Non-Population Industrial Schedule, Union Bryarly Mill took in 3,500 bushels of wheat valued at $3,675 and produced 700 bushels of flour for sale valued at $4,000, and 2,000 bushels of corn and rye valued at $1,400.

Comparing the price of the flour to that reported by other millers in the area, it appears wheat flour sold for around $6.00/bushel at that time.[236]

There are approximately forty-one pounds of flour in a bushel. One bushel of wheat weighs sixty pounds and yields about forty-two pounds of white flour and approximately sixty pounds of whole wheat flour.

I had the opportunity to visit with John and Karen Bryarly Trenary, who met me at the homeplace and took me on a tour of the mill. Much of the equipment is still in the building, and I got my first look at a flake augur, which would have been used to move grain from one step in processing to another, and some wooden wheels with lattice designs that piqued my curiosity.

Though the waterwheel is long gone, the main driveshaft and gears remain in the lower level.

After the tour, we pored over mill ledgers dating back to the 1840s, which show the mill was known as Middle Creek Mill for a time in the 1800s. Numerous entries for "stuff" led Karen to wonder if the term was code for liquor from the family's distillery. The ledgers show the Bryarlys sold a variety of goods in addition to grain and liquor, and "stuff" was recorded across the columns so often that we determined it referred to miscellaneous items, just as it does nowadays.

The Trenarys have no children and expressed concern about who will be the mill's next steward.

BERKELEY COUNTY

1867 Middle Creek Mills

John Aikens

Date	Entry	Stuff	flour	wheat
Aug 12"	To 100 of flour 21st To 100 of flour		200	
31st	to 100 of flour Sep 14" To 100 flour		200	
Sep 28"	To flour		200	
1868 Mar 6"	By Wheat To flour To Stuff	389	392	31 40
June 4"	To 100 flour July 15" To 125 of flour		225	
July 28"	To flour Aug 7" By Wheat		100	8 04
Aug 7"	To flour To Stuff	176	196	
22nd	To flour		100	
Sep 1st	By Wheat To flour		294	5 48
5"	By Wheat To flour		196	7 00
Oct 7"	To flour To Stuff	65	100	
1869 Feb 4"	By Wheat By J J Lowery			30 00
March 30"	By Wheat To flour To Stuff	30	98	1 30
April 9"	To flour To Stuff	60	196	
May 1st	To flour To Stuff	57	196	
20"	To flour		100	
24"	By Wheat To flour To Stuff	127	392	5 20
June 8	To flour		100	
July 8	To flour To Stuff	60	100	
19"	To 65 of flour 27" To 50 of flour		115	
Sep 25"	To flour		98	
Oct 11"	To flour To Stuff	50	98	

Page from Union Bryarly Mill ledgers
Photo by Tracy Lawson

Page from Union Bryarly Mill ledgers
Photo by Tracy Lawson

Jefferson County
Formed from Berkeley County in 1801

37. BEELER'S MILL

Jefferson County
Address: 6517 Kabletown Road (CR 25), Charles Town, WV 25414
Coordinates: 39.2509546, -77.8410457
Year Built: 1878
Period of Significance: 1761-1946
Added to the register of Jefferson County, West Virginia, Historic Landmarks in 2015

© Google Maps

Beeler's Mill's 22-foot Fitz wheel - Photo by Tracy Lawson

Just the wheel? That's it?

If that thought crossed your mind, I guarantee you won't think about what's missing when you behold the twenty-two-foot-high Fitz wheel in Tom and Barbara Ingersoll's front yard. There's no better way to gain an appreciation for the size and construction of a waterwheel than when it's not dwarfed by an adjacent building. At twenty-two feet in diameter by four feet wide,[237] this wheel is considered of above-average size, but standing alone on the Ingersoll's lawn, it appears huge.

First, a little background on what's missing over at Beeler's—the mill that once derived its power from the wheel. Christopher Beeler purchased the property in 1752 and built a wool carding mill on the site by 1761. This type of mill mechanized the labor-intensive process of combing out all the tangles in wool fibers prior to spinning it into thread, which sped up the process of making clothing and other textiles for home use.[238]

In 1789, Christopher's son Benjamin acquired the mill and operated a carding mill and gristmill on the site. Benjamin's will, dated 1827, directed that the mills be repaired and left as a portion of the dower to his widow, Sarah. When Sarah remarried Abraham Isler, the property became part of his estate. By the end of the Civil War, the mill was over a century old. J. B. McElroy bought the mill for $2,800 from the Islers' heirs in 1869, and within ten years it was falling into disrepair.[239]

William F. Weirick and John Weller, two prominent businessmen in Charles Town, purchased the mill for $600 through Jefferson County Chancery court and built a four-story gristmill on the site. The new mill was powered by the extant Fitz Overshoot Wheel, one of thousands mass-produced at the Tuscarora Iron Works in nearby Martinsburg and used in small mills in eastern rural America into the twentieth century.[240]

Within the next few years, Weirick and Weller build a sawmill on the property, and Robert J. Weirick was listed as the proprietor of a flour mill four miles south of Charles Town in the 1904 *West Virginia Gazetteer and business directory*.[241] A fire destroyed the gristmill in 1907, which was rebuilt by the Clipp family, who purchased the property around 1920. They reused the Fitz wheel in the new mill.

In 1946, T. Wilmer Clipp dismantled the mill and used the lumber to build the Children's Haven orphanage in Bloomery, which operated from the mid-1940s through the 1960s. Clipp sold the Beeler's Mill property to D. Edgar Stultz.[242]

Sheila Birnbach, who owned the property from 2000-2007, and the Ingersolls, the current owners, are responsible for significant restoration and repairs to the property.

The original millrace has been altered over the years, and though water can be piped out of nearby Evitts Run to power the wheel, the wheel is currently immobilized, awaiting excavation and repair of the north wall of the tailrace. The drystone wall is failing, and the vibration from the rotation of the wheel could further destabilize it.

52. FEAGANS MILL

Jefferson County
Address: 175 Wheatland Road, Kabletown, WV 25414
Coordinates: 39.24203 -77.92174
Year Built: 1940
Period of Significance: 1794-1944
Added to the National Register of Historic Places in 2017

© Google Maps

Feagans Mill - Photo by Elmer Napier

In 1748, then-sixteen-year-old George Washington surveyed the Eastern Panhandle for Lord Fairfax. Impressed with the region, Washington bought land along Bullskin Run in 1750. He continued to acquire land and at one time owned more than 2,300 acres in the Eastern Panhandle.[243]

Early Quaker settlers in Jefferson County left a legacy in Feagans Mill, which rose from the ashes twice. Today, it is owner Danny Lutz's dream to restore the mill to its World War II-era glory. Lutz is the Jefferson County supervisor for the Eastern Panhandle Conservation District, which provides services to farmers and homeowners using various cost-share programs, equipment rentals, and conservation education activities.

The mill is a gable-roofed, two-story, three-bay rectangular structure measuring forty-four feet wide by thirty-four feet deep. Its wooden exterior is covered in sheets of ornamental pressed metal.

The foundation of randomly laid stone and brick may be the original and date to around 1795, as records show all the mills built on this site have been of the same dimensions.[244]

Feagans is the only mill in Jefferson County that could, with repairs, be made operational. Its Fitz waterwheel, two run of buhrstones, sifters, elevators, bolter, a leveler, and bagger remain in place from the 1940 iteration of the mill.[245] A gasoline-powered engine located on the mill's first floor was used to supplement waterpower during dry spells or when the water in the millpond was frozen.[246]

From the 1760s to the 1880s, wheat was a major export crop for the lower Shenandoah Valley.[247] The favorable climate and ample available land attracted farmers from eastern colonies as well as from Europe.

Abraham Haines, a Quaker from New Jersey, moved west to what was then Frederick County, Virginia, around 1745.[248] He and his brother Joshua were among the original settlers in the region and, between them, purchased about a thousand acres in the Bullskin Run area. Abraham returned to New Jersey, where he died in 1758. His son, Nathan, who reached the age of majority in 1775 on the eve of the American Revolution, moved west and took possession of his inheritance.[249] In 1784, Nathan purchased additional land adjacent to "Col. George Washington's line," and added to his holdings again in 1797.[250]

The first known record of the Haines Mill that stood on this site dates to 1804, when Nathan Haines applied for an insurance policy on his "Brick Mill – Three story high – 44 feet by 34. Covered with wood – One water wheel, two pair stones with Seating and other machinery. Within 40 feet of a sawmill."[251]

The mill appears to have remained in the Haines family through the first half of the nineteenth century and passed to Edward B. Haines, a grandson of Nathan's.

During the Civil War, Union forces captured or destroyed over seventy flour mills in the Shenandoah Valley while carrying out the scorched-earth policy ordered by General Ulysses S. Grant during the Valley Campaign of 1864. According to local lore, Union General David Hunter ordered the Haines Mill burned.[252]

The Southern Claims Commission (SCC) was created by an Act of Congress on March 3, 1871, to receive, examine, and consider claims submitted by Southern Unionist citizens for compensation for supplies that had been confiscated by or furnished to the US Army during the Civil War. The SCC certified the Union loyalty of the claimant, determined the appropriate value of the lost property, and recommended that the US House of Representatives allow, disallow, or bar the claim.

While the documents pertaining to Edward B. Haines's 1872 claim are not available in the archives, the Southern Claims Commission's index shows his was approved and he did receive compensation. It is not known if it was for damages or for supplies that had been confiscated, but local lore seems to suggest that the mill was at least partially burned.[253]

Of the 22,298 claims filed for compensation, only 7,092 satisfied the rigorous sworn statements and cross-examination used to prove both the sustained Union loyalty of the claimant throughout the war and the validity of the claim.[254]

Within three years, it appears Edward had the mill up and running again, perhaps with the financial help of his cousin, Nathan Walker of Loudoun County, Virginia. In 1867, Nathan and his wife, Jane, sold their interest in the Haines Mill property, ten acres of land, on which there was a "valuable Brick mill and Saw Mill," to Edward B. Haines and Silas H. Feagans.[255]

In April 1884, another fire destroyed the mill. The *Sprit of Jefferson County* newspaper reported:

> The valuable Head Spring Mill of Mssrs. Feagans & Haines, on the Bullskin Run, near the Jefferson Woolen Mill of Mssrs. J.J. Jobe & Co, was destroyed by fire Thursday night, together with several thousand bushels of wheat and other stock. Loss probably $7,000 to $8,000, upon which there is an insurance of $3,000, we understand, in the Loudoun Mutual. The gentlemanly and esteemed proprietors have the universal sympathy of the community in their loss.

The Jefferson County Land Book reduced the appraised value of the mill by half—to $2,000—due to the damage suffered by the fire.[256]

Though the partners were able to rebuild the mill quickly, in September 1885, E. B. Haines sold the property to his partner, Silas Feagans. The deed described the property as a "valuable frame mill and frame house, together with a steam sawmill, engine and boiler."[257]

When Silas Feagans died in 1889, his son Wilder Clayton Feagans purchased the mill from his parents' other heirs and took over operations. The 1904 *West Virginia Gazetteer* lists W. C. Feagan [*sic*] as the proprietor of the flour mill and grain business in Wheatland.[258] He took steps to modernize the mill, replacing the wooden waterwheel with a Fitz Overshoot Wheel manufactured in nearby Martinsburg and purchasing a Haggenmacher Plansifter for separating different grades of flour.[259] He did not, however, choose to upgrade to a roller mill system. In the 1880s, many millers considered the roller mill a phase that would pass, as stone-ground meal was believed to be more healthful. Roller mills also required a steady stream of water to provide a reliable power source, which was lacking at Feagans Mill.[260]

After Wilder's death in 1937, one of his sons, Cecil, who had spent the early part of his career working as an engineer at Bethlehem Steel Company in New Castle, Delaware, returned home at age forty-two to run the mill. Cecil installed a 50-foot steel forebay to concentrate the flow of water to the wheel.

Just two years later, in January 1940, a third fire destroyed the mill.[261] This time, the mill's loss was estimated at $12,000—and again, its owner began rebuilding right away. Within two months, Feagans hosted a "Mill Dance, Round and Square," which was open to the community with no admission charge.[262]

Though he rebuilt the mill from the foundation up, Cecil must have shared his father's opinion about the merits of stone-ground flour, because he also eschewed a roller mill system and stuck with the tried-and-true Overshoot wheel and two sets of buhrstones.

Cecil worked in a cutting-edge field—aeronautics—at Fairchild's Aircraft Corporation in Hagerstown, Maryland, yet he restored the mill using outmoded equipment.[263] It is unclear whether that decision hastened the demise of the business, but for whatever reason, the business did not rebound after the last fire. In November 1943, Cecil Feagans closed shop and sold the mill to Jacob Keller. Though the last chapter in the mill's long history was brief, it did contribute what it could to the global war effort and continued the lower Shenandoah Valley's tradition of producing grain for broader markets until its doors closed for good. In April 1944, Jacob opened a creamery in the building but kept the property less than a year before turning over the building and all the equipment to Charles R. Keller.[264]

In 1949, Charles Keller sold the mill to Percy Drury, who in 1954 sold the mill to James and Martha Mason, the maternal grandparents of Danny Lutz, the current owner. Upon his grandmother's death in 1993, the mill passed to Danny and his sister, Karen. Full title transferred to Danny in 2010.[265]

Feagans Mill - Photo by Tracy Lawson

The Fitz wheel at Feagans Mill - Photo by Tracy Lawson

JEFFERSON COUNTY   137

16. POTOMAC MILLS
THE SHEPHERDSTOWN CEMENT MILL RUINS

Jefferson County
Address: River and Trough Roads, Shepherdstown, WV 25443
Coordinates: 39.4280577, -77.7786149
Year Built: 1826
Period of Significance: 1826-1901
Added to the National Register of Historic Places in 2014

© Google Maps

Potomac Mill Ruins - Photo by Tracy Lawson

Potomac Mill Ruins
Photo by Tracy Lawson

The Potomac Mill ruins stand as a reminder of the area's role in westward expansion and commercial development via waterway. The first half of the nineteenth century saw improvements in the nation's infrastructure, with turnpikes like the National Road and slack water navigation like the Erie Canal. The Chesapeake & Ohio Canal, also known as the "Grand Old Ditch," operated from 1824 to 1931 between Washington, DC, and Cumberland, Maryland.[266]

Potomac Mills began as a gristmill and was owned by physician Henry Boteler and businessman George Reynolds. In 1828, six months before work began on the section of the canal that would run from Point of Rocks to Harpers Ferry, Shepherdstown mill owner Henry Boteler wrote to the president of the C&O Canal Company and identified what he believed to be the proper kind of limestone for natural cement production in the hills around his gristmill. Just three years after the business opened, Potomac Mills was converted to produce hydraulic cement.

Natural cement is made from limestone, which is calcined (oxidized) by heating it to 1,300 to 1,500 degrees Fahrenheit, a slightly higher temperature than is used to produce quicklime. The mill then pulverized the calcinated rock into a fine powder using the same kind of buhrstones used to grind grain. When combined with water, this powder produced a hydraulic paste which would harden underwater—perfect for the building of canals.[267]

"The mill grew with the natural cement business, and beginning in 1829, the gristmill did double duty during harvest season, alternating between grinding grain and cement stone."[268]

This leads one to wonder if the customers who brought their grain to be milled discovered bits of gravel in the finished flour. Fortunately, circumstances changed when, late in 1829, new buhrstones made specifically for grinding calcinated limestone arrived and were installed in the mill.

By 1834, C&O Canal construction had reached Shepherdstown. Nearly all the traffic on the canal was agricultural produce, with flour topping the list.[269] The mill had contracts to supply cement for building the canal through 1837.

Though Boteler and Reynolds's enterprises grew rapidly in their first decade in business, in 1835 the two dissolved their partnership and Reynolds bought out Boteler's interest in the mill. Reynolds also owned and operated a canal packet boat, but when the canal contracts dried up, Reynolds found himself thousands of dollars in debt. In 1842, he mortgaged everything he owned to try and salvage his business, but despite his efforts, he defaulted in 1846 and was ordered by the Chancery Court to sell off his property, including Potomac Mills. A newspaper advertisement in 1846 described the "Very Extensive and Valuable Milling Establishment known as the 'Potomac Mills,' with 10 or 12 acres of land adjacent thereto."

The Mill-House is of Brick and very well built. It has Six Pair of Buhrs and commands the entire water-power of the Potomac River. Besides the Merchant Mill, there is a sawmill, of the most approved construction, a Plaster Mill, and several large and well-constructed permanent Lime Kilns, situated immediately on the River and near the Mill, with every convenience for manufacturing the Hydraulic Cement upon the most extensive scale. Upon the premises are a large and well-built Smoke House, Blacksmith's Shop, several Work-Shops, with a convenient Dwelling-House.[270]

Alexander Boteler, son of Dr. Henry Boteler, purchased the property for $15,000.[271] In 1861, Union troops burned the mill complex and dealt a death blow to Alexander Boteler's business. In 1865, the property was again for sale at auction.[272]

Major Harry Blunt leased the property through the 1870s, but alternating floods and drought plagued his attempts to conduct business. The 1882-1883 *West Virginia Gazetteer* has no listing for Blunt's cement mill,[273] and other sources indicate the mill closed in 1884 due to low water levels in the Potomac. Blunt installed a steam engine to power the turbine wheel, but after the improvement a record flood in 1889 washed out the canal and railway and reached the second floor of the mill. Though the mill was back in operation within a week, the canal did not recover until 1892, and it was 1896 before cement could be delivered by boat.[274] As a result, the mill operated only sporadically through the 1890s. When Major Blunt died in 1901, his son took over the business, but by 1904, the property went up for sale again. A flood in 1924 that closed the C&O Canal for good also damaged the vacant mill beyond repair.[275]

The Potomac Mills ruins, the warehouse, and one of the lime kilns are part of an 18-acre site and are visible from the road, with historic markers placed nearby. Visitors may park on the side of the road and hike up to the kiln, but warning signs discourage entry, as the ruins are not stable. On the opposite side of the road, the vantage points above the mill ruins offer excellent views of the remaining stone walls and the Potomac River. Again, the ruins are not stable, so enjoy them from a safe distance!

Potomac Mills is unique among the mills included in this book, not only because it is a ruin, but also because one of its multiple functions helped create transportation routes to serve the agricultural community.

Furnace, Potomac Mills
Photo by Tracy Lawson

2. SHEPHERD'S MILL

Jefferson County
Address: 207 East High Street, Shepherdstown, WV 25443
Coordinates: 39.4316206, -77.8024236
Year Built: c. 1738
Period of Significance: c. 1738-1939
Added to the National Register of Historic Places in 1971

© Google Maps

Shepherd's Mill - Photo by Shannon Purvis Thomas

Shepherd's Mill, one of the oldest in West Virginia, is now a stunning residence owned by Adam and Shannon Purvis Thomas. The mill retains its forty-foot waterwheel, which is the largest known freestanding waterwheel in West Virginia and one of the largest in the world, manufactured at the Martinsburg branch of the Fitz Water Wheel Company around 1894.

First known as Pack Horse Ford, Shepherdstown is the oldest community in what is now West Virginia. Settlers arrived in the area as early as 1719,[276] and Thomas Shepherd, who acquired the town site in 1734, named it Mecklenburg in honor of British King George III's wife, Charlotte of Mecklenburg, and began selling lots. Shepherd was a man of vision, "enterprising, energetic, philanthropic, with a large wealth."[277]

The Thomas Shepherd Grist Mill, built around 1738, was likely the first of its kind in the valley of Virginia[278] and is the reason Shepherdstown developed as a commercial and manufacturing hub. It was the largest milling operation in the area, favorably situated near the banks of the Potomac River, along the Indian trail that led to Pack Horse Ford. This road later became the Philadelphia Wagon Road, and residents of Maryland could easily access the mill to grind their grain. Shepherd ran it as a merchant mill from the beginning, buying grain at local market prices and selling flour locally and to distant commercial markets.[279]

As the town grew, local businesses included a pottery, gun works, a busy ferry, and the nearby Potomac Cement Mill, which produced hydraulic cement used on the locks of the C&O Canal from Georgetown to Cumberland.[280] *(See Potomac Mills, page 137)*

Thomas Shepherd, born 1705, married Elizabeth Van Meter, ten years his junior, in Monocacy, Maryland around 1733.[281] She was a daughter of John Van Meter, "the Indian fighter," who settled in what is now Berkeley County in the early 1730s. *(See Old Fields Mill, page 195)*

The newlyweds patented a 222-acre tract of land on October 3, 1734, divided it into town lots, and sold it the way land developers do today.[282] After Thomas built a saw and gristmill on that original tract, he purchased another 457 acres adjacent to his father-in-law's land.[283]

In December 1762, his application for a charter was approved by the Virginia House of Burgesses, giving him ownership of the town and the right and responsibility to establish a local government. Mecklenberg officially became a town in the colony of Virginia, with Thomas Shepherd as its sole trustee.[284] As anti-British sentiments rose, the town became known as Shepherd's Town.

Thomas and Elizabeth had five sons and five daughters,[285] and the Lafayette Chapter of the Sons of the American Revolution placed markers in memory of the couple on the fence of the Shepherd Family Cemetery in Shepherdstown, which note that all five of their sons served in the Revolutionary War.[286]

Thomas, Jr. and Abraham, were with Henry Bedinger in Hugh Stevenson's militia company.[287] *(See Bedinger Mill, page 77)* The young men took part in the Beeline March from Shepherdstown to Cambridge, Massachusetts, covering 600 miles in twenty-four days, one of the first two southern militia units to respond to George Washington's call for riflemen to fight in the American Revolution.[288]

When Thomas Shepherd died in 1776, he willed the town to his youngest son, Abraham, who was away at the war. The town's only trustee was absent, and it had no government.

Even without an active trustee, the town was so prosperous that its residents were able to raise $20,000 in cash to support its bid as the site for the location of the new national capital in 1790.[289] By 1793, the townspeople decided it was time to govern themselves. "After [Thomas Shepherd] died in 1776 and until 1793 there does not seem to be anyone in authority, and it became necessary to have a new charter from the State of Virginia at Richmond. During the life of the first charter there had been the French and Indian War also the Revolutionary War and the establishment of a new National Government."[290]

Thomas Shepherd Jr., (1743-1793), inherited the gristmill when his father died in 1776, and by 1813-14, the mill was owned by his heirs.[291]

The original mill, which had one set of stones and measures sixty feet by forty-five feet, is the wing that now houses the home's kitchen. Some of the gears on the mill's bottom are original to the building.[292]

The frame upper stories were built sometime in the 1890s to accommodate a roller mill system.

This pre-1894 photo shows the original wheel, which was located 100 feet downstream from the current wheel's location. Image in public domain, Historical Architecture and Engineering Record File WV 5-12

In the first half of the nineteenth century, Shepherd's Mill's heyday, it had eight run of buhrstones and employed twenty to twenty-five people to handle the accounting, shipping, and milling duties. Its products shipped to all major port cities in the Mid-Atlantic states by rail and canal, and from there, around the world, mostly to Europe and the West Indies. Though it was well over one hundred years old by the mid-nineteenth century, improvements made during the second half of the 1800s make it more representative of mills built during that period.[293]

The mill continued to be a profitable enterprise through the Civil War, but with the roller mill production method's rise in popularity and the increase in efficient shipping routes, larger mills began to squeeze out the older, smaller mills that had served communities since decades before America's birth.

Shepherd's Mill's chain of ownership in the early to mid-nineteenth century is incomplete. In the 1882-1883 edition of the *West Virginia Gazetteer and business directory*, Shepherdstown had three flour mills. John H. Duke ran saw and gristmills. John D. Staley was also a miller.[294] In 1870, twenty-year-old Shepherd Gattrel was John H. Duke's apprentice in the mill.[295] In 1880, Duke, a thirty-nine-year-old bachelor, was boarding with the Gattrel family and working as a miller, though the available records could not confirm Gattrel and Duke operated Shepherd's Mill.[296]

The 1891-1892 *Gazetteer* shows Legge & Reynolds (John F. Legge, A. S. Reynolds), as proprietors of the Shepherd Roller Mills.[297]

Sometime in the late nineteenth century, the mill's owner made improvements to keep pace with changing technology and installed a roller system that increased the mill's capacity.

In 1894, Upton S. Martin replaced the original waterwheel, also forty feet in diameter, which was located one hundred feet downstream from the current wheel's location.[298] The first wheel used an endless cable and a transfer station to send power to the lineshaft inside the mill. Martin engineered the current wheel's placement on the east side of the mill, and historical accounts say fourteen men rolled the wheel into position, as a child would roll a hoop along the sidewalk.[299]

After the mill ceased production and closed in 1939,
it fell into a state of disrepair.
Image courtesy of West Virginia & Regional History Center.
Used with permission

Martin reported working as a miller in the 1910 Census.³⁰⁰ He leased the mill to Luther Thompson, Jr. in 1923, and went on to serve in the state legislature in the 1930s.³⁰¹

Even with the improvements, Shepherd's Mill was destined to become obsolete. Known in its last years as Thompson and Carter Mill, it was too large to exist as a local supplier and too small to compete in wider markets and ceased production in 1939.³⁰² After more than 200 years of continuous operation, Shepherd's Mill fell into a state of disrepair.³⁰³

Former Shepherdstown mayor Silas Starry purchased the mill in the late 1960s and took steps to see the property placed on the National Register of Historic Places in 1971.

Minimal repairs on the property made through its idle decades weren't enough to keep up with natural decay, but when Ira and Nancy Glackens purchased the property in 1973, they financed a full-scale renovation to turn the mill into a private residence. They decorated the space with paintings by Ira's father, William Glackens.

The Glackens, who were both in their eighties when they died in 1990, had no immediate survivors and left the mill to Patrinka Kelch, who had been their caretaker in their declining years.

Kelch, who sometimes opened the mill to the public for community events, left provisions in her will that the property was not to be sold to either the city of Shepherdstown or Shepherd University.³⁰⁴

In 2017, former mayor Jim Auxer tried to buy the property at public auction, with hopes of using it as a community arts and events center. The property was zoned for single-family residential use only. The mill sold to a private businessman at public auction.³⁰⁵

In 2020, Adam and Shannon Purvis Thomas purchased the mill, which is currently configured with three bedrooms and about 3,000 square feet of living space.

The wheel is described in a Fitz company bulletin published in 1928: "40 ft. diameter by 2 ft. face Fitz Steel Overshoot Water Wheel in mill of Thompson and Carter, Shepherdstown, W. Va., driving 35-barrel mill with 90 cu. Ft. of water per minute. There is no storage dam here. The water comes straight from a large spring. A turbine wheel would be absolutely worthless here."

It may have been installed by Thomas and Josiah Matthews, who bought the former Fitz foundry.[306] *(See Tuscarora Iron Works, page 109)* The wheel and its reduction gears are set in bronze-lined, self-oiling bearings produced by the Fitz company.[307]

Shannon said living in a historic structure is a new experience, and they're committed to maintaining the historic integrity of the mill while making it a functional living space. They've had to add plumbing and an HVAC system, but they're doing everything to install modern updates with as little footprint as possible, even in areas of the property that aren't historically regulated.

Projects high on their to-do list include adding a master suite and guest room upstairs, modernizing the kitchen and bath on the main floor, and taking steps to protect and refinish the pine floors. Outdoors, they'll be landscaping, repairing fence, and improving the platform near the waterwheel.

Later, they hope to update the utility room, bury the propane tank, and renovate the barn into a storage and workshop space.

Though neither Shannon nor Adam admits to being a history buff, owning a piece of Shepherdstown's history has sparked their interest because they feel connected in a personal way. The couple loves to entertain and looks forward to hosting dinner parties and other gatherings in their stunning home.

Shannon, an artist, is thrilled to set up her studio upstairs, where she has all the sunlight she could want and can listen to the rushing waters of Town Run as she works.

The mill is on private property, so if you visit in search of a photo opportunity, please be respectful. The waterwheel side of the mill is best viewed from Mill Street, the next side street to the east, from outside the fence.

Gears manufactured by the Fitz Wheel Company
Image in public domain,
Historical Architecture and Engineering Record File WV 5-12

The 40-foot Fitz wheel as it appears today.
Photo by Tracy Lawson

Chapter 2
Potomac Highlands

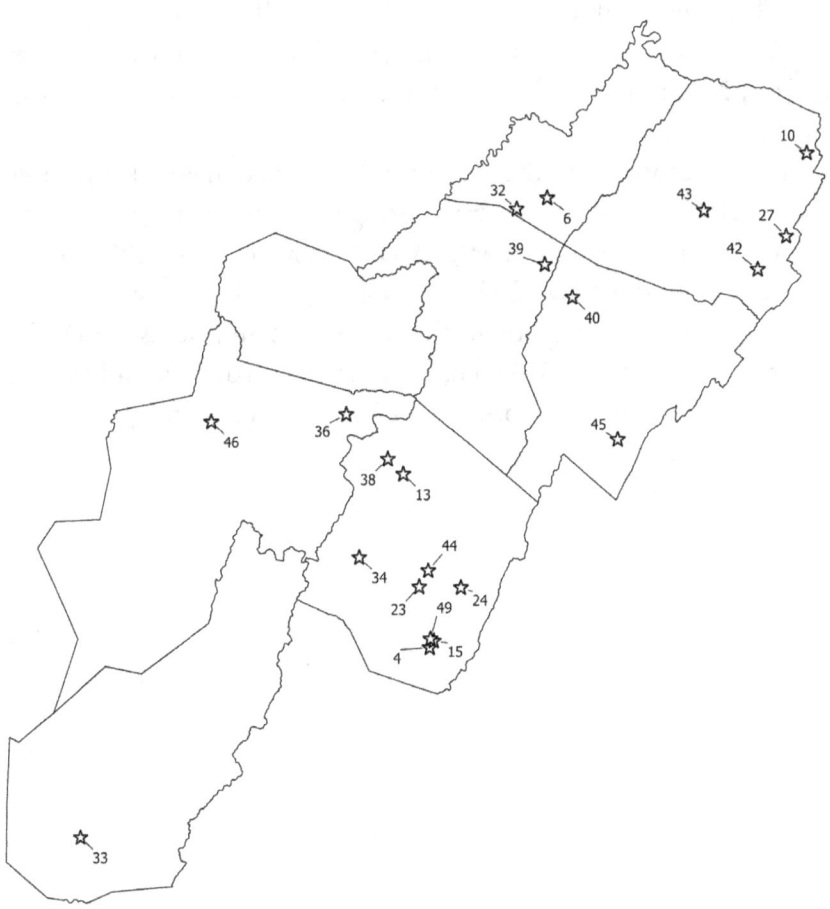

The Potomac Highland region's mountains and ridges are frequently topped with high, residual sandstone hills known as knobs. Its valleys are floored with limestone and shale. Spruce Knob in Pendleton County, at 4,861 feet in elevation, is the highest point in the state.[308] The region drains into the Potomac River by many of the same streams that run through the neighboring Eastern Panhandle, including Patterson Creek, the South Branch of the Potomac, the Cacapon River, and the Shenandoah.

George Washington established forts there during the French and Indian War, some of which are still standing.[309] Braddock's Trail cuts through Hampshire County. Federal and Confederate armies repeatedly invaded the region during the Civil War, with Romney changing hands fifty-six times, Keyser fourteen times, and Harpers Ferry eight times.[310] In 1866, Mineral and Grant counties were created from sections of Hardy and Hampshire.

These counties retain the remote and rural vibe that makes hitting the back roads so appealing. Be sure to bring a map, because you can't count on good cell service, and most service stations don't stock paper maps anymore, no matter how much they might come in handy.

It seems nearly everyone in the region has an interest in local lore. Folks tell stories of frontiersmen, Revolutionary patriots, and those who engaged in the struggle of brother against brother as though they knew them personally.

The largest concentration of mills in the state is found within this region.

GRANT COUNTY
Formed in 1866 from Hardy County

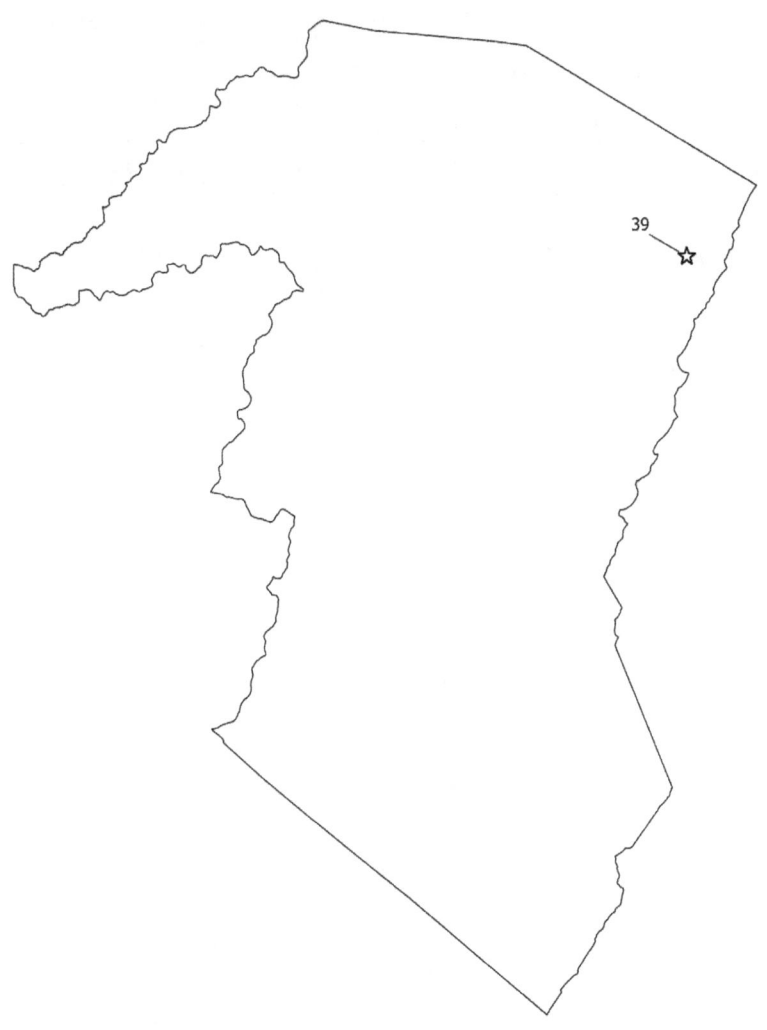

GRANT COUNTY   159

39. LYON'S MILL

Grant County
Directions: Upper Patterson Creek and Williamsport Roads, Old Fields, WV 26845
Coordinates: 39.20205, -79.02831
Year Built: 1882
Period of Significance: before 1812-1966

© Google Maps

Lyon's Mill - Photo courtesy of the Society for the Preservation of Old Mills

Lyon's Mill, once an important element of everyday life in the Grant County countryside, now stands as a monument to bygone days. The two-and-a-half story frame structure, painted red with white trim, boasts a twenty-four-foot steel Fitz Wheel mounted in the rear, which ties with one other mill for the third-largest waterwheel in the state. *(See McClung Mill, page 353)* The mill's inner workings, which include both a roller mill and buhrstones, remain in place.

The diary of W. H. Arehart of the Sixty-Seventh Virginia Cavalry, CSA, tells of Union troops burning the mill at Williamsport on January 4, 1864.[311] Though the mill was within West Virginia's borders, the area's residents held divided allegiances, and the Union commanders considered it prudent to destroy infrastructure, like the mill, that might later benefit the enemy.

An 1822 map of Hardy County shows Abraham Van Meter's Mill at Williamsport, which was then located in Hardy County, and ties that mill to another built by the Van Meter family in nearby Old Fields.[312]

Lyon's Mill's chain of ownership during its productive years exemplifies the connections forged between rural families over generations, and at one point, the Lyon family owned both mills on sites that had originally belonged to members of the Van Meter clan.

The Mill Creek, known locally as Mill Run, joins Patterson's Creek at Burlington, about twenty-eight miles north of Williamsport, and is one of the creek's larger tributaries. Mrs. G. H. Ebert, Sr., a local historian, recalls a sawmill, flour mills, and woolen mills operating in the vicinity of the town. At Antioch, about six miles above Williamsport on Mill Run, a woolen mill operated until well into the twentieth century,[313] as did the subject of this profile.

According to George R. Padgett, the mill's current owner, John Day built the mill in 1882 and sold it to John McDonald, who improved the property by installing a Midget Marvel, a self-contained roller mill system for wheat grinding, while retaining the buhrstones for grinding corn and buckwheat.

An article in the 1908 *Inter-Potomac Industrial Edition* newspaper gave a description of Eagle Roller Mills:

The Eagle Roller Mills, located at Williamsport, W. Va., are producers of flour, meal, buckwheat flour, and feed. The mills are equipped with the best appliances for the producing of the best flour and feed that can be made. Its capacity is fifteen barrels a day with storage room for two thousand bushels of grain. On account of the construction of the plant and the nature of the power used, a minimum of labor is required. The power is furnished by a mountain stream and a twenty-six-foot overshot wheel.

The owner and manager of these mills is Squire H. A. Alt.... In 1904 he bought the Eagle Mills of J. S. McDonald and has since supplied the surrounding country with the very finest quality and feed. About the time he took over the Eagle Mills, he was elected Justice of the Peace.[314]

Ault sold to David Cassady around the time the above article was written, and Cassady operated the mill until his death in 1927.

Tracking the relationships between the families who had a hand in the evolution of the mill—the Cassadys, Lyons, and Hilkeys—led back to the decade before the start of the Civil War.

William Cassady and his sister Margaret married siblings Elizabeth and Hiram Lyon. In 1850, the young couples lived near one another on farms in the Williamsport area. Hiram and Margaret Lyon and their five-month-old daughter, Sarah Elmira, lived next to Jacob and Nancy Hilkey, whose son, William, was about twelve years old.[315]

In the 1870 Census, William Hilkey and Sarah Elmira Lyon, now thirty and twenty-one years old, respectively, were married and living on a farm near her parents and Sarah's uncle William Cassady and his family.[316]

William Cassady's son David was then a lad of two. David Cassady was four years old when existing histories state John Day built the new mill on the ruins of the one burned by Union forces in 1864.

William Hilkey's brother Jacob moved to neighboring Mineral County around 1879, where he bought a mill in Laurel Dale and served as postmaster. *(See Laurel Dale Mill, page 209)*

When William died in 1899, David, then just nineteen years old, assumed responsibility for his widowed mother's care and took over the family farm. He purchased the mill from Squire Alt around 1907-1908.

In 1927, David died at age forty-nine of an infection following cataract surgery, leaving his widow with two young sons. His obituary headline reads, "Taken in his Prime," and the tribute states that "no one stood higher as husband, father, or friend."[317]

David C. Lyon, Hiram Lyon's first cousin once removed, first appears in the neighborhood in the 1920 Census. When David Cassady died in 1927, David C. Lyon served as an administrator of his will and later purchased the mill.[318]

Under David Lyon's ownership, the wooden waterwheel was replaced by a steel Fitz Wheel measuring twenty-four feet in diameter and three feet wide. When in operation, it makes only four and a half revolutions per minute. David Lyon passed the mill on to his son Arnold S. Lyon and though the mill changed hands again since Arnold owned it, it still bears the name Lyon's Mill. Excerpts from a 1976 article entitled "County's Last water-Powered Mill" read:

> The old Williamsport Mill is silent now. The water rushes over the fifty-foot fall while the wooden chute that used to divert it to the massive wheel has turned gray with age and begun to fall apart. David and his son, Arnold, operated the mill until Charles Bonar, the present owner, purchased it from Arnold Lyon. The mill has been out of use since 1966.
>
> Although the water wheel moves very slowly, the inside gears reduce the distance traveled by getting smaller, which increases the speed until the drive shaft hums when the mill is operating. The ground floor has the offices, the roller mill, the receiving area for grain, and, at the present, the burr [*sic*] mill for corn. The other levels and floors house the chutes for vertical transportation of grain and the augers that move the grain horizontally.

The roller mill is powered by the water mill, and it can run around the clock. During World War II it was operated 24 hours a day and put out about 25 barrels of flour daily.[319]

James Spicer, who owned the mill in the 1980s, revived it to grind corn and buckwheat during the county's annual Heritage Weekend and by appointment.[320]

George Padgett's grandfather had an interest in mills and passed that interest along to George, who recalls his grandfather gave him a copper windup toy of a gristmill. He bought the mill as a retirement project and place for family gatherings and told me he now owns "pretty much the whole town," which includes the mill, the cottage, and the big house purchased from Spicer, as well as the general store, the school, and a house purchased from Lois Lyon Cassady. He keeps his collection of antique farm equipment in the mill and has hopes of making it into a museum. He retains the old water rights—for both the stream and the spring—which have conveyed with each sale of the property.

The mill can be found at the intersection of Upper Patterson Creek and Williamsport Road, to the rear of the white cottage. Use due caution, as Patterson Creek Road curves and has poor visibility. When visiting this or any mill site, be respectful of private property.

While the front view of Lyon's Mill gives no clue to the size of the building, on the opposite side, a mountain stream powered the 26-foot wheel. Photo courtesy of the Society for the Preservation of Old Mills

Lyon's Mill
Photo courtesy of the Society for the Preservation of Old Mills

HAMPSHIRE COUNTY
Formed in 1754 from Augusta and Rockingham Counties

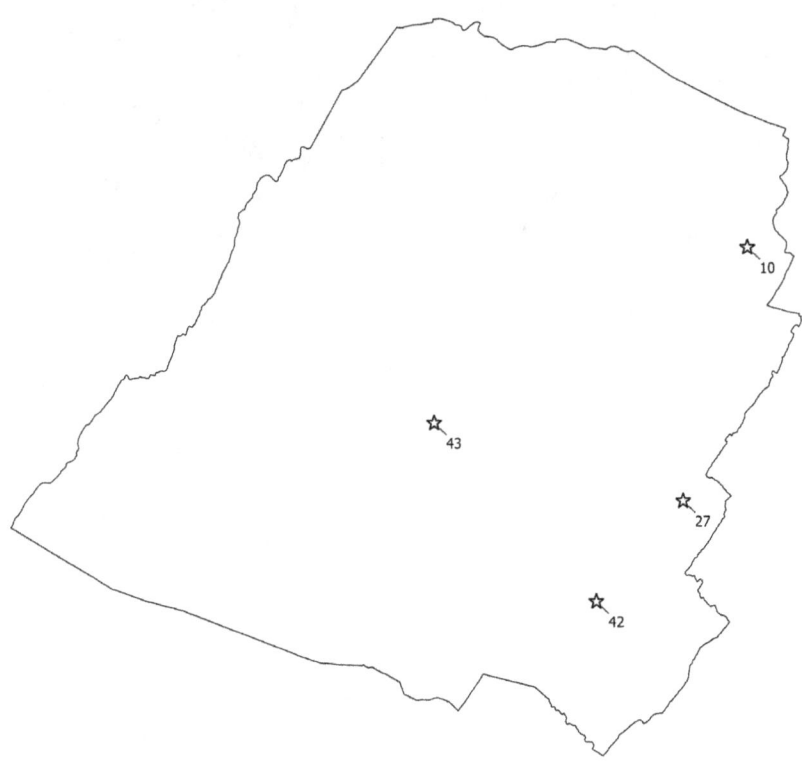

10. BLOOMERY MILL

Hampshire County
Address: 16264 Bloomery Pike, Bloomery, WV 26817
Coordinates: 39.3947266, -78.3810682
Year Built: 1800
Period of Significance: 1800-1936

© Google Maps

Bloomery Mill - Photo by Tracy Lawson

The Bloomery Mill, and its Dutch door, date to 1800.
Photo by Tracy Lawson

The Bloomery Mill, built around 1800, is a two-and-a-half-story stone structure with a tin roof. It has clapboard siding in the gable and on the east side where the waterwheel once stood. The original waterwheel was inside the building, but photos from the 1920s show the replacement iron wheel was mounted on the exterior east wall. The inner workings of the mill, including two run of buhrstones and the bolter, remain in place. The Dutch door is original to the building.

Bloomery's history is chock-full of drama that predates the American Revolution through the Civil War.

In the 1730s, Hampshire County was frontier, lying far beyond the settled area of the northern neck of Virginia that ended around present-day Stafford County. The robust men and women who ventured to the area during that time relied on Forts Enoch and Edwards for protection. Among these pioneers was Henry "James" Caudy, from Holland.

According to historian Charles Hall, the area that would become Hampshire County was, in the 1730s, Indian hunting ground controlled by the Iroquois Confederation, with a trail running through it used by the northern tribes to make war with the Catawba and Cherokees to the south. Many historical events of that period, like the tale of Caudy's Castle, were not documented but were handed down for generations. Their anecdotal nature means details will vary. You may have heard a different version of the tale that follows.[321]

James Caudy was either returning from a stay at the fort or out hunting when he encountered a party of Indians. Some versions of the story say the natives had just come from murdering his family, and when Caudy fled, they gave chase. His long rifle had but one bullet. He could not kill all his pursuers with one shot, nor could he reload fast enough to be certain of fending off all of them.

He headed for the rocky precipice known as The Castle, which rose over a thousand feet in the air, and took cover in a depression in the rocks. The trail he had ascended was so narrow that only one man could come up at a time. When the Indians advanced, Caudy braced himself and used the butt of his rifle to push the leader off the trail and sent him plunging down the cliff. The late Kenneth Glenwood Johnson, whose family owns the land on which Caudy's Castle stands, gave his own two

Caudy's Castle rock formation rises above Bloomery.
Image courtesy of West Virginia & Regional History Center
Used with permission

The Leith homestead and mill with the water wheel intact.
Author's private collection

cents' worth about the legend in a video interview in 2009. He reckoned that Caudy may have pushed a few of his pursuers off the cliff to their doom and the rest of the party likely called it a day and turned back.[322]

Hampshire County was authorized by an act of the General Assembly of Virginia in 1753, carved out of Frederick and Augusta Counties, and the first county established in what is now West Virginia. Part of Braddock's Trail runs through Bloomery. Local historians are proud to point out that a young George Washington worked as a surveyor in the area. He supposedly spent the night at James Caudy's home in 1748 while on a surveying assignment. Washington returned a few years later as a colonel in the British Army, when General Edward Braddock chose a road that wound through Bloomery Gap. This was the route by which his forces made their march to Fort Duquesne in 1755, during the French and Indian War.[323]

The village of Bloomery got its name from the cut-stone iron furnace established there two and a half centuries ago, when iron and lumber were sent to market down the Cacapon and then the Potomac. Iron furnaces of this style were called bloomeries because at one point in the melting process the furnace appeared to flower out, called the "bloom phase." When the furnace opened, the area was known as Sherrard's Store and, in its prime, had two tanneries, an iron maker, a gunsmith, a woolen mill, a shoemaker, and two mills.[324]

Glenwood Johnson stated that the furnace "provided jobs for about eighty men and put Bloomery on the map as an industrial area."[325]

Local historian Rob Wolford was kind enough to drive around with me while I was in Hampshire County in June 2020. When he told me the furnace required so much fuel that crews clear-cut the rolling hills in the area, I had a hard time imaging all the forest shorn away.

Robert Sherrard, a prominent local businessman who had achieved the rank of colonel in the Continental Army, is credited with building a woolen mill, a sawmill, and the surviving stone gristmill now known as the Bloomery Mill.[326] Other sources say Samuel Foltz was the builder. It is likely, but unknown, whether Sherrard hired someone to build the mill buildings.[327]

I found Samuel Foltz, a miller, in the 1880 Hampshire County Census. He was born around 1813, and so could not be the individual who built Sherrard's mills around 1800.[328]

When Robert Sherrard died in 1845, his son Robert B. took over the businesses.

As tension grew between the North and the South, Hampshire County's residents' loyalties were divided. Even though the county became part of West Virginia and was, therefore, Union territory, most of the residents were Confederate sympathizers. Col. Robert Sherrard was the largest slaveholder in the area,[329] and his son was an ardent supporter of the Southern cause. At the outbreak of the Civil War, his woolen mill manufactured cloth for the Confederate Army— until Union Army raiders destroyed it. It was never rebuilt.[330]

Bloomery was visited by raiding parties of both Union and Confederate soldiers during the Civil War.[331] Food and other provisions were often hidden in the gristmill.

By war's end, Robert B. Sherrard's businesses had suffered irreparable setbacks. Both Rob Wolford and Bloomery Mill owner Ken Johnson said Sherrard's property was repossessed and sold on the courthouse steps in the years following the Civil War.

After the war, Hampshire County—now a part of West Virginia by choice—turned toward restoring its economy and infrastructure. Bridges and highways were rebuilt. Public buildings and institutions were repaired and reestablished.[332] Mills, repaired or rebuilt, went back into service.

Jefferson Davis Leith was born in 1868, and his name provides a clue to his family's sympathies in the late war. He ran the Bloomery Mill beginning around 1910. The iron waterwheel fell to ruin around 1930 and was sold for scrap. The mill ran on a gasoline engine until 1936, when it ceased operation.[333] George Johnson, listed on the 1920 Census as the stepson of Jefferson Davis Leith, operated a sawmill from 1948 to 1976 and founded the Lazy J Ranch in 1956.

George's son, Kenneth Glenwood Johnson, continued the legacy and passed it on to his children. The Johnson family's 10,000 acres are the largest private landholdings in the county and include Caudy's Castle, the Bloomery Furnace, Bloomery Mill, and the Sherrard barn, recently restored by the Johnson family.

Ken Johnson, Glenwood's son, kindly showed me the ancient barn and opened the mill, where he spent a great deal of time as a boy, to give me a tour. Bloomery Mill, like the other historic landmarks under the care of the Johnson family, is a cherished and protected part of their legacy.

Bloomery Mill can be viewed from the street but use caution. The road is narrow and busy. Contact the Johnson family for permission to come on the property.

43. FRENCH'S MILL

Hampshire County
Address: 54 Fairground Road, Augusta, WV 26704
Coordinates: 39.2940834, -78.6366780
Year Built: before 1891
Period of Significance: 1891-2000
Added to the National Register of Historic Places in 2014

© Google Maps

French's Mill is now home to an entrepreneurial project started by two homeschooled teenagers. Photo by Elmer Napier

French's Mill, a three-story frame building with gray shingle siding, dominates the turnoff that leads to the Hampshire County Fairgrounds. For over a century, the mill was part of everyday life in the crossroads community of Augusta.

The mill, which changed hands in 2021, is now home to RDSWV, LLC, an entrepreneurship project spearheaded by siblings Victoria and J. D. Croucher, two area homeschooled teenagers.

Their business plan for Recycle, Discover, Support West Virginia LLC encompasses a little of each. They take donations of newspapers, cardboard, and shopping bags which can be used to package items sold at their thrift store in the smaller adjacent building on Fairground Road. The public will be encouraged to donate unwanted items for the thrift shop. Sale of thrift shop treasures and fresh produce will go to support renovations on the mill and other programming.

The "discover" aspect of the business promises science, art, and history activities that will promote the Department of Environmental Protection's youth programs. Their plans include a model train display, a wildlife collection, and an art gallery. The Croucher kids are award-winning nature photographers.

* * *

Though the oldest mills in Hampshire County date to the late eighteenth century, the first mention of this mill appeared in the *WV Gazetteer and business directory of 1891-1892*.[334] As the agricultural interests near Augusta grew, the mill served nearby farmers, saving them the time or trouble of transporting their crops to be processed at mills in Romney, Bloomery, or North River.

Known in its early days as the Augusta Milling Company, historic maps and aerial photographs show evidence of a creek that once ran north of the mill but no longer exists.[335] It is likely the original mill on the site ran on waterpower.

After fire damaged the original mill sometime between 1907 and 1910, members of the community invested in the Augusta Milling

Company, which incorporated in 1911 with $10,000 in capital stock.[336] Charles French, one of the investors, would later purchase the mill.

The structure exhibits a mix of old and new building techniques and machinery one would expect to see in a mill that has evolved over time.

Its post-and-beam construction resembles that found in mills a century older. Even though roller mill technology was readily available and already in use in mills such as the nearby Yellow Springs Mill, the Augusta Milling Company's investors chose to install a run of buhrstones four feet in diameter.

Other mills in the area still ran on waterpower, but the Augusta Milling Company chose a woodburning steam boiler instead of a waterwheel. By 1912, the Augusta Milling Company was up and running again, capable of producing sixty barrels of flour a day.[337]

In 1939, Charles French bought the mill and sold it in 1949 to his nephew Marshall French, who modernized the mill by covering the original wooden siding with asphalt shingles and replacing the boiler with first a car battery, and then electricity.

He also removed the equipment dedicated to processing wheat and focused on cornmeal, buckwheat, and animal feed.

According to an article in the *Hampshire Review*, Marshall French regretted removing the wheat grinding machinery, however necessary it was for business. "People stopped buying wheat flour," he said. "Women just didn't bake bread anymore. I guess it was easier to buy the bread."[338]

Marshall changed the name of the mill to French's Feed Store, which changed hands when Dave Moulden purchased the mill in 1982. In the first decade of 2000, the mill ceased operation. Dan and Cathi Hartsook purchased the property in 2013 and submitted it for inclusion on the National Register of Historic Places in 2014.[339]

Sacks that decorate the walls of the first floor advertise some of French's Mill's products, including yellow cornmeal, pure buckwheat flour, and self-rising wheat flour.

Before the Crouchers bought the mill, Historical Hampshire website featured it on its list of endangered sites in the county:

"French's Mill in Augusta was not long ago a working feed mill supporting small farmers…who wished to have their own grain ground for feed."[340]

French's Mill, ever a mix of old and new, exemplifies the transition away from water-powered buhrstone mills to more industrialized operations, yet retains much of its original equipment, including the stones, chutes, and elevators, all of which will give a glimpse at the mill's past while the energetic youngsters forge ahead to create a new attraction and gathering space for their community.

The thrift store adjacent to French's Mill
Photo courtesy of Carola Croucher

27. SPAID-EATON MILL

Hampshire County
Address: 106 Mountain View School Road, High View, WV 26808
Coordinates: 39.2418638, -78.4384441
Year Built: before 1845
Period of Significance: before 1845- c. 1950

© Google Maps

This mill's owner knew nothing of its history. There was a wealth of information to discover. Photo by Elmer Napier

Early in 2020, before my first research trip to West Virginia, I went through Elmer's photographs, identifying and familiarizing myself with the dozens of mills on my list.

One of them could not be identified from available sources. There was no record of it in the Society for the Preservation of Old Mills database, and no one had profiled it in blog posts or articles. It was a mystery, and I emailed Elmer to ask about it.

Elmer told me he'd met Henry Manson, the man who owned the little mill in High View, Hampshire County. Manson knew almost nothing of the mill's history but was eager to have it included in the book. He'd heard it used to be on the other side of the Virginia state line, but when the line moved in 1907, the owners, none the wiser, continued paying taxes to the state of Virginia into the 1950s. Manson said he'd heard there was once a sawmill on the property that was washed out in a flood.

It wasn't much to go on, but I was ready to put my research skills to the test and see what I could discover.

Hampshire County's deed records have not all been digitized, but I was able to access information about the two most recent owners. Henry and Dana Manson had purchased the property in 2012 from William E. Davis, who bought it in 1969. I would have to do a lot of research once I arrived, but there was still plenty I could do.

Assuming the mill was active in the mid-nineteenth century, I searched through the 1850 and 1860 Census records for millers living in the vicinity of High View in eastern Hampshire County. There were two: Joseph Hannum and Michael Spaid.

On my first research trip to West Virginia, I stayed three days in Hampshire County. I visited all four mills but spent the bulk of my time in the courthouse poring over old deed books.

I worked my way back from William E. Davis, the last known owner. He was a nephew of Carson and Caudy Davis, who owned the Yellow Spring Mill[341] *(See Yellow Spring Mill, page 187).* Henry and Goldie Seldon sold the land to Davis in 1968. A survey attached to the deed showed the location of an "old grist mill."[342] I was thrilled to be on the right track.

The Seldons bought the land from J. E. and Hattie Eaton in 1932.[343] About six weeks later, the Seldons bought land from N. L. and Laura Morris. That deed references "thence S. W. with the course of said [Old Man's] Run to the ford N. E. of J. E. Eaton's Mill."[344]

This was great! I had proof that J. E. Eaton had owned the mill on the site. I kept working backward, reading earlier deeds referenced in each document.

In 1924, the Morrises bought the land from A. C. and Minnie Oates, which parcel was conveyed to the Oatses by the executors of C. N. Garvin, deceased, by an undated and unnumbered deed, which was to be recorded by an unspecified clerk in an unspecified County Court.[345]

It looked like I might be stuck—until I noticed in the deed that the land parcel was partly in Hampshire County and partly in Frederick County, Virginia.

C. N. Garvin had to be the key to the mill's early history. But there was no death record for that individual in Hampshire County.

Back in my hotel room that night, I got on Ancestry.com and put together a dossier on the individuals in the deeds.

Henry Seldon, (1863-1938) who lived in High View in 1940, listed his occupation as "miller."[346] His wife Goldie's maiden name was Eaton. Here was a connection. I was on the trail!

Joseph Edward Eaton, Goldie's father, listed his occupation as "owner of a flour mill" in 1920.[347]

In 1910, Henry Seldon's family's neighbors in Frederick County, Virginia, were members of the Spaid family—and C. N. Garvin.[348]

The 1900-1901 and 1904-1905[349] *West Virginia Gazetteers* show Lee Johnson running the flour mill, while Cephas Garvin was the postmaster and owner of the general store. In 1900, Fred Seldon, Henry's father, was running the sawmill.[350]

The 1900 Census shows Lee Johnson's family living next door to the Eaton family.[351]

I found records of Cephus Newton Garvin, born in High View, Frederick County, Virginia, in 1851. His parents were David John Garvin and Margaret Spaid.[352]

In the 1870 Census, Lee Johnson's father, William S. Johnson, was a farmer and miller.[353] This connection to the Spaids was significant, as Michael Spaid was one of the potential owners of the mill from the 1860 Census. The research put me squarely in the appropriate time.

Ancestry.com had a link to a published genealogy of the Spaid family[354] that established the connections between the Spaid, Garvin, and Capper families. The introduction explains High View becoming part of West Virginia:

> When the Spaids settled in Hampshire county it was a part of Virginia, and remained so until during the Civil War, when the state of West Virginia was struck off. In speaking of the older Spaids we almost invariably say they were born in Virginia, but of those born since the war we have tried to be explicit.
>
> Frederick county is still a part of Virginia, and along the Frederick-Hampshire line there are many little post offices, and it has been very confusing to know just which county the office is in. High View was in Virginia for many years, but lately was moved to a building a few rods away and that transferred it to West Virginia.[355]

Hampshire County historian Rob Wolford reported High View became part of West Virginia in 1907.[356]

Cephus Newton Garvin—bless his unusual name—would be the key to connecting the mill's twentieth-century owners to its nineteenth-century owners. I continued my research using Ancestry and the Spaid family genealogy.

Margaret Spaid (1816-1892) third of Frederick and Margaret (McVicar) Spaid's daughters, was born and reared in Hampshire County. She had the usual life of a pioneer child. September 20, 1832, she married David John Garvin, b. October 14, 1810, and they settled on a farm in High View, Virginia. Here eleven children were born to this worthy couple. George and Courtney, both fine specimens of manhood, were killed in the Confederate Army, the former in his twenty-fifth year, the latter under twenty…Sarah Jane and Cephus never married but after their parents' deaths continued to reside together until her death in 1915…Cephas is a rich farmer and businessman and though he has reached the Biblical age he looks like a much younger man. A competent judge has called him "the prince of schoolteachers" so that was evidently his calling in early life.[357]

Cephus's mother, Margaret Spaid Garvin, was a first cousin of Michael Spaid. The 1860 Federal Census Non-Population Schedule shows Spaid running a flouring mill that ground wheat, rye, corn, and buckwheat. He had invested $1,500 in the one-man operation, which produced about 2,000 bushels of meal worth $1,650.[358]

"Michael Spaid, the youngest son of John and Hannah Spaid, was born and reared in Hampshire county. When thirty years old he married Mary Elizabeth Kline and settled on a farm on the west bank of Capon river, where three of his children still live. After eighteen years of married life the father died in January of 1868 and left six minor children to be reared by the mother alone."[359]

Numerous connections between the milling families in Hampshire County emerged. Mary Elizabeth Kline Spaid was a second cousin of Asa Cline, who owned the Yellow Spring Mill.[360] Asa's mother, Elizabeth Spaid Cline, was Michael Spaid's cousin.[361]

After Michael Spaid died in 1868, David John Garvin, Cephus's father, was one of the administrators of Spaid's estate.[362]

Michael Spaid and Meredith Capper, his brother-in-law, purchased 200 acres from Jonathan Simmons in 1856, which included "the same mill and sawmill property and water and water privileges conveyed to the said Jonathan Simmons by Thomas Hook and Elen his wife."[363]

Simmons married Thomas and Eleanor McVicker Hook's daughter Nancy around 1844, and it stands to reason that Hook sold them the mill property shortly thereafter. The Simmonses were living in Hampshire County in 1850,[364] and sold the property to Spaid and Capper when they moved to Lafayette, Missouri, in the mid-1850s.

The deed between Simmons and Spaid and Capper states Simmons bought the property with the mill on it, so I concluded Thomas Hook was either the builder or one of the early owners of the mill on the site.

Because the mill does not appear in Wilmer Kerns's article "Mills of Old Frederick County, Va.," I further conclude it was built sometime after 1813 and before 1845.

When I visited Henry Manson with my findings from the Hampshire County Courthouse in hand, I greeted him with, "Should we do the mill tour, or do you want me to tell you a story first?"

He opted for the story, so we sat on the front porch and went over the deed records. I'm not sure who was more delighted, he or I, with what I could tell him about his mill.

During the mill tour, Henry said that after he bought the mill, he asked one of the area old-timers if he knew its age, but the man shrugged and said, "It's always been there." Henry also ruefully told of how he cleaned out the entire mill soon after he bought the property but overlooked a window with no glass in it. No sooner was the mill spick-and-span than a flock of birds came in through the window and messed it up again.

He believes the mill is the second mill built on the site, but a lot of the lumber and beams used are from the original mill. He pointed out that the nails inside the mill are square cut, a type used between 1810-1900, which further supports the estimated age of the structure. The roller mill system inside the mill dates to the latter part of the nineteenth century. A millstone is used as a pier for one of the support posts, evidence of the mill's evolution.

The mill's known history has been submitted to the Society for the Preservation of Old Mills so it can be accessed and added to by individuals who may have additional information.

42. YELLOW SPRING MILL

Hampshire County
Address: WV-259 and Capon River Road, Yellow Spring, WV 26808
Coordinates: 39.1824620, -78.5100667
Date Built: c. 1896
Period of Significance: c. 1896-1990
Added to the National Register of Historic Places in 2014

© Google Maps

The Yellow Spring Mill's remote location allowed it to remain a productive part of its community longer than most other mills in the state.
Photo by Elmer Napier

The 30-foot Fitz wheel once powered the inner workings of the mill. Photo by Tracy Lawson

The raised sluice directed water to the wheel. Image courtesy of West Virginia & Regional History Center. Used with permission

Yellow Spring Mill, which has the distinction of being among the last water-driven mills to operate in West Virginia,[365] also stayed in operation decades longer than most mills profiled in this book. Its transitional appearance is an excellent example of a rural, industrial, twentieth-century roller mill, with the steel waterwheel and millrace coexisting with evidence of modern electric power.

Though the village of Yellow Spring is located a mere ten miles south of the Northwestern Turnpike (US Route 50), the region's mountain terrain hindered development. Winchester and Romney, the nearest major towns, were each at least thirty miles away and often inaccessible. This made it necessary for the hamlet of Yellow Spring to develop self-sufficiency.

Self-sufficiency, of course, required a mill. Frederick Secrist reportedly built the first mill at Yellow Spring around 1796, which was operated by his son Abraham. The original mill was unlikely to have any of Oliver Evans's innovations, but a second run of buhrstones, installed later, was used with a bolter that sifted and graded the flour.[366] According to the 1860 Federal Non-Population Schedule for Industry in Hampshire County, Abraham Secrist's flour mill was a one-man operation that ground wheat, rye, corn, and buckwheat and produced two thousand bushels, worth $1,650, that year.[367]

Abraham and his wife, Catherine, deeded the mill to their son, Morgan Secrist, in 1867, and Morgan, in turn, sold the mill to Asa Cline in 1870.[368]

Cline operated the existing water-powered buhrstone mill, and though he sold it to his son-in-law, Leonidas Aiken, around 1882, he seems to have stayed involved with the business. The structure was destroyed by a suspicious fire in January 1888, and when Aiken and Cline rebuilt it they installed a modern roller mill system and a large waterwheel. Once the mill was up and running again in 1889, they added a circular saw.[369]

A general store and post office were established nearby, and the community's industrial interests included a distillery, an ink factory, and a parlor organ factory. Roads and transportation to the area improved, though it was still "more accessible by balloon than otherwise." When another fire destroyed the mill in July 1895, Aiken and Cline sold the property to D.W. Griffith and Ashby Frank. It is likely the new owners rebuilt the mill between 1896 and 1899, using the same setup—roller mills and a large waterwheel.[370]

In 1914, brothers Caudy and Carson Davis bought the mill for $1,975 and established another link in the familial connections between millers in Hampshire County.

You may recognize Caudy's unusual first name as the surname of the fabled Henry "James" Caudy, Hampshire County's Indian fighter and subject of the story of Caudy's Castle *(See Bloomery Mill, page 169)*.

While attempting to establish a connection between Caudy Davis and the early settler James Caudy, I did note that an 1813 listing of mills in Hampshire County included "James Caudy & Co."[371]

A little more digging revealed that James Caudy IV and Samuel Gard owned and operated a "Merchant's Mill" at Capon Bridge in the first half of the nineteenth century. Samuel was married to Sarah Caudy, James IV's sister.[372] Samuel Gard also owned an extensive tannery at Capon Bridge prior to 1820.[373]

Two early communities in the area were known as Caudy's Mill and Gard's Mill, which suggests the family enterprise may have expanded to include more than one mill. Gard's Mill later became known as Capon Bridge when it established its first post office in 1856.[374]

I was able to establish an even closer familiar connection between the Spaids and Davises, names associated with the High View mill that, until recently, had no known history and has been dubbed the Spaid-Eaton Mill *(See Spaid-Eaton Mill, page 181)*.

Caudy Davis's mother, Hannah Caroline Spaid, was a daughter of Hiram and Jemima Spaid and a niece of Michael Spaid, who owned and operated the High View mill in the 1860s.

He and his wife Ada Spaid Davis, who was a daughter of Nicholas and Angeline Spaid and a second cousin of Caudy's, operated the mill and nearby general store.[375]

Caudy Davis installed the thirty-foot overshot iron Fitz Wheel to increase the mill's efficiency. Like the large wheels at Shepherd's Mill and McClung Mill, the main wheel connects to a large iron-toothed gear that turns a smaller gear and shaft, transferring power to a vertical shaft inside that powers the equipment.[376]

The mill is a three-story building of frame construction with a gable roof and a one-story ell, has a Fitz Wheel thirty feet in diameter, the second largest in the state. The main building measures forty-three feet by thirty-eight feet, and the ell measures sixty feet by twenty-one feet.

Caudy's son Charles Sr. took over running the mill in 1934 and later bought it for $8,500. He converted it to gasoline power in 1940, and then to electricity in 1951.[377]

In the late 1940s, Caudy Davis brought the "clearest spring water in the gap" to the community. Over a mile of iron pipe brought the water downhill, where, as of 2004, several homes and businesses were still served by the seventy-year-old system.

The constant flow of water has consistently arrived with enough pressure to release a fountain-like spurt high into the air at the old mill pond.

Though many small milling operations were closing by the mid-twentieth century, Yellow Spring Mill's remote location worked in its favor. As commercial poultry farms became popular in the region, the mill increased production and eventually hired ten people to produce thirty to forty tons of animal feed a day. Grain arrived from the Midwest by rail to Winchester, where it was transported to the mill by truck for processing.

The same modern transportation networks that helped keep the mill in business also allowed residents to access goods and supplies from distant locations, and over time, residents' dependence on locally processed flour and feed decreased.

Charles Sr. died in 1987, and the Yellow Spring Mill ceased operation around 1990. Charles Jr. sold to Kenneth Seldon, the owner of Riverside Service, in 2007. Seldon refurbished the mill for historic preservation, and after his death in 2011, Guy Davis, a grandson of Carson Davis, bought the mill at public auction. In response to my inquiry for information, Mr. Davis noted that he plans to do structural repairs to the property, which is currently being used for storage. He has no plans to open it to the public.

From US 50, take Capon River Road to the mill site. This scenic drive winds along the river.

The Yellow Spring Mill is conveniently located near the intersection of WV-259 and Capon River Road. When I visited the site, I parked in a gravel lot across the road. You can get a good view of the building for photos from the edge of the property, including the enormous Fitz Wheel.

HARDY COUNTY
Formed from Hampshire County in 1786

40. OLD FIELDS MILL

Hardy County
Address: 841 Old Fields Road, Old Fields, WV 26845
Coordinates: 39.1398488, -78.9633068
Year Built: 1890
Period of Significance: before 1812-1943

© Google Maps

Old Fields Mill is a private residence. Photo by Elmer Napier

Old Fields Mill is a private residence, recently purchased by two families to share as a weekend getaway spot. Though it was built around 1890 to replace an earlier mill on the site, its history begins decades before the American Revolution, in the earliest days of white settlement in the area.

Isaac Van Meter (1692-1757) brought his family to the area known as Indian Old Fields in 1744. His brother John also came west with his family and settled in what was then Berkeley County. John's daughter Elizabeth married Thomas Shepherd,[378] the founder of Shepherdstown and Shepherd's Mill. *(See Shepherd's Mill, page 143)*

During the escalating hostilities with Native Americans and the French in 1756, a youthful George Washington, then a colonel in the provincial militia,[379] directed a fortification be built to protect the area settlers. Originally called Fort Van Meter, and then Town Fort, the stone walls of the fortification no longer stand, but the area is known to this day as Fort Pleasant. The early history of the fort is anything but pleasant, however. The following year, Isaac, then sixty-five years of age, was working unprotected in his fields a short distance from the fort when he was killed and scalped by members of the Delaware and Shawnee tribes.[380] His murder came just four days after his family welcomed a new baby, born to Isaac's son Garrett and his wife, Ann Markee Sibley Van Meter.[381]

Garrett's younger brother, Colonel Jacob Van Meter (1764-1829), inherited the Fort Pleasant property after his father's death, and he and his wife, Tabitha Inskeep Van Meter, raised their family there. Later, he built another home he named Traveler's Rest, about 200 yards away from the old fort, for himself and his wife. It is also known as the Rebecca Van Meter House. Fort Pleasant was placed on the National Register of Historic Places in 1973.

Colonel Jacob Van Meter was a pillar of the local Presbyterian church and an enterprising businessman. For years he and Chief Justice John Marshall raised thoroughbred horses.[382] He built the first mill in Old Fields before 1812, called "the finest flour mill that had ever been erected up to that time in the South Branch Valley."[383] His was included in an inventory of mills made in old Frederick County, Virginia, during the War of 1812.[384]

A map, surveyed and drawn under the direction of John Wood in 1822, shows Jacob Van Meter's Mill near the location of the present mill, and McNeal's [sic] Mill in Moorefield, approximately five miles south.[385] This mill was also included in the 1812 inventory of mills in Old Frederick County[386] and may have been known as Daniel's Mill, Bean's Mill, and Wilson's Mill at various times. It was located on the corner of Main Street and Rohrbaugh Lane in Moorefield and closed in 1949.[387]

The 1822 map also shows Abraham Van Meter's mill in Williamsport, (*See Lyon's Mill, page 159*) which was also included in the 1812 inventory.[388]

Ann, Rebecca, and Susan, three of Colonel Jacob's daughters, remained unmarried. They lived at Travelers Rest after the death of their mother, Tabitha Inskeep Van Meter, in 1851.

Rebecca Van Meter (1798-1882) kept a personal journal, making entries about twice a week from 1855-1865. Her entries indicate frequent contact with Daniel Renick McNeill and his wife, Mary Jane McClung, who hailed from Greenbrier County, where that proliferate clan had settled about the same time. (*See Beaver Mill, page 393*)

Daniel (1802-1881), whose lands adjoined the Van Meter family's, owned Willow Wall, a U-shaped building in the Georgian-Tidewater style, built around 1811. The house is a private residence and was also placed on the National Register of Historic Places in 1973.[389]

The Van Meters and the McNeills were close friends and neighbors with mutual business interests. The Van Meters do not appear to have run the mill themselves. Local lore says the McNeills owned and operated the mill for many years. My research yielded a sheaf of deed records and a long paper trail of owners and millers.

Many of Colonel Jacob's family moved west to Kentucky, leaving the homeplace and mill in the control of his nephew Isaac (1757-1837). From there, the property passed to nephew Jacob Inskeep Van Meter (1802-1882), and then his son Isaac II (1845-1909) inherited the original Fort Pleasant tract. His obituary says he "possessed a fine farm and Colonial mansion, where he dispensed hospitality with a free hand."[390]

Local historian Kelly Williams stated a second mill was built less than a mile from the first mill around 1828, and records indicate the Van Meter mill was damaged in a flood around 1887. The current mill structure was built around 1890, likely by Isaac II (1845-1909).[391]

In a deed made March 17, 1890, trustees purchased land on behalf of Isaac Van Meter from the estate of Jacob Van Meter. This land was bounded on the south and west by Mill Run, and the deed states that Mill Meadow is a tract of approximately 275 acres.[392]

George William McNeill, a first cousin three times removed of Daniel Renick McNeill,[393] married Sarah "Sadie" Van Meter in 1895, one of many marriage alliances over the years between the two families. In 1900, the young couple and their two children lived next door to her parents. The men in both households listed their occupations as farmers and livestock dealers.[394]

In 1908, Isaac Van Meter and Sadie and George McNeill sold a parcel of land "adjoining the said Baldwin's mill lot" to William Henry Baldwin. The parcel contained ninety square poles and fetched a price of twenty dollars.[395]

Two parcels of land at the mill's location changed hands throughout the first decades of the twentieth century. In 1911, James Van Meter, Jacob Van Meter, and George and Sadie McNeill, all heirs of Isaac II, divided the land, rather than sharing several parcels. George and Sadie received the Sheep Pasture and the Mill Meadow.[396]

Ava Leatherman Aylor (1917-2008) stated in an interview that she grew up nearly in sight of the mill and used to accompany her grandfather, George T. Leatherman, to have grain ground. She would ride horseback, "standing behind him and holding on tight." She remembers Mr. Baldwin, who worked at the mill and lived in a house just below. When she was very young, she was afraid of him because he had a long, white beard. She had pleasant memories, too, of playing on the rocks below the mill with friends.[397]

In 1921, William Henry Baldwin sold the mill to Homer P. Baldwin for $3,000.[398] Homer sold it to Geo. W. Miller and Mont P. Miller in August 1923, and in 1928, they sold B. C. Liggett the property for

$3,500.³⁹⁹ In 1930, Homer Baldwin was renting a house next door to the McNeills and was working for wages as a miller.⁴⁰⁰

In January 1936, B. C. Liggett and his wife, Ethel, sold to G. R. Miley, "that certain lot with Mill and tenant house located thereon, containing one acre, more or less, situate in Moorefield District."⁴⁰¹

When a judgment went against Miley in a suit in chancery in 1938, he was forced to sell the mill. David C. Lyon, who owned another mill in nearby Williamsport, bought the mill on its one-acre parcel for the bargain price of $805.⁴⁰² In February 1939, Lyon purchased an adjacent property with a dwelling house on the land.⁴⁰³ Lyon's Mill in Williamsport was almost certainly built on the foundation of the Abraham Van Meter Mill. *(See Lyon's Mill, page 159)*

On December 4, 1943, David and Cora Lyon sold the Old Fields Mill and the adjoining nine-and-three-eighths-acre tract to Lemuel and Alice Combs for $3,250.⁴⁰⁴ Combs sold it again three weeks later to John William and Ada McNeill.⁴⁰⁵ Nancy Nolen, who lived in the area as a child, remembered visiting her Aunt Ada and Uncle Bill and swimming at the mill in the late 1940s and 1950s. She said the mill was not in operation at that time.⁴⁰⁶

The property passed out of the McNeill family in 1968,⁴⁰⁷ then through several other owners before Mitch and Rhonda McNeill purchased it in 1989.⁴⁰⁸

In a phone interview, Mitch reported that after Bill bought the mill in 1945, he had the building wired for electricity and removed the mill equipment. Bill distilled whiskey in the mill's basement, at a time when it was not unusual for people to sell or barter with homemade liquor to acquire staples.

Mitch stated that while most of the mill's interior is white pine, there are a few hand-hewn oak beams that may have been salvaged from an earlier structure. After Bill's death, the next owners fixed up the mill to use as a hunting camp.

Mitch McNeill owned the mill property from 1989-2007, and served as its property manager until October 2020, when David and Rebecca Raina and John and Mary Pitts became the latest owners of the Old Fields Mill property.

McNeill's Rangers

McNeill's Rangers was an independent Confederate military force commissioned under the Partisan Ranger Act of 1862,[409] a push to recruit troops to operate as guerrilla fighters. Its captain, John Hanson McNeill,[410] was a brother of Daniel Renick McNeill.[411]

After the repeal of the Act on February 17, 1864, McNeill's Rangers was one of two partisan forces allowed to continue operation, the other being Mosby's Raiders. Both guerrilla forces operated in the western counties of Virginia and in West Virginia. Many Union generals considered Captain McNeill and his men to be bushwhackers, akin to terrorists and not entitled to protection when captured, as was the case with other prisoners of war.

McNeill's Rangers had pro-Union irregulars to contend with in western Virginia. Pendleton County was pro-Union and organized itself into the Pendleton Home Guards, which frequently confronted the roving Confederate bands. On July 19, 1864, a detachment of McNeill's Rangers attacked about thirty Home Guards under Captain John Boggs near Petersburg. Boggs's company was known as the "Swamp Dragons."[412] *(See Boggs Mill, page 217)*

McNeill's Rangers were often in the area, and Willow Wall was used as a hospital to tend to the wounded.[413]

Rebecca Van Meter noted in her diary on October 11, 1864: "We hear that Capt. McNeill is still living." She wrote again on November 15, 1864: "Captain McNeill died last week in Harrisonburg of his wound had his family with him."[414]

45. A.M. SNIDER MILL

Hardy County
Address: Upper Cove Road and Hill Road (CR 20/2), Mathias, WV 26812
Coordinates: 38.8743514, -78.8618307
Year Built: unknown—possibly early 1900s
Period of Significance: unknown, estimated 1900-1936

© Google Maps

The history of A. M. Snider Mill has mostly been lost to the ages. Photo by Elmer Napier

Brothers Albert Moze "A.M." Snider and Arthur Snider built the mill, which was later primarily owned by A. M., according to his granddaughter Annabelle Vance daughter of A. M.'s daughter Clarice.

The two-and-a-half-story frame structure has cantilevered second stories in the front and over a loading bay in the rear. The building is in an extreme state of disrepair. Part of the south side has collapsed, and Upper Cove Run has undermined the foundation on the north. Its appearance befits a structure whose history is shrouded in uncertainty.

Though little information is available about the mill, I estimate it was built in the early 1900s, since the builders, A. M. and Arthur Snider, would have been in their late twenties and early thirties respectively at that time. I've been relying on information gleaned from the *West Virginia Gazetteers*, and in this case, the information in their listings indicated this was probably the second mill in Mathias at the turn of the twentieth century.

In both the 1882-1883[415] and 1891-1892[416] *Gazetteers*, J. T. Mathias owned the grist and sawmill.

The 1900-1901 *West Virginia Gazetteer and business directory* lists Mathias & Jenkins as running the flour mill and Mathias & Snider operating the general store.[417]

It wasn't until 1904-1905 that Snider & Bright owned a planing mill.[418]

Kenneth Hawse, A. M. Snider's great-grandson and part owner of the property, reported that his grandmother Gussie Snider married E. B. Souder and that's how the mill came into the Souder family.

The Mathias Brethren Church, located a short distance away at the corner of Upper Cove Run Rd. and Hill Rd., was built in 1908. A. M. Snider was one of the church founders, and Samuel Mathias, a cousin of A. M.'s wife, Eliza Catherine Mathias Snider, was the first pastor. As the story goes, A. M. would sit in the front pew during services and, when he felt the preaching had gone on long enough, would hold up his pocket watch as a signal to his brother Arthur.

No records were available to confirm whether the mill continued in operation after A. M. Snider's death in 1936.

MINERAL COUNTY
Formed in 1866 from Hampshire County

6. ANTIOCH MILL

Mineral County/Hampshire County
Address: Grayson Gap Road (CR 6) and Knobley Road (CR 9), Antioch, WV 26710
Coordinates: 39.325107, -79.018985
Year built: 1787
Period of Significance: 1787-1968

© Google Maps

After nearly two-and-a-half centuries, the Antioch Mill's new owners are getting ready to relocate the building. Photo by Tracy Lawson

After nearly 240 years of serving its community as a saw, grist, and woolen mill, the Antioch Mill is getting a new lease on life in Romney, in neighboring Hampshire County.

Mills were once a large part of Mineral County's economy. The Mill Creek Country Club, Mill Run, and The Millstone Restaurant serve as reminders that there were once as many as eighteen mills in the area.[419] At this writing, just two remain—and the Antioch Mill is slated to relocate soon.

Kandise and Larry Berkel of Romney have had their eye on Antioch Mill for years, and according to Kandise, it was love at first sight. Originally, the couple planned to renovate the mill at its current location, but after they bought it in 2020, they decided to dismantle and move it to neighboring Hampshire County and plan to adapt it to serve as their residence.

Built around 1787 and owned first by Samuel Barker Davis, the Antioch Mill has been a sawmill, a flour mill, and most recently, a woolen mill. When Davis and his family moved to the area, he found a densely wooded wilderness with trees so bound to one another with a network of grapevines that clearing the land required climbing up to hack away the vines so individual trees could fall to the ground.[420]

A contract between Samuel B. Davis and carpenter John Bussey for constructing a log house survives, with the quaint spelling preserved: "A bargain between Davis and John Bussey, for said Davis of the dimensuns as follwrs 16 feet square, 8 feet below justs (joists) three logs about and outside chimbly 6 feet wide, with one dure (door) 6 by 3 and one winder. The said Davis agrees to give Bussey Ten Dollars when the work is finished. Signed: John Bussey, Samuel B. Davis."

The log house, which was standing in 1971, was considered a fine example of pioneer construction. The four-story Antioch Mill measures thirty by sixty feet with hand-hewn pegged beams and boasts a twenty-four-foot by four-foot waterwheel, which makes it part of a three-way tie for the third-largest wheel in the state. It is structurally sound after more than 230 years, so it is possible Mr. Bussey also built this mill. Samuel B. Davis married Margaret Harrison, and for the first century of its existence, members of the Davis and Harrison families owned the mill.

Brashear Rogers, who purchased the mill in 1880, married Mary Evelyn Dye, a Harrison granddaughter, and the familial connection remained intact. Brashear Rogers did much to modernize the mill, removing the buhrstones and installing a roller system while continuing to operate the sawmill.[421] In 1890, Isaac Rogers, Brashear's nephew, was killed in the mill while unloading logs.[422]

Brashear experienced financial difficulties, and in 1897, he sold the mill outside the family to A. P. Roberts. D. W. Billmeyer purchased the mill from Roberts in 1918, and continued to grind wheat, corn, and buckwheat for local farmers while adding machines to card and spin, and looms to make cloth, rugs, and blankets.

At that time, the Markwood Woolen Mill was located just three miles away, evidence that carding and processing wool was a profitable business in the area. A reel for warping bars later purchased from the defunct Markwood Mill had already been in use for more than 150 years when it was moved to Antioch.

James Billmeyer took over ownership of the mill in 1923 and sold to Ira Parker Shreve in the 1920s, and in 1936 Scott and Lacey Rotruck acquired the mill and used a gasoline engine to power the equipment. During the later years of the Great Depression, Rotruck said they sold locally and in surrounding cities like Charleston, Wheeling, Clarksburg, and Parkersburg. Shrewd customers would buy cloth from their mill and take it to a tailor. In this way, a man could get an overcoat that would cost a hundred dollars in a store for about twenty-five. The wool for the mill was obtained from sheep raised in the surrounding communities and was either purchased outright or worked "on shares" into blankets, rugs, cloth, and yarn for knitting.

It was washed, dried, and carded by hand, and then put through three bolting machines, from which it was spun and twisted and made ready for weaving. There were three batting machines, one hundred spindles and three looms in the mill.

As with many other mills profiled in this book, Antioch Mill was a community gathering place. News in the county might travel by way of the grapevine, but the ancient mill was the center from which it was dispatched.[423]

In a 1964 newspaper article, Rotruck stated that he and his wife hadn't run the woolen mill since 1942, when the government cut off the wool supply during World War II.[424]

In their later years, the Rotrucks ran the weaving equipment only sporadically,[425] and after Mr. Rotruck's death in 1968, the Merrimack Valley Textile Museum bought several pieces of equipment from the mill. A spokesman for the museum said the purchase was the most important acquisition made by the museum in a decade.[426]

32. LAUREL DALE MILL

Mineral County
Address: Burgess Hollow/Laurel Dale Post Office Rd. (CR 5/2) New Creek, WV 26743
Coordinates: 39.3059295, -79.0948545
Year Built: c. 1867
Period of Significance: c. 1867-1949

© Google Maps

Laurel Dale Mill - Photo by Tracy Lawson

Laurel Dale Mill is a favorite spot for prom, engagement, and senior photos.
Photo by Tracy Lawson

Laurel Dale Mill is an unaltered mid-nineteenth century mill with a buhrstone grinding apparatus and a wooden overshot wheel. It is a two-and-a-half-story frame structure with three bays and sits atop a stone foundation. It is a popular spot for locals to take prom, senior, and engagement photos.

Laurel Dale Mill's history exemplifies how rural neighbors' isolation increased their likelihood to work together and intermarry.

Mineral County resident Betty Dzubba, who provided an unpublished manuscript about the Antioch Mill written by Pearl Berg, dated September 1971, stated in a letter: "Laurel Dale or McNeill Mill dates to 1879. Its waterwheel generated power for electrical plants before and up to 1953."[427]

Seymour Whipp's article, "The Passing of the Old Mill Wheel," states: "The old mill is still standing at Laurel Dale. The water wheel does not turn, but there is water in the mill race. It is owned by a man named Kuhns [Kuh]."[428]

Laurel Dale's post office on New Creek at Pokejoy Run was established in 1878. At the time, the names Big Springs and Laurel Dale were considered for the community, but Big Springs was already being used for another town. Laurel Dale got its name from the first free school in the area, which sat on a hill that was covered by three different growths of laurel plants.[429]

Members of the Hilkey, O'Neill, and Kuh families operated the mill and the post office, two community hubs, for nearly one hundred years.

According to a deed dated June 12, 1867, "William Warner Thomas is at this time building a water grist mill on the lands of Mary and William Thomas…"

That deed goes on to specify water rights: "…the said William Warner Thomas can at his pleasure…take the water from the New creek at or near the line crossing the same of Jesse Davis's, lay out and open a canal…so that the water from the said New Creek may be used in propelling the grist mill, the said Wm. W. Thomas is hereby authorized to locate said canal…and to have the full control of the same after it is made."[430]

Jacob Hilkey was well-established in the milling industry before he became the second owner of the Laurel Dale Mill. In 1860, while living in Hardy County, he listed his occupation as "Mill Wright."[431] In 1870, he and his family are found in the Grant County Census. Grant had been formed from Hardy County in 1866, so the Hilkeys were likely in the same locale. He listed his occupation as "miller."[432]

In 1878, the Hilkey family relocated to New Creek district in Mineral County, and Jacob Hilkey became Laurel Dale's first postmaster. The record indicates his son-in-law later took over the position.[433] 1880 Census records indicate Jacob was working as a miller in Mineral County.[434]

The 1882-1883 edition of the *West Virginia Gazetteer* shows Jacob Hillig [*sic*] running a water-powered mill with two run of stones in Laurel Dale.[435]

In 1884, William Warner Thomas and his wife, Sarah, sold the property that included the Thomas Mill to Jacob Hilkey and Charles McNeill, "the first being a miller and the second a farmer of Laurel Dale, WV."[436]

Charles McNeill, the son of Scottish immigrants, was not living with his parents in New Creek at the time of the 1880 Census, but he must have been acquainted with the Hilkeys, his parent's nearest neighbors. He and Mary Jane, Jacob's daughter, married in November 1883.[437] It appears they, like many others profiled in this book, may have purchased the mill with the intention of starting a newlywed couple off with land and a business.

The West Virginia Genweb article about Laurel Dale calls Hilkey's Mill a point of central interest, and noted, "Water races from New Creek slopes to power [a] giant wooden waterwheel in [the] process of converting saddlebags of homegrown grain...owned and operated by William "Billy" Hilkey, oft quoted as saying, 'When Mag Fout can't make good bread I'll think it's my flour!'"[438]

This folksy quote illustrates how easily details can become confused. William Hilkey was a younger brother of Jacob.[439] Billy was also a miller, who appears to have operated a mill near Williamsport, in Grant County, around the time Jacob ran the Laurel Dale Mill. I'm not sure if the man who uttered the quote was Jacob or Billy—but doesn't it make you wonder about Mag Fout's bread?

Jacob Hilkey died on November 22, 1889, at age seventy-one. His widow, Betty, and her children sold the mill to Charles McNeill, who operated the post office and general store.[440,441]

William Warner Thomas, who built the mill, remained in the area. His family lived next door to Charles McNeill in 1900.[442] In the 1910 Census, the McNeills' neighbors were the John Kuh family, and in due time, the Kuh name would also be associated with the mill.

John Kuh owned a blacksmith shop located at the junction of Dolls Gap and Burgess Hollow Road. He handled wagon and buggy repair work, horseshoeing, and other tasks typical of a blacksmith.[443] The McNeills' daughter, Margie Helen, married John Kuh's son Lewis in 1919.

After Mary Jane McNeill died in 1927, Lewis and Margie lived with Charles until his death in 1936. Charles, in turn, left the mill to his daughter Margie Kuh.[444] She and her daughter Mary, were the last two postmasters at Laurel Dale until the branch closed in 1960.

The mill came back to the Thomas family when Margie and Lewis Kuh sold to twin brothers Willard and Wilson Thomas in December 1949.[445] The pair were grandsons of William Warner Thomas and had inherited a farm in New Creek from their uncle, J. T. Thomas, in 1945.

Rhonda Layton, who was the mill's owner when I visited the property in July 2020, purchased it from Edward and Sherree Pickford in 1994.

Rhonda said she fell in love with the isolated spot, which included the mill, a barn, and the five-bedroom farmhouse that she has since restored. The mill has not been restored, but most of its inner workings, as well as the wooden waterwheel, remain intact. The bolter had remains of the rotted silk inside.

In February 2021, Tyler Parker and Laura Brown purchased the property.

PENDLETON COUNTY
Formed in 1788 from parts of Augusta, Hardy, and Rockingham Counties

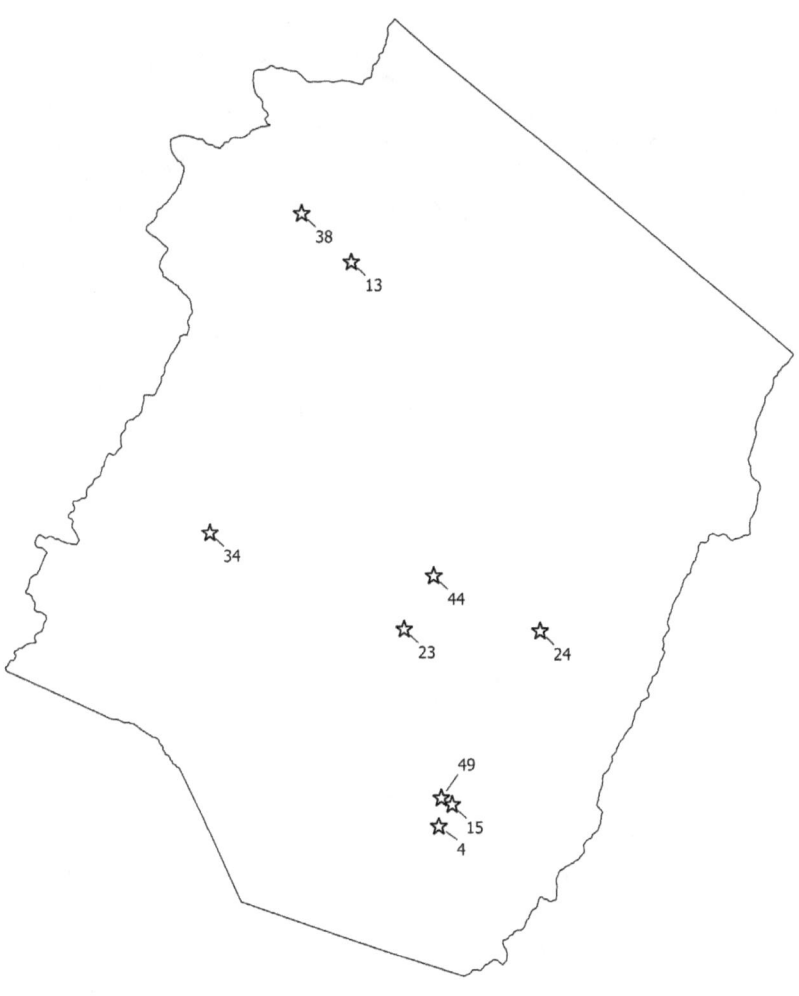

13. BOGGS MILL

Pendleton County
Address: Mountaineer Drive (US 33 and WV 28) and CR 9, Seneca Rocks, WV 26884
Coordinates: 38.8196448, -79.3857333
Built: before 1820
Period of Significance: 1797-1966
Added to the National Register of Historic Places in 2004

© Google Maps

Boggs Mill near Seneca Rocks - Photo by Elmer Napier

Nestled in the valley below Seneca Rocks, Boggs Mill is only slightly evolved from its 1820s appearance. The Seneca Valley in Pendleton County, known for its pastoral scenery, was settled by German and Irish immigrants. The area boasts one of the most productive agricultural regions in West Virginia. Some sources report a mill stood on this site as early as 1797, which was likely built by Jacob Carr Sr. (1750-1814). When Carr sold the property to John Boggs Sr. in 1820, the mill was mentioned in the deed.[446]

Boggs Mill is a rectangular, gable-end building, constructed using mortise and tenon, braced frame construction. It has clapboard siding, a standing seam metal roof, and a stone foundation.[447] Originally two stories high, a third story was added to the mill in the mid-nineteenth century, and three roller mills were installed there around 1906. The machinery inside the building was reportedly in good condition when the National Register of Historic Places Registration Form was filed in 2004. The mill served the community as a grain mill, retail store, and gathering place.[448]

The mill operated continuously for 136 years and survived inclement weather, a Civil War battle fought nearby, and a severe flood in 1985 that damaged the west wall and waterwheel badly enough that the wheel was removed.[449]

Boggs Mill drew power from the North River until after World War II. It is believed the Allis-Chapman engine on site powered the mill from the mid-1940s until its closing in 1966. Presently, the structure is in fair condition.

This mill, like others profiled in this book, remained in the family for generations. John Boggs Jr., the youngest of John and Margaret Boggs's children, married Elizabeth Carr, a great-granddaughter of the original owner, Jacob Carr, in 1842, and took over running the mill.

John Boggs Jr. listed his occupation as "farmer" on Federal Census records in 1850-1880, and this unassuming quality—in which he does not credit himself with the specialized skills needed to maintain and run a mill—was characteristic of his modesty about his many accomplishments.

Though John Jr.'s brothers James and Aaron and his nephew Charles all enlisted in the Confederate Army, John Jr. marched to his own drummer. He organized an independent militia unit which fought for the Union.

His independent militia, the Swamp Dragons, patrolled the area and skirmished with Confederate forces. John served as a delegate to the West Virginia Constitutional Convention in 1863. The following profile, which portrays him as much more than the owner of a country mill, appeared in the Wheeling *Intelligencer* on July 17 of that year:

> JOHN BOGGS, the delegate from Pendleton, was born in that county, October 15, 1815, and is near 48 years of age. His father was a native of Ireland. Mr. Boggs was trained a farmer and when he was old did not depart from it. He was married at the age of 25. Has lived a quiet, unpretending life. Has been magistrate several years, since the adoption of the amended constitution of '50, but always refused to hold any kind of position previously, believing the old regimen aristocratic and anti-republican.
>
> He has always been at war with the eastern aristocracy and its oppressions. Opposed secession with all his efforts and influence and voted against the ordinance along with nearly all the voters in his section of the county. When hostilities broke out, he raised a company for home protection, call the "Swamp Dragons" or "Swampers," and this little band of mountaineers has ever since been a sort of Swiss independence up there in the mountains of Pendleton, and defied John Letcher and the southern Confederacy. No rebel can set his foot inside the domain of the "Swampers" with any assurance of getting out alive. Mr. Boggs commanded the "Swampers," and drilled and fed them from his own means, for about six months. The rebels have ever since had a special enmity against him. He has been frequently waylaid, and shot at, and they offer a standing reward of $2,000 and exemption from military service during the war to the man who will take him, dead or alive.

Frank Boggs, the mill's last owner, rests on the porch.
Older brother Wilbur drives the horse in the foreground.
Image courtesy of West Virginia & Regional History Center.
Used with permission

He has been in a number of skirmishes with them and has laid out for weeks at a time without ever changing his clothes. Mr. Boggs represented Pendleton in the second session of the Constitutional Convention, held last February. The county would have been represented here in the restored government but being cut off from the rest of mankind, with seventy miles of hostile country between it and the federal outposts, the people there did not even know what was being done here or elsewhere.

For this reason, no election was held in Pendleton on the ordinance for a division of the state, submitted in October 1861, but they voted on the adoption of the Constitution in April '62, and the amended Constitution last May. In politics Mr. Boggs has always been a Whig and never voted for a Democrat in his life. Voted Bell in '60 but wouldn't do it again. Up to the time of the rebellion he was not specifically hostile to slavery but always favored its abolishment by gradual means. Now he is willing it should be extinguished by any means that may be found necessary to affect the object and may be set down as a pretty thorough anti-slavery man.

Religiously Mr. Boggs is not a member of any church. He was reared under Presbyterian influences, but, individually, is partial to the Dunkards. In person, he is six feet, rather sparsely built, and stoops very slightly. His hair, which has been black, is quite gray, face smoothly shaven, eyes grayish blue, nose Roman, general appearance of face shrewd and wide awake. In manners he is unobtrusive but possesses the openness and frankness peculiar to frontiersmen. Makes few speeches, brief and to the point. Is always in his seat and attentive to business and is a respected and useful member.[450]

John Boggs Jr. went on to serve in the first, second, third, and ninth legislatures of West Virginia. He was elected Sheriff of Pendleton County twice in 1865-1866 and 1867-1871.[451] He and his wife, Elizabeth Carr

Boggs, raised a family of seven children. He appears on an 1890 Schedule of Surviving Soldiers, Sailors, and Marines and Widows. At the age of seventy-five, he suffered from rheumatism and was nearly blind.[452] He died in 1893.

Aaron Carr Boggs, one of their sons, took over the mill around 1880.[453] Aaron turned the business over to his son, Frank, between 1910 and 1920.[454] So, all four men who owned and operated the Boggs Mill were members of the Boggs and Carr families. Continuing the tradition of generations of millers before him, Frank Boggs did custom grinding for local farmers for a toll. He also sold flour and feed by the pound.[455]

Frank reported the mill's value as $3,000 in 1940, the last date that Federal Census data was available.[456] By the 1960s, commercial flour was inexpensive and readily available in stores in rural areas, and most of Frank's milling business was animal feed.

Frank and his sister Ona both of whom never married, continued to live in their parents' home throughout their lives. When they grew elderly, their neighbor, Louise Bowers, cared for them.

Frank sold the mill to Louise and her husband, Ward, in 1966. Louise's niece and nephew, Vickie Skavenski and Sonny O'Neill, are the current owners of the mill. Vickie recalled that Frank was well-known in the community. In addition to his duties at the mill, he was a feature writer for the *Pendleton Times* newspaper, founded by William McCoy in 1913 *(see McCoy Mill, page 245),* and a Sunday School superintendent. Ona used to dye Easter eggs traditionally with onion skins for Vickie when she was a girl.

Boggs Mill, which has been part of the Pendleton County landscape for two centuries, is well-steeped in local history. Vickie and Sonny are interested in preserving the mill and are considering opening it to the public as a museum, a coffee shop, or as a gallery for local artisans.

34. CIRCLEVILLE MILL

Pendleton County
Address: 211 Chantilly Dr, Circleville, WV 26804
Coordinates: 38.6674302, -79.4956627
Year Built: before 1882
Period of Significance: before 1882- c. 1920

© Google Maps

Idelta Lambert unlocks the mill's door. Photo by Elmer Napier

The history of the Circleville Mill seems to have been stripped away over time. Idelta Sponaugle Lambert, the current owner, said a man named Harry Wolf sold the machinery inside the building to a miller in Pennsylvania sometime in the 1940s, before she and her husband bought the property. Other than that, she remembers little about the mill's history.

The waterwheel was destroyed by a flood in 1985 that also undermined the foundation in the rear of the building. The millrace that runs parallel to the river is now dry.[457] Without much to go on, I began my search for clues to the Circleville Mill's past.

Circleville, on the North Fork of the Potomac River, was originally named Zyrkleville after John Zyrkle, who ran a dry goods store in the town.[458] By 1910, Circleville had more the genuine appearance of a village than any other place in Pendleton except the county seat itself. It had two stores, a mill, a church, a two-room schoolhouse, and about ten homes.[459]

Henry Wymer bought the land on which the mill now stands from Philip Teter in 1869.[460] It is not known if the mill was already standing on the property when Wymer (later spelled Wimer) purchased it, but the Circleville Mill's location, four-tenths of a mile from the center of town, supports the theory that it was the mill mentioned in the 1910 village profile.

The Teter, Wimer, Dove, Sponaugle, Raines, and Lambert families are associated with the property and with milling in the Circleville area.

Absalom Dove (1803-1877) was a millwright, and his sons Nimrod and Jacob both entered the same trade. A Northern sympathizer, Absalom was from Dovesville, located near the West Virginia border in Rockingham County, Virginia.[461] He moved to the "Union side" of Hardy County to live on Flat Mountain at the outset of the Civil War. This created a rift between him and his brother Abel, who supported the Confederacy.[462]

Nimrod Dove, who served in the Confederate Army for five months before obtaining a disability discharge,[463] appears to have had mixed feelings about which side he was on. Though he fought for the South, he named his daughter, who was born a few months after his discharge, Americus. A son, born in February 1865, was named Abraham Lincoln.

Nimrod and Jacob were both working as millers in 1870.[464] Though we can't be certain where Nimrod worked at that time, his name appears in issues of the *West Virginia Gazetteer and business directory* that span twenty-two years, from 1882-1904.

The 1882-1883 *Gazetteer* listing for Mt. Freedom states that the village is also known as Circleville. Subsequent editions refer to it only as Circleville. The village's population increased from 125 to 150 by 1904. It had daily mail service and a telephone connection by 1900. Nimrod Dove ran the flour mill for the twenty-two-year period covered by the available *Gazetteers*. By 1904, the flour mill was being run by the partnership Dove and Bennett.[465,466,467,468]

Nimrod listed his occupation as miller in 1900 and reported that he owned a mortgaged farm. His son William was working in a grist mill.[469] His partner Bennett in the 1904 *Gazetteer* may have been Elijah Bennett, a son of Moses Bennett, who was a miller in the Dry Run area of Pendleton County in 1850.[470] Elijah was a first cousin of Nimrod's wife, Elizabeth Bennett,[471] and was about seventy years old when he listed his occupation as miller in the 1910 Census.[472]

Stewart Raines, who lived near the elderly Elijah Bennett in 1920, reported his occupation as miller in that Census.[473] Raines's mother was a Bennett, and he was related to the Lambert family by marriage.

By 1930, no one in the Circleville district reported working as a miller or in a flour mill.[474] This suggests that the Circleville Mill may have ceased operations between 1920 and 1930.

In his will, dated 1904, Henry Wimer, (son of Jacob) left property to his two nephews, Jacob L. and Isaac C. Wimer, the sons of his brother George.[475] The brothers petitioned the circuit court to partition certain tracts of land, amounting to approximately 296 acres. The commissioners appointed to examine and divide the land in August 1913 did so, and in their report allowed for Jacob L. Wimer to "build and maintain a dam about 325 feet in length at a place where the river breaks over its banks south west of where the Noah Teter Gap Run enters the river and a right of way from his lands through the lands assigned to Isaac C. Wimer to said dam, and that Jacob C. Wimer was not to damage any crops while working on said dam."[476]

It is evident from the wording in the commissioners' recommendation that Jacob L. Wimer received the parcel with the mill on it. A comparison of a sketch included in that document with a current satellite map of the area confirms the mill stands on what was once Jacob L. Wimer's land. Upon his death, the land passed to Isaac Wimer's daughter Effie and her husband, Isaac Cook. They sold the land to Harman Sponaugle, and upon his death, his heirs sold the land to Roy Keith and Idelta Sponaugle Lambert.[477] The Lamberts already owned the Isaac C. Wimer parcel.

Though the mill has not been in operation for around eighty years, the Lamberts maintained the structure, and relatives say Idelta, whom age has not slowed, talks of making the mill useful again, perhaps as an event venue.

15. HOMAN MILL

Pendleton County
Address: 10413 Sugar Grove Rd, Sugar Grove, WV 26815
Coordinates: 38.5097249, -79.3186217
Date Built: before 1824
Period of Significance: before 1824- c.1970

© Google Maps

Homan Mill is one of three remaining mill structures in the tiny village of Sugar Grove. Photo by Elmer Napier

Though a mill has stood on the site for two centuries, time came to a standstill inside the Homan Mill in the 1970s. If you ignore fifty years' worth of accumulated dust and a few broken windowpanes, it's easy to believe the miller has just stepped away for a spell.

Sebastian Hoover/Huber, a German immigrant, brought his family to Pendleton County and purchased 300 acres on the South Fork of the Potomac River sometime before the Seven Years' War (1756-1763). Sebastian, who was known as Bastian or Boston Hoover, bought an additional 200 acres from Robert Green in 1763. He was killed during the Tory disturbances in 1780.[478]

One of Sebastian's sons, Jacob (1751-1835), purchased a 325-acre tract that encompassed the present community of Sugar Grove.[479] Jacob built a mill on the site sometime before 1824, when a deed of a real estate transaction between Christian Eye and Ester Buffenbarger mentions Jacob Hoover's mill race in its description.[480]

Jacob was a brother of Peter Hoover, whose descendants built the Hoover Mill just up the road in Brandywine *(See Hoover Mill, page 235)*.

William and Barbra Wise Kiser came to the area in the 1830s and settled in Sugar Grove, on land that had belonged to Jacob Hoover. Some sources say William's father, Jacob Kiser, had a mill at North River, so William may have been trained in the art of milling as a young man.

Behind Jacob Hoover's mill and across the river was the Daniel Probst farm. The Probsts were one of the area's most prominent families, and Daniel was related by marriage to Jacob Hoover. Daniel's daughter Polly married John Kiser, one of William and Barbara's sons, in 1836.[481]

John and Polly settled on the land with the mill site that same year, when William deeded his property to his sons John and David.[482] The Kiser family's numerous descendants intermarried with Mitchells, Rexrodes, Hoovers, and Waggys—all milling families in Pendleton County.

Three of William and Barbara Kiser's daughters married into the proliferate Rexrode clan: Mary Ann, (Henry) Elizabeth (Augustus), and Sarah (Joseph)[483] *(See Rexrode Mill, page 311)*.

Another daughter, Susannah (sometimes given as Susan), married William Lewis Waggy.[484] William, Jr. George, and Edward, their sons, all had an interest in the third mill in Sugar Grove, which Edward built in 1917 *(See Waggy-Mitchell Mill, page 277)*.

It is unknown whether John Kiser continued to use Jacob Hoover's mill, expanded it, or built another, but the Kiser Mill is mentioned in a list of county school districts in 1846.[485] Family lore recalls that John ran the mill while his children were young.

The 1850 Federal Non-Population Census for Pendleton County shows both father and son were running separate mills. William had a water-powered saw, grinding, and carding mill. He had invested $5,500 into his business, which produced 3,000 barrels of flour worth $8,000, 30,000 feet of lumber valued at $300, and 4,000 pounds of wool valued at $1,400 in 1850. John had invested $1,000 in his flour mill, which produced 300 barrels of flour valued at $900.[486]

Three of John and Polly's sons served in the Confederate army during the Civil War. Harvey died of wounds sustained in the battle of New Market. After the war, Harrison was the miller, and James Pleasant, or "Pleas," as he was known, ran the store that is now owned by the Bowers family. Harrison and Pleas never married.

The youngest Kiser daughter, Mary Jane, married Sylvester Mitchell in 1888.[487] Sylvester was a son of George Washington Mitchell and a nephew of Benjamin Mitchell, another Sugar Grove miller[488] *(See Mitchell Mill, page 251)*. Mary Jane and Sylvester Mitchell lived at the homeplace for a time and, in 1908, built the house that currently stands next to the mill. They had seven children, but only Leafy, their youngest, survived to adulthood.

In 1920, Leafy married Virgil Homan Sr., a veterinarian from nearby Ruddle,[489] who brought yet another milling connection to the family. He was a descendant of James William Byrd, a noted millwright from the Shenandoah Valley who built the McCoy Mill in 1845 *(See McCoy Mill, page 245)*.

When Harrison grew old, Sylvester took over running the mill. Harrison died in 1918, Sylvester in 1932, and Mary Jane in 1934. Leafy, now the matriarch, raised her family of six sons and cared for Pleas until his death in 1937. In 1936, the Homan family expanded the mill from a four-story, gambrel-roofed structure to what it is today. The work was done by Ike Simmons, a local millwright.[490] Originally water powered, in its later years, the mill ran on a diesel engine.

Richard Homan, Virgil and Leafy's second son, took over the milling business in 1946 after his return from World War II. Despite being a man of extraordinary experiences and accomplishments, his granddaughter, Hannah Byrd DuPoy, says that running the mill was one of his purest joys. He was proud of the mill's buckwheat and enjoyed peddling it across the state.

Hannah wrote, "My grandfather passed when I was fifteen. My mom and I talk frequently about how much we regret not asking him more about his time running the mill. He was a fantastic storyteller and shared many tales, but we have so many questions about what would have been mundane tasks. Folks always say he could hear, from whatever floor he was on, if something was malfunctioning, and could correct the problem just as quickly."

Regarding the mill, she wrote, "It's as if, one day, everyone walked out and left things just as they were. It's such a treasure to our family."[491]

Richard Homan attended Sugar Grove Elementary School and graduated as salutatorian from Franklin High School in 1941 and from Bridgewater College in 1950 with a BA in math.

A World War II US Army veteran, Homan served with the 610th Tank Destroyer Battalion in Europe in the Rhineland and Central Germany Campaigns and was promoted to sergeant. He was assigned to the International Military Tribunal at Nuremburg, Germany, during trials of top Nazi leaders. After the war, he worked for Kiser Roller Mill, Sugar Grove,[492] and his commitment to serve his community seemingly knew no bounds.

He was a member of Francis Asbury United Methodist Church in Sugar Grove, where he was teacher and Sunday school superintendent.

Civic-minded Homan served as president of the Pendleton County Board of Education, a member of Pendleton County Board of Health, the Town Council of Franklin, the Pendleton County Extension Service Committee, served four six-year terms on Veterans Council of West Virginia Department of Veteran Affairs, and was a Corridor H supporter.[493]

He was a charter member of VFW Post 9666 at Sugar Grove, which he helped to organize and where he served through all the chairs to Commander (VFW Department 1957, Jr. Vice Commander-in-Chief 1966, Sr. Vice Commander-in-Chief 1967, Commander-in-Chief 1968). He served two terms as District Commander, served as chairman of every major committee in the West Virginia Veterans Department, and was then elected Department Commander in 1957, where he served six years on the National Council of Administration, National Legislative Committee, National Security Committee, National Awards and Citations Committee, National Budget and Finance Committee, and as chairman of the National Loyalty Day Committee.[494]

In addition, he was active with the American Legion, Disabled American Veterans, West Virginia Bankers Association (past president 1991-1992), the Pendleton County Industrial Development Authority, Area Three Governor Caperton's Partnership for Progress, and was a Thirty-Second Degree Mason of the Pendleton Lodge 144 F&AM.

An elected member of the Pendleton County Bank Board of Directors from 1952-2010, Homan served as president from 1969-2010 and CEO from 1972-2000.

It must come as no surprise that he was also a recipient of the Distinguished West Virginian Award.[495]

During the years Richard Homan served the VFW at the national level, the mill's business began its decline, though it continued in operation until the 1970s.

Homan Mill in Sugar Grove is a substantial, aesthetically pleasing structure. It stands four and a half stories, is built of frame construction with a seamed metal gambrel roof. The main part of the building dates to the early to mid-nineteenth century. It was expanded in 1936 to include additional storage and workspace on the lower floors, with gable peaks, shed dormers, and plenty of windows to let in the light.

Cara Homan Mitchell, who is married to Dr. Brandon Mitchell, the seventh-generation owner of another Sugar Grove mill *(See Mitchell Mill, page 251)*, and a great-niece of Richard Homan, took me on a tour of the Homan Mill with her two youngest kids in tow. They were obviously used to trekking around the mill, because as soon as she opened the padlock on the door, her little boy scampered off to play.

Upstairs in the main grinding area, we examined the buhrstones for grinding cornmeal and buckwheat that occupy one end of the main room, the row of chutes and elevators with glass observation windows, and two roller mills for processing white flour. A burlap grain sack, half full, lay abandoned between the two sets of buhrstones. Cara opened the door on one of the roller mills and said, "There's still flour in here."[496]

Shelves full of paper sacks with colorful illustrations and brand-names like Indian Chief Cornmeal and Mountain State Bleached Flour confirmed that Homan Mill was run, at least in part, as a merchant mill in which the miller purchases grain from farmers wholesale to process and sell in retail markets.

In the office, unfulfilled order tickets dating back as far as 1957 remained clipped to a metal organizer, and a 1959 calendar hung on the wall. A bicycle, possibly used to run errands on the property, stood propped in a corner.

It seemed the past was hovering just at my elbow. The people who should have been there to run the machinery were the only thing missing. Still, with caring and interested descendants like Amy and Hannah DuPoy and Cara Mitchell, the Homan Mill is sure to be a fixture in Sugar Grove for at least another hundred years or so.

Cara insisted I take a few of the paper flour sacks as souvenirs. The hundreds that were left behind, many still in their paper wrappers, stand in testament to Richard Homan's plans for the future of his once-prosperous business.

Unfilled order tickets remain in the office at Homan Mill half a century after it was closed. Photo by Tracy Lawson

Hundreds of unused flour sacks give the impression that it was a spontaneous choice to close the mill.
Photo by Tracy Lawson

24. HOOVER MILL

Pendleton County
Address: Dickinson Mountain Road/Fultz Gap/Fritz Run Road (CR 21/2), Brandywine, WV 26802
Coordinates: 38.6071966, -79.2506790
Year Built: before 1850
Period of Significance: before 1850 - c. 1930

© Google Maps

Hoover Mill in Brandywine was instrumental to liquor production in the area from its earliest days. Photo by Elmer Napier

The Hoover Mill's exterior is in a state of decay.
Photos by Tracy Lawson

The late Eston Teter, who hailed from a Pendleton County milling family, believed the original Hoover Mill in the village of Brandywine had an undershot wheel and ground grain both for bread and for moonshine.[497] Sources within the Hoover family say the mill was the first built in the area. One historian claims it's so old that "John Miller who lived opposite the Hoover Mill was a deserter from the Army of Cornwallis."[498]

Local historian Paula Mitchell supplied a list of names known to be associated with the Hoover Mill, among them a man with the surname Miller who was supposed to have built the mill. A search of Federal Census records yielded a John Miller, age twenty-five, living with his young family near the Hoovers in 1850.[499] Another John Miller, seventy-three, was the Hoover family's next-door neighbor in 1860,[500] and was listed again, then a venerable eighty-three years old, in 1870.[501] While the elder John Miller could have either built or supervised the building of the mill, neither of these men was old enough to have served in the British army during the American Revolution. Though I was unable to substantiate that bit of local lore, records show someone with the name Miller first lived in Brandywine around 1757.[502]

Roy Bowers, a Hoover descendant and the mill's current owner, estimated that the mill was built before the Civil War. My efforts to pinpoint an approximate date of the mill's founding led to Henry Williams, a twenty-seven-year-old miller and native of the District of Columbia. According to census records, Williams was living with the William Hoover family in 1850.[503]

William Hoover's mill is present in the 1850 US Federal Census Non-Population Schedule for Industry. It was a water-driven saw and flouring mill. Hoover reported $3,100 invested in the business. The mill operated with two mill hands and turned out 1,000 barrels of flour and meal and 15,000 feet of lumber.[504] This suggested the mill was established well before 1850.

The mill's size and configuration could accommodate an Oliver Evans-style system, and photos of the interior show wooden chutes that would have moved the grain from one step in the processing to the next.

According to descendants Roy Bowers, Greg Hoover, and Olin Hoover, the family held one of, if not the first, whiskey distilling license in the state of West Virginia. This sets the Hoover Mill apart from any of the others profiled in this book, and I was eager to see what more I could bring to light.

The History of Pendleton County, West Virginia says that at the turn of the twentieth century the community of Brandywine had "the only thoroughfare from the east of any importance,"[505] over Shenandoah Mountain to Harrisonburg, Virginia.

The village of Brandywine was named by Continental Army veterans in remembrance of the battle by that name fought in Pennsylvania in 1777.[506] But there's more to every story, and some locals claim the name Brandywine truly alludes to a wreck on that Shenandoah Mountain pass that involved a wagon full of Hoover hooch.

The visual image of wooden casks bouncing away down a mountain road enhances the tale, and the Hoover Mill's story is not complete without examining the battle for temperance that led to the nationwide period of Prohibition from 1919-1933.

The movement to abolish West Virginia's alcohol trade began within a year of the state's founding in 1863.[507] Despite the ongoing Civil War, in which each half of the divided nation wrestled to bend the other to its will, most West Virginians did not believe they had the right to control the habits of their neighbors.[508]

At the state's first Constitutional Convention in Wheeling in 1863, Governor Arthur Boreman advocated a license system that would enable the state to take an active role in the management of vice. The 1863 legislature took the governor's advice and passed a law to license intoxicating liquors.[509]

The national temperance movement, driven by tension between social ideals and practical realities, was doomed to a long, arduous fight. Prohibition historian David Kyvig wrote, "A new wave of temperance agitation began with the formation of the Prohibition party in 1869 and the Women's Christian Temperance Union in 1873, two organizations which put prohibition at the top of a list of desired social and political reforms."[510]

In the 1870s, county after county in West Virginia voted to go dry. Of the fifteen that still allowed liquor sales by the summer of 1881, twelve bordered at least one other state that wasn't dry.[511]

As the new century dawned, industrialization, immigration, and the rise of a more progressive power structure convinced most Mountain State residents that controlling—and eventually abolishing—the alcohol trade was necessary.

Politicians salivated at the thought of the extra revenue to be gained by increasing alcohol retail license, production, and selling fees. According to the license bill's supporters, the increased rates were "estimated to create from $100 to $150,000 per year."[512]

With the West Virginia budget tied to the alcohol business, fees and taxes applied to the West Virginia liquor industry generated the bulk of license revenues. Under a law which went into effect on May 1, 1905, distilleries and breweries were required to pay a $100 distilling or brewing fee. Whether inside or outside West Virginia, makers of beer and spirits had to pay for a "manufacturer's selling license" to carry on a wholesale liquor business within West Virginia borders. Distillers paid a fee of $500, and the levy for brewers ranged from $600 to $6000, depending on annual production.[513]

Despite the onslaught of efforts to curtail liquor production, the Hoovers carried on their business. The following was filed in Pendleton County Court in 1897:

> Upon the motion of William Hoover who the Court certifys [sic] is a man of good moral character is given permission to sell ardent spirits wine, bear [beer] and drink of like nature at his ware room in Bethel District in this County from the 13th day of December 1897 to the 1st day of May 1898. Thereupon the said William Hoover came into open Court and together with J. T. Harold, J. T. Kile, B. S. Havener, and William B. Anderson his sureties entered into and acknowledged a bond in the penalty of $3,500.00 conditioned according to law, which said bond is approved by the Court and ordered to be recorded.[514]

A license and permit bond such as this protects consumers from harm by guaranteeing businesses will adhere to laws and regulations set by federal, state, and local government agencies. This type of bond can be assured by posting as little as 1 percent of the amount of the bond,[515] so perhaps William Hoover was required to pay only $3.50 for the license, unless he was later found to be in violation of the law.

The license tax-related revenue collected by the state between July 1898 and July 1899 totaled $225,107. Of that, $210,327 came from fees and taxes on beer and liquor.[516] By the eve of the vote on state prohibition in the summer of 1912, that amount had tripled.[517]

Other restrictions on the liquor trade were put into play during this period. US Representative James R. Mann, a progressive Republican from vice-ridden Chicago, sponsored the 1906 Pure Food and Drug Act, which removed patent medicines from drugstore shelves. The law regulated product labeling and paved the way for the implementation of the US Food and Drug Administration.[518] Drugs, defined in accordance with the standards in the United States Pharmacopoeia and the National Formulary, could not be sold unless the specific ingredients were plainly stated on the label.[519]

An article in the Highland County, Virginia, *Recorder* dated March 13, 1908, read:

> The law as to distilleries has been greatly improved. The small country distilleries are brought under the provisions of the Mann law, that is to say, the small distilleries in the country districts must show to the court that a majority of qualified voters of the district or town are in favor of the application; that there is adequate police protection, and that the establishment of said distillery shall not be contrary to sound public policy or injurious to the moral or material interest of the community. The new law prohibits the sale of liquor in any quantity at the place where the distillery is located, if the distillery is located in a territory where retail liquor license cannot be granted.[520]

West Virginia went dry in 1914,[521] five years before the National Prohibition Act was ratified by the requisite number of states on January 16, 1919.[522]

As state legislators continued to tighten the noose, West Virginians found alternative ways to quench their thirst. The government responded with harsher enforcement, which led to increasingly aggressive violation, and West Virginia remained awash in illegal hooch.

Under national prohibition, a citizen was either a teetotaler or a criminal. One West Virginia judge uttered the following in 1923:

> I care not what your individual opinion of the law may be, you cannot say that intoxicating liquor has ever benefited anyone in a substantial way, except in those who traffic in it. It is a law and it is not a matter of whether we are personally in favor of it or against it – it must be enforced. It is said that it interferes with our personal liberty – but bear in mind that there is no such thing as personal liberty. Liberty consists in doing such things as may suit our own convenience so long as it does not interfere with the rights of another or with the public.[523]

Lester Hoover, who worked in the mill as a teenager, was interviewed for a magazine article around the time of his hundredth birthday. Lester recalled the last few years before Prohibition went into effect in West Virginia, when his family's main source of income came from applejack, or apple brandy. All the neighbors would bring their apples to be pressed at the Hoovers' cider mill. The pomace, or crushed remains of the apples, would be left to ferment until it disintegrated when squeezed. Then it was poured into the still's copper kettle, which had an airtight lid with a coiled copper pipe that led outside the stillhouse and through a barrel of cold water, which caused the alcohol-laden steam to condense. When the liquor was run through the apple mash a second time, the resulting applejack came out 86 proof.[524]

A government agent would come by about once a month to sample and stamp the barrels of whiskey. Once this was done, the Hoovers would haul the barrels to logging camps to sell. They drank a lot themselves too. When they went to the fields to work, they always brought a jug along.[525]

How long the Hoovers held their liquor license is uncertain, but Lester reported that his dad was the only licensed liquor refiner in the area before Prohibition and that he held "license number two."[526] Neither the state's Alcohol Beverage Control Association nor the Department of the Arts, Culture, and History keep records back far enough to confirm the date or the number of the license.

Compelled to cease production when West Virginia went dry in 1914, the family's distilling days came to an end during Prohibition when someone stole their idle still and carried it away to another part of the county to make moonshine. Lester's brother, a sheriff's assistant, saw the destroyed remnants of it after it was cut up during a government raid on a moonshine operation in the Smoke Hole.[527]

* * *

According to local historical accounts, the Hoovers had the first gristmill in the area, and Lester Hoover stated that the mill was built by his great-grandfather, William Hoover (1817-1889). However, evidence shows his grandfather Peter Hoover may have built an earlier mill on the site.

Peter (1746-1807) was a son of Sebastian Hoover, an early settler, and brother of Jacob Hoover *(See Homan Mill, page 227)*.

Peter left land to his sons William and George. William (1785-1835) married Barbara Probst in 1806 and bought George's portion of the land in December 1820.[528]

The land passed to William's son, who is called William Sr. (1817-1889) in genealogy records. He was appointed postmaster of Brandywine in 1877. With his second wife, Elizabeth, William Sr. deeded the land to his son William J. (1855-1917) and his wife, Mary Jane Rexrode, in 1885.

In the late 1800s, the mill may have been expanded to accommodate a Barnard and Leas roller mill system.

On the 1910 Census, William J. listed his occupation as miller in a custom mill. His son Lester, then seventeen years old, was working as a miller.

When automobiles came to Pendleton County there were no bridges across South Fork River, and there were two river crossings, located at each end of the William Hoover property. Model Ts had problems fording the river due to the slick rocks, so Raymond, one of the Hoover kids, would hitch horses to the cars and pull them through the river. He was usually given a quarter for his services.[529]

The Hoover family understood the art of the side gig. William Jr. made chicken coops, and when he had a wagonload full, they would leave early in the morning, cross Shenandoah Mountain, and deliver them to Harrisonburg. Then they would proceed to the Dry River area to camp for the night, get up early the next day, and come back to Brandywine. On one trip, William Jr. drank tainted water while at the campsite, contracted typhoid fever, and died unexpectedly at the age of sixty-two.[530]

William J. and Mary Jane had eleven children, and their sons George, William W., and Raymond worked at the mill.

When Paula Mitchell interviewed Raymond Hoover, the youngest brother, he recalled that the mill closed around the time of the Depression. He used to assist in the mill and did a lot of the grinding.

The mill had likely ceased operation by 1943, when Virgil and George inherited and divided the property. George received the tract with the mill. As George never married or had children, upon his death the property passed to his brother Lester, who left the mill to the children of his sister Erma Hoover Bowers.[531]

Exterior of Hoover Mill during its heyday
Photo courtesy of Jana Reichelderfer

23. MCCOY MILL

Pendleton County
Address: 293 Thorn Creek Road, Franklin, WV 26807
Coordinates: 38.6101324, -79.3515719
Year Built: c. 1845
Period of Significance: c. 1757-1945
Added to the National Register of Historic Places in 1986

© Google Maps

McCoy Mill has been a bed-and-breakfast inn and a student dormitory.
Photo by Elmer Napier

McCoy Mill near Franklin, owned by three generations of statesmen and gentlemen farmers, is now owned by Professor Daniel Taylor, who considers it the perfect place to showcase modern sustainability practices.

Ulrich Conrad, a pioneer settler from Switzerland, came to Pendleton County around 1757 and built a mill at the mouth of Thorn Creek on the South Branch of the Potomac. He received a patent for the land on May 12, 1770. Conrad's son Ulrich Jr., inherited the property in 1777, which had "six acres with [a] mill seat thereon erected."[532]

Ulrich Jr. supplied flour and meal to the soldiers in Lord Dunmore's War, a 1774 precursor to the American Revolution,[533] and again for Continental troops in 1782.[534]

General William McCoy (b. 1768) purchased the Peninger and Ulrich Conrad sections at and below the mouth of the Thorn and established himself in the mercantile business in Franklin. He likely hired someone else to run the mill. His prominence as a public man in his own county resulted in his election to Congress for eleven consecutive terms beginning in 1811. He was a trusted friend of President Andrew Jackson, and for many years he held the important post of chairman of the Committee on Ways and Means. He was also a member of the Constitutional Convention of 1829. His Congressional career was brought to a close by a stroke that left him paralyzed.[535]

William McCoy (b. 1800), nephew of General William McCoy (b. 1768) and son of the general's brother Benjamin came to Franklin as a youth to assist in his uncle's business while General McCoy was serving in Congress. An attorney, he held the positions of justice and deputy sheriff and served in the state legislature. He married his first cousin, Caroline McCoy, General William's daughter, in 1829, and they had one son, William (b. 1830). Caroline's death the same year, at age twenty-six, was likely due to complications from childbirth.

William McCoy (b. 1800) inherited the mill after General William McCoy's death in 1835 and found the business so profitable that he decided to replace it with a larger mill.[536] He kept some of the original foundation when he tore down the original mill in 1845 and retained a log cabin that dates from the 1700s. When the cabin fell into ruin in the early 1900s, the original stone chimney was saved and now graces a log cabin built in the 1980s.[537]

Captain William (b. 1830), a graduate of the Virginia Military Academy, was an attorney like his father and served in the state legislature.[538] At the outbreak of the Civil War, he was made captain of the Twenty-fifth Virginia Infantry Regiment Company F. Within months, he contracted measles and returned to his father's home, where he died of pneumonia.[539] Edward W. Boggs, a son of General James Boggs, succeeded him in command[540] *(See Boggs Mill, page 217)*. Captain William's half-sister, Caroline, married William Harrison Boggs, another son of General James Boggs, in 1868.[541]

Because Captain William died a bachelor without children, the mill passed to yet another William McCoy (b. 1878) after the death of William (b. 1800) in 1886. William (b. 1878) was a grandson of William (b. 1800), the son of John McCoy. William McCoy (b. 1878) continued the family tradition by studying law and serving in the West Virginia House of Delegates, but he forged his own path in 1913, when he founded the *Pendleton Times*, the area's first newspaper. His son William, (b. 1921), took over the *Times* in 1952, and after his death, John Wright McCoy, a grandson of William (b. 1878), a significant local farmer who owns land adjacent to the mill, assumed ownership of the newspaper.

The adjacent miller's house was built around 1920. After World War II, when William (b. 1878) sold the property to the American Legion for use as a Legion Home, an addition was built to connect the mill house to the mill. The equipment inside was removed in the 1950s.

The mill was nearing its 150th year when Glen and Iris Hofecker adapted it to a furniture workshop and bed and breakfast inn.[542] The Hofeckers added the current waterwheel and used it to generate electric power for the building. After Glen's death in 2006, the bed and breakfast ceased operation, and the mill was listed for sale in 2010.

Enter Daniel Taylor.

When Taylor purchased McCoy Mill in 2010, it had not been used in several years and was in a state of disrepair, with a leaking roof and a sagging porch. He replaced about a quarter of the siding, scraped, repainted, and renovated the kitchen and bathrooms. The old chestnut split rail fence, which was rotting and damaged in places, could not be restored as chestnut trees no longer exist. Taylor brought large rocks from the cliff to fill in gaps with a rock wall fence.

The 1845 mill has notable structural features, including sixteen spruce beams that measure forty-two feet by twenty feet by ten feet. According to Taylor, no known spruce trees that size grew within thirty miles of the mill site. The posts supporting the massive beams are chamfered, a Dutch design used from the 1600s, in which corners are cut away to make symmetrical sloping edges. According to Taylor, this building technique was not just ornamental; it was believed posts with less exposed edge would catch fire more slowly, so that the beam structure might survive even if the walls burned. The interior paneling is all poplar, chosen because it burns relatively fast and not too hot—another preventive choice.

He believes the original 1757 mill was a sawmill, and presumes the current mill was also used first as a sawmill and later adapted to grind wheat, corn, and buckwheat.

The river confluence has provided a remarkable abundance of wildlife that actively use this joining of rivers, including bear, otter, deer, muskrat, mink, beaver, bald eagle, golden eagle, osprey, and eels. The shores have also provided intriguing Native American arrowheads and other artifacts.

Taylor, who lives in the mill and rents the attached miller's house to his son and his family, is president and professor at Future Generations University, which is based in Franklin and specializes in applied community development and implementing programs that advance just and lasting change.

The Future Generations Global Network, a separate parallel group, coordinates programs in Afghanistan, China, Haiti, India, Peru, and the United States.

Taylor is adapting the mill into an example of hyper efficient hydroelectric power by harnessing the power generated by the Thorn River's twelve-foot waterfall—and it's no stretch to say the project is well within his wheelhouse.

Learn more about Future Generations University at www.future.edu, and the Global Network at www.future.org.

The wheel at the rear of McCoy Mill
Photo by Tracy Lawson

McCoy Mill in winter
Photo courtesy of Tina Bowers

This chamfered post, found in Union Bryarly Mill in Berkeley County, is indicative of the technique used in many other mills of the period, including McCoy Mill. Photo by Tracy Lawson

PENDLETON COUNTY   251

4. MITCHELL MILL

Pendleton County
Address: 11684 Sugar Grove Road, Sugar Grove, WV 26815
Coordinates: 38.4973984, -79.3288486
Year Built: before 1784
Period of Significance: before 1784-1949

© Google Maps

Mitchell Mill, with the family homeplace in the background
Photo by Tracy Lawson

Mitchell Mill
Photo by Tracy Lawson

Many of Pendleton County's early settlers were of German ancestry, and their folklore included hex signs to ward off evil spirits.

Circular motifs common in Pennsylvania Dutch hex signs have been used in diverse applications across Europe for millennia.[543] The six-pointed rosette, carved on artifacts dating back to 400 BCE, is said to be a symbol of Christ's resurrection and life everlasting. In modern hexerei, it symbolizes both protection and prosperity.[544] Traditionally, each design was considered a painted prayer.[545]

Mitchell Mill, located in Sugar Grove, a hamlet at the edge of the Virginia State Line in southeastern Pendleton County, has several six-point rosettes carved in its interior.

First settled in prerevolutionary times, Sugar Grove gets its name from a large grove of sugar maple trees in the area. By 1900, Sugar Grove had two stores, a church, a post office, a blacksmith, mills, a resident doctor, and six houses. Only four more houses have been added to the community since.[546]

Milling was the predominant industry in the area, and three mill structures, one of which was constructed in the early twentieth century, survive today. Their owners and descendants are related to one another by blood and by marriage.

The Hoover family was the first to settle in Sugar Grove. The oldest surviving home was built by Daniel Kiser before 1870 and is now owned by the late Bill Bowers's family.[547] Keep an eye out for the surnames Mitchell, Homan, Kiser, Botkin, and Rexrode, too. You'll meet them all in the Pendleton County chapter of this book. *(See the following for more: Homan Mill, page 227, Botkin-Simmons Mill, page 305, Rexrode Mill, page 311, Waggy-Mitchell Mill, page 277, and Hoover Mill, page 235)*

In 1774, Georg Puffenbarger III bought the land on which the Mitchell Mill stands today. The exact date of the mill's construction is unknown, but oral tradition states that in 1784, George Washington and his nephew Bushrod surveyed what is now the George Washington National Forest. While they were in the area, Bushrod dined with the Puffenbarger family, and the surveying party bought cornmeal at their mill.

This six-pointed rosette hex symbol carved into the stair stringer is one of many found in Mitchell Mill.
Photo by Tracy Lawson

A randomly placed mantel inside the Mitchell Mill has been saved and treasured by generations of the Puffenbarger and Mitchell descendants because, as the legend goes, the great Washington—or maybe it was his nephew—laid his corncob pipe there during their visit.[548] So this family can claim, not that George Washington slept here, but that maybe, just maybe, George Washington smoked here! After his two terms as president ended, Washington continued surveying work until a month before his death in December 1799.[549]

For generations, it was common to name male Puffenbarger and Mitchell descendants George Washington in tribute to the family's connection to the Father of our Country.

The family homeplace near the mill dates to that same year, and the first legal document to reference the mill is an 1821 deed. Through the years, the mill's operation supported as many as four households of the Mitchell-Puffenbarger clan at a time. The family also farmed together and ran a sawmill and threshing business.

Each succeeding owner was expected to maintain and update the mill, a four-story, frame structure that stands forty-seven feet high over a raised stone foundation measuring approximately thirty by thirty-one feet. Over the years, the mill has been re-sided four times and its gabled, shingle roof changed to tin, but the beams inside the mill, built in the old way, remain unaltered and are pegged rather than nailed.

Georg's son Christian married Mary Mitchell in 1828. Though the couple had no children of their own, they cared for and raised nephews from both sides of the family.

For over a century after Christian took over running the mill, its buhrstones ground corn and buckwheat, and a toll taken for payment was recorded on a toll board. Some customers stored their grain in bins on the third floor and had it processed as it was needed. People waited their turn while the mill worked its way through its daily capacity of 125 bushels, and the miller's wife often served meals to the waiting folks.

After Christian's death in 1855, the mill passed to members of the Mitchell family. The first was Benjamin Mitchell (1829-1904), a son of Mary Puffenbarger's brother Jacob.[550]

The mantel is a tangible tie to George Washington's 1784 surveying trip to the area. Photo by Tracy Lawson

During the Civil War, Yankee soldiers were camped across the river from the mill. Tired of their steady diet of rice, the commander and several of his men crossed the river early one morning and advanced to the mill. They woke the inhabitants of the homestead and ordered Benjamin's wife, Hannah Swadley Mitchell, to fix a breakfast of pancakes and other foods. She didn't have time to dress properly before she fixed a delicious breakfast for the hungry men.[551]

Benjamin was still working as a miller at age seventy,[552] but his son Samuel (1863-1932) took over operations around the turn of the century. He reported his occupation as miller in a custom mill in 1910,[553] 1920,[554] and 1930.[555] He made coffins in the upper story of the mill when he wasn't busy milling.[556] Many of his tools remain in the building.

Samuel's son Hugh (1898-1955), who united the two original families again when he married Gertrude Puffenbarger in 1921, listed his occupation as a postal carrier in the 1920 Federal Census.[557]

Hugh and Gertrude's daughter Margene Moore shared some childhood memories that suggest both Samuel and Hugh worked in the mill in the 1920s. They were likely the ones who bought the Fitz Wheel from the defunct Hiner Mill in 1932.[558] The wheel is twenty-four feet in diameter and two feet wide, with seventy-two buckets. Fitz Wheels were specially designed to break down for easy transport.[559] Margene wrote:

> The first thing I remember is the large wooden wheel. Grandpa (Samuel Mitchell) and Daddy (Hugh Mitchell) only ground buckwheat, corn, and rye. I remember that our bread was very dark. We kids loved to ride on the wheel when they weren't grinding. But that stopped when one time we got the wheel going round so fast that we had a hard time stopping it.

> The mill had four floors, machinery on all floors and large bins on the top floors for some of the farmers to store their grain. The wheel was run by water coming from a dam about 500 yards above the house and mill. It collected water from several springs in the gap. From the dam to the waterwheel was a long trough (sluice) that carried the water to the forebay on top of the wheel

that controlled the water that went over to run the wheel. The wooden wheel then turned several large, wooden cog wheels in the lower floor of the mill. They, in turn, ran the 'rocks' that crushed the grain coming from the first floor. The rocks were two large round stones that had a hopper over each of them to hold the grain. My grandfather and daddy took several days out of the year, sitting bent over, using a sharp-edged tool to 'pick' the rocks to sharpen them.

The ground buckwheat and rye went into a bin on the lower floor, and was then hand-carried upstairs and dumped into another hopper that went into a long batiste bolter downstairs that separated the bran from the flour.

When I was six or seven (around 1926-1927), Grandpa and Daddy hired an engineer from Ohio to install all the machinery that was needed to grind wheat using a tractor to run the machinery. I remember Daddy mixing some substance that looked like cornstarch with flour that made our bread white for the first time.

My mother told me that when she married my daddy, she had $2,000. That money went into "making over the mill."[560]

Margene's remembrance serves to confirm that Hugh Mitchell had two run of buhrstones for corn, rye, and buckwheat grinding, and installed two roller mills to process wheat flour in the 1920s. It currently has one run of buhrstones. The second run was removed to make room for the rollers. The remaining buhrstones were used to grind buckwheat and cornmeal.

After the 1947 flood, Hugh took out the sluice and dam and converted the mill to run on a McCormick gasoline engine. In time, the combination of damaging floods and the significant cost of the government's regulations requiring the flour to be bleached ended the mill's operation in 1949.

Descendants of the Mitchell-Puffenbarger clan are proud stewards of the mill and well-steeped in its 200-year history. Though the mill has not been active since Tom Mitchell was nine years old, it passed to him and Hugh's other children. They, like every preceding generation, maintained the property.

Recently, a new generation has shouldered the responsibility for the mill's upkeep and preservation. The legacy now rests with Tom and Paula Mitchell's son, Dr. Brandon Mitchell. Brandon, who owns a general dentistry practice in Franklin, juggles the demands of a young and growing family while refurbishing his family's mill. Under his ownership, the entire rock foundation has been rebuilt by world-renowned stonemason James Floory, who used the original stones, some of which weighed between 700 and 900 pounds.[561] Brandon has also hired help to rebuild stairways, repair basement flooring, and reset the main beams, and hopes to get the mill back to full operation.

Brandon's wife, Cara Homan Mitchell, comes from another Sugar Grove milling family. While I was visiting, Brandon joked that his kids, with their long pedigree of millers on both sides of the family, will grow up to be the "best millers ever."

Tom, Paula, and Brandon met me at the mill to give me a tour, and as we explored the different levels, one question dominated our conversation: "What do you suppose that machine/tool/unidentified object is for?" Brandon's obvious enthusiasm for the task ahead of him was catching, and we passed an enjoyable afternoon admiring the ongoing restoration and surveying machinery and objects that had once served a purpose and are now quaint, a little dusty, and ready for a return to usefulness.

Paula, a local historian, shared stories about the mill that have been passed down through the generations.

In times past, families in Sugar Grove believed a cure for childhood asthma and whooping cough was to put the child in the hopper with the grain and let them remain there until all the grain was ground out. Some area old-timers who recalled sitting in the hopper of grain insisted that afterward, their cough was either cured or, at least, the severity reduced.

When a Dr. Smith, a physician in Augusta County, interviewed locals about this practice, none of them could offer explanations for why or how this treatment helped ease coughs, but one woman suggested the buhrstones' gentle vibration shook the cough out of the afflicted person.[562]

But the cure didn't have anything to do with the hex symbols—or did it?

38. ONEGO MILL

Pendleton County
Address: 2930 Allegheny Drive, Seneca Rocks, WV 26884
Coordinates: 38.8472812, -79.4216917
Year Built: b.1880
Period of Significance: b.1880- c.1920

© Google Maps

The Onego Mill's origins are not readily apparent.
Photo by Tracy Lawson

The village of Onego, pronounced "one-go," lies in Pendleton County within the Monongahela National Forest.

Onego is a Seneca word meaning *pool*, but some folks claim the village is called that because the old bridge that crossed Roaring Creek was so narrow that it only allowed one car to go at a time,[563] a moniker that pokes fun at the size of the community.

If you're not watching for the Onego Mill, it's easy to miss. Its location near Roaring Creek is the only clue to its past function. As of this writing, the two-story building is well maintained and appears to be used for storage.

In the 1970s, parts from three mills were used to build the Glade Creek Grist Mill at Babcock State Park in Fayette County. Several published sources mention the Onego Mill as among those that provided the transplants. But the unassuming little structure perched on the edge of Roaring Creek is not that mill.

The 1882-1883 *West Virginia Gazetteer and business directory* lists two mills in Mouth of Seneca, one run by A. C. Boggs, the other by A. H. Dolly.[564]

The little white building in Onego is just a few miles from Boggs Mill in Mouth of Seneca, but could I prove it was the mill run by A. H. Dolly?

Julie Taylor, who descends from family in the area, stated that her great-grandfather John R. Adamson ran a general store and post office near the mill, and sure enough, the Adamsons were present in the area, with G. W. Adamson & Bro. running the general store in 1882.[565]

1880 Census data showed Joseph Adamson living next door to Amby Dolly, a miller.[566] Just a few pages away I found Aaron Boggs, also a miller, which was enough evidence to establish the two mills' proximity. I concluded that Amby Dolly (1836-1915) was the miller at Onego at that time.

What else could I learn about him?

Amby's paternal grandfather, Johann Dahle, was a miller, though his mill was located near the Pendleton-Grant County line.[567] Dahle (Dolly) came to America as a Hessian soldier in the services of the British army under General Cornwallis. He was captured at Yorktown and imprisoned at Winchester, VA, for a time. Family tradition maintains he was advised by General Washington himself to remain in Virginia, and around 1780, he settled on the North Fork in what would become Pendleton County. He was known by the nicknames Cornyackle and Barleycorn and lived to the ripe old age of one hundred years. The Dolly family's landholdings, which increased over time to several hundred acres, may have included the upland grassy area known as Dolly Sods.[568]

Johann's eldest son, Andrew, settled on a farm deeded by his father near what is now the Pendleton-Grant County line.[569] He owned a mill there, which may have also been his father's.[570]

One of Johan's grandsons, Amby Harper Dolly, (1836-1915), the son of George Washington Dolly, married Phoebe Davis in 1859[571] and served in the West Virginia State militia during the Civil War from July 2, 1863, to June 1, 1865.[572] He listed his occupation as miller in the 1880 Census.

In the 1891-1892 *Gazetteer*, J. K. Dally is the miller in Mouth of Seneca,[573] and the 1900 issue lists J. R. Dolly, which may have been a typographical error and refers to the same individual.[574] I was unable to determine the exact identity of this person. Amby did not have a brother or son living in the area, so it was likely a cousin or nephew.

J. R. Dolly is listed again as running a flour mill in the 1904-1905 *Gazetteer*, but in this edition, Adam Kisamore appears for the first time as a miller.[575] Kisamore, a nephew of Amby Dolly, was a miller and farmer in Onego.[576] His mother, Margaret Dolly Kisamore, was Amby's sister.

Kisamore was working as a miller in 1910,[577] but in 1920[578] and 1930,[579] he reports his occupation as farm laborer.

Unfortunately, the trail goes cold there, with no indication of when the mill ceased operation. What I did learn has been shared with the Society for the Preservation of Old Mills, in the hopes it may lead to more information.

44. PRIEST MILL

Pendleton County
Address: 131 Priest Mill Lane, Franklin, WV 26807
Coordinates: 38.6400106, -79.3290667
Year Built: 1900
Period of Significance: 1900-1950
Added to National Register of Historic Places in 2000

© Google Maps

The Priest brothers honed their skills as mechanics in the Confederate Army. After the war, they returned home and opened a furniture factory.
Photo by Tracy Lawson

In the years following the Civil War, members of the Priest family harnessed the power of the South Branch of the Potomac River to run a furniture- and wagon-making enterprise. Their fascination with technological innovations—particularly electricity—led them to modify their business to provide power to the village of Franklin nearly two decades before it became available in other remote parts of the state.

In 1860, Samuel Priest was a twenty-five-year-old master mechanic. His brother, Thomas, three years younger, was a journeyman,[580] signifying he successfully completed an apprenticeship qualification and was considered competent to work in his field.[581]

These mechanically-inclined brothers enlisted early in the war— Samuel with the Twenty-Fifth Virginia Infantry, Company E, where he rose to the rank of First Sergeant. He was wounded at Second Manassas, August 29, 1862. In January 1863, his skill as a mechanic led to him being detailed to make cloth for the Confederate Army.[582] It is possible he was keeping the machinery in good repair for the task. Thomas, a Fifth Sergeant, was taken prisoner in October 1864 and detained at Camp Chase in Columbus, Ohio. He was released in June 1865 after taking the oath of allegiance.[583]

After the war, Samuel and Thomas reunited in Franklin and opened a cabinetmaking business. In 1895, Samuel and his sons Robert and Paul rented a site on the banks of the South Branch of the Potomac. In their woodworking and wheelwrighting mill, the Priest family made furniture, flooring, molding, and architectural details for many Franklin homes and churches, including some now listed on the National Register of Historic Places.[584] They also built a variety of conveyances, from heavy lumber and farm wagons to carriages and buggies. Their thrift is evident in the wood shavings saved from their furniture manufacturing and lumber planing to be used to insulate the outside walls.

When the building caught fire in 1899, the Priests used a team of horses to drag their three-sided planer out of the flames. They reinstalled it when they rebuilt the following year.[585]

Thomas appears to have continued in the woodworking business with Samuel and his sons for a few years, and in 1910, he listed his profession as undertaker,[586] so perhaps he was building coffins as well. Thomas never married, and resided with his sisters Mary and Sadie, both of whom also remained single. Both women predeceased him, Mary in 1911 and Sadie in 1912. Thomas died in 1916.

Since then, the mill has retained its original footprint and shape, except for a 1916 shed-roof addition on the north side of the first floor, built to accommodate the Bullock generator and control panels for the hydroelectric power plant. The mill was in continuous operation from 1900 through the 1950s, with wool carding, the process used to prepare it for spinning or use as batting for quilts and comforters, as its final function.[587]

The millrace measures 988 feet from the headgates at the dam to its entrance under the mill, which supplies a twelve-foot head, or drop, to power the turbine. Its governor controls and adjusts the amount of water entering the mill's Leffel Turbine to controls its speed.[588] The turbine is located beneath the first floor. Water from the race flows through an L-shaped channel to the turbine pit and exits below the turbine into the tailrace.[589]

Samuel Priest and his sons were fascinated by electricity and Thomas Edison's invention of the light bulb. Electricity was transforming the daily lives of individuals in populated areas. By harnessing the power source that powered their factory, the Priests brought the modern convenience to Franklin.

After Edison developed the first practical incandescent light bulb in 1879, which was supported by his own direct-current electrical system, hydroelectric plants built to generate power in cities across the United States guaranteed Edison a fortune in patent royalties. But direct current was difficult to transmit over distances without a significant loss of energy.[590] An Edison employee, Nicola Tesla, had a background in mathematics that his inventor boss did not, and he redesigned Edison's DC generators to use alternating current, which could transmit high-voltage energy over long distances using lower current. Edison dismissed Tesla's ideas as "splendid" but "utterly impractical."[591] Tesla left Edison in 1885 and set out to raise capital. Industrialist George Westinghouse purchased some of Tesla's patents, and within a year, Westinghouse Electric began installing AC generators around the country, focusing mostly on the

A governor regulates the amount of water that enters a mill's turbine and controls its speed. Photo by Tracy Lawson

The Priest Mill generated hydro-electric power for the city of Franklin, WV. Photo by Tracy Lawson

less-populated areas that Edison's system could not reach. By 1887, after only a year in the business, Westinghouse already had more than half as many generating stations as Edison. The concern at Edison was palpable, as sales agents around the country were demoralized by Westinghouse's reach into rural and suburban areas.

In 1893, Westinghouse won the contract to light the Chicago World's Fair and had all the positive publicity he would need to make alternating current the industry standard.

Edison, attempting to halt Westinghouse's takeover of the fledgling industry, claimed the AC system was more dangerous, with all that voltage passing through the wires. "Just as certain as death," Edison predicted, "Westinghouse will kill a customer within six months after he puts in a system of any size."[592]

The AC-versus-DC power debate was settled by the time the Priests put their mill to work generating electricity. In 1911, Paul Priest's home became the first in Franklin to have electric lights. The house also served as a model home, with each of its four sides displaying a different style of siding, shingles, and trim, to aid customers in choosing what they wanted for their own houses.[593]

When Colonel John McClure, a Franklin merchant, donated $4,000 to create a town power plant, the Priest Mill took on an additional role as the Franklin Central Electric Station. In 1916, two streetlights on Franklin's main street were electrified for the first time. The mill also served as the Municipal Water Works and, in October 1917, charged 1,883 kilowatt hours and 500,000 gallons of water to the city.[594]

Edison had not been wrong about the dangers of AC current. Samuel's son Robert, who moved to Pittsburgh and took a job as an electrician at the Westinghouse Power Company in Pittsburgh, was forty-one years old when he met with a tragic end in 1918.

The people of our town were both shocked and grieved to learn on Friday that Robert Priest, son of our townsman, Samuel P. Priest, had been fatally injured while working in the powerhouse of the Westinghouse Company in Pittsburgh. The young man came into contact with some live wires and was terribly burned but walked across the street after the accident happened. He was taken to a hospital and died six hours later being conscious to the last. He realized his condition and had a message sent to this brother, Paul Priest, to come to his bedside. Death came before his brother reached him. Mr. Priest's remains were brought back to his boyhood home, and on Wednesday afternoon after impressive funeral services in the Methodist church, they were laid to rest in Cedar Hill cemetery, followed by a large concourse of sorrowing friends. The Masonic Order of this place had charge of the burial. The young man is survived by his aged father, three sisters, Mrs. Mason Boggs and Mrs. Roy L Campbell, of our town, and Mrs. Stiles of Kansas, and one brother, Paul Priest. The floral emblems sent with the body by the Westinghouse Company and Masonic Lodge were beautiful.[595]

Samuel Priest died in 1921. In 1930, Paul Priest's son, S. Elliot, was an electrician working with the "light system" in Franklin.[596] In 1940, Paul listed his occupation as "planing mill operator," so it appears he was still working in the mill toward the end of its operations.[597] Paul, the last of the original Priest Mill partners, died in 1946 at age seventy.[598]

After the mill closed in the 1950s, it remained idle through two owners. In 1986, Vincent and Shirley Budris bought the mill and began renovations.[599] Vincent, a retired carpenter and millwright, was proud that he generated his own electric power for his lathes and other machinery from the mill.[600]

The Priest Mill property, which also includes a house, a modern cabin, and a guesthouse converted from a shed once used for painting wagons, was sold after Vincent's death in 2012 to Jake and Darla Young, and sold again in 2021 to Tom and Teresa Calhoon, who bought the cabin four years before purchasing the rest. Tom and Teresa plan to offer the guesthouse and a modern cabin on the property as short-term rentals for vacationers.

Above: This house above the mill, once owned by Paul Priest, showcased the different styles of siding and trim available from the mill, each side bedecked in a different combination.

Left: Now a guest house, this was once the shed where wagons were painted.

Photos by Tracy Lawson

17. TRUMBO MILL

Formerly in Pendleton County
(now dismantled, in storage in Lynchburg, VA)
Year Built: c. 1831

Trumbo Mill before it was dismantled
Photo courtesy of Robert Hiller

Wanna Buy a Mill? Some Assembly Required.

When Robert Hiller purchased the vacant Levi Trumbo Mill around 2012, he had it disassembled, with photographs and two- and three-dimensional drawings created. Each piece of wood was labeled by a member of the Timber Framers Guild before it was stored in a warehouse in Lynchburg, Virginia. Hiller envisioned transforming the historical structure into a home he could enjoy during his retirement.

Now, his plans have changed, and he's searching for a buyer who is as passionate about timber frame buildings as he. You just have to put it back together.

When assembled, the structure is a two-and-a-half-story frame structure, four bays, measuring twenty-six feet by forty-six feet. It is made of oak and pine with an undershot wheel. The original machinery for the two run of stones includes portions of the hopper boy, face, gear, lantern and pinion gears, and manual sieve. The flooring is a mix of heart pine and oak.

A metal barrel stencil was found inside a wall during the disassembly and has been retained with the rest of the salvage.

Approximately sixty tons of hand-hewn sandstone foundation blocks were also salvaged from the mill.[601]

If this piques your interest, Hiller suggests a visit to millwright Ben Hassett's website at www.hassettmillwrights.net. Hassett is a reputable source for anyone considering undertaking such a project.

Levi Trumbo (1790-1859) is believed to be the original owner of the mill. Upon his death in 1859, his heirs conveyed his land to Allen Dyer: "The first tract contains 100 acres or less and lies on West side of the South Fork [of the Potomac] joining and above Cowger's land includes the Mansion House, the Grist Mill and Saw mill and is bounded as follows ..."[602]

Dyer and his wife conveyed parcels of land totaling about 344 acres to William Adamson in 1870.[603] The land on which the mill stood remains in the Adamson family to this day.

PENDLETON COUNTY 275

Every board was numbered before it was put in storage.
Photo courtesy of Robert Hiller

This barrel stencil, to mark 196 lbs. of superfine flour,
was found in the mill. Photo courtesy of Robert Hiller

49. WAGGY-MITCHELL MILL

Pendleton County
Address: 8951 Moyers Gap Road, Sugar Grove, WV 26815
Coordinates: 38.5136559, -79.3265707
Year Built: 1917
Period of Significance: 1917- c. 1950

© Google Maps

The Waggy-Mitchell Mill is now a private residence.
Photo by Tracy Lawson

The white frame farmhouse on Moyers Gap Road is a private residence, and its appearance gives no indication that it is Sugar Grove's third remaining gristmill. Built in the early twentieth century, the Waggy-Mitchell Mill's story is brief and punctuated by war, disease, and personal loss. Brenna Mitchell, a granddaughter of Ben Hurl Mitchell, the mill's last operator, wants to see it remembered along with the nearby Mitchell and Homan Mills.

Edward Waggy was one of seven children born to William Lewis Waggy and Elizabeth Puffenbarger of Sugar Grove. As a young man, he worked as a schoolteacher.[604] Both his parents died in 1911, and after that Ed, a bachelor, lived with an older brother, William Lewis Waggy, Jr.

In 1917, at age thirty, Ed reported on his WWI draft card that he was in the process of "installing a flour and feed mill and also insurance agent part time with International Life Insurance in Pendleton County, WV."[605] Nowhere does it state whether Edward built the structure or simply installed milling equipment in an existing building. He enlisted in the Naval Reserve as a yeoman on March 25, 1918, and worked for the Bureau of Ordnance, stamping letters and telegrams as they came into the Bureau. He contracted the Spanish Flu in December 1918 and did no sea duty because of his illness. After his discharge in June 1919, Ed returned to Sugar Grove.

Ed's health may have been compromised by that bout with the flu—so much so, that his brother George ran the mill while Ed worked as an office clerk.[606, 607]

Their next-door neighbor was Benjamin Hurl Mitchell and his wife, Hattie Eye Mitchell.[608] Ben was a grandson of Benjamin Mitchell, who owned the nearby Mitchell Mill. He was a corporal in Battery A of the 313th Field Artillery of the Forty-Second Division during World War I and was also discharged in June 1919.[609]

In 1922, tragedy struck the Waggy family three times. An outbreak of flu, typhoid fever, and pneumonia early that year sickened many in Sugar Grove and claimed the life of Edward's brother William. Just forty years old at the time of his death, William left behind a wife and four children under the age of eight.

A few months later, in June, George Waggy, Ed's miller brother, died of his injuries after an accidental fall from a rock cliff, leaving behind a wife and one ten-year-old daughter.[610]

That November, Edward died at the age of thirty-four. His death certificate could not be located, but it is likely he also succumbed to the flu or some other communicable disease in that time before the availability of antibiotics. As an insurance agent, he likely handled his brothers' life insurance policies before and after their deaths. His will leaves specific instructions for the distribution of the insurance money to William's and George's widows and children, and leaves more to their surviving brother, John Marshall Waggy, and their two sisters, Martha Simmons and Mina Waggy, and to Robert L. Eye.[611]

It made me wonder if Edward had a premonition that he would not live long after the deaths of his two brothers.

The Waggy's neighbor, Benjamin Hurl Mitchell, bought the mill. Brenna Mitchell, his granddaughter, stated in an email that he built a house, which is no longer standing, behind the mill. "Granddad died when I was eight, so I didn't have a long time with him. I don't remember him talking about the mill. He spent most of the time with me ensuring I could recite all my granddads back to the one who first came to America. He also taught me how to count in Dutch, as that was all most people spoke in this community until World War I. Finally, he talked about his experience [as a soldier]. My dad didn't talk about the mill operation either."[612]

Brenna stated that her granddad ran the mill only as a sideline and served the community as a deputy sheriff. The mill had a gasoline engine, and when her grandfather wanted to gas up his car, he would pull alongside the house and fill his car's tank from inside—something she found entertaining when a child.

Brenna's interest in local history and the life and times of her beloved grandfather led her to author the book *Pendleton's Boys of '17*, which commemorates and tells the stories of Pendleton's World War I through letters, articles from the *Pendleton Times*, and regimental histories. The book is available through the Pendleton County Historical Society.

POCAHONTAS COUNTY
Formed in 1821

33. MCNEEL MILL

Pocahontas County
Address: US 219 and SR 39, Hillsboro, WV 24946
Coordinates: 38.1575365, -80.1817662
Year Built: 1868
Period of Significance: 1791-1948
Added to the National Register of Historic Places in 1985

© Google Maps

Isacc McNeel, a descendant of the area's earliest settler, purchased and rebuilt a mill on this site in the 1860s. Photo by Elmer Napier

Around the time the highway numbering system came into effect in 1926, the stretch of country road that ran past the McNeel Mill in Pocahontas County joined with the 200 miles of highway through Pennsylvania to the New York state line as the original US Route 219.[613]

Today, US Route 219 stretches 535 miles from its southern terminus at the New River in Rich Creek, Virginia, through West Virginia, Maryland, Pennsylvania, to West Seneca, New York. Other than a short stint as a major city expressway just outside Buffalo, Route 219 carries the traveler past smaller towns and rural scenery.[614]

* * *

The community of Mill Point once had a fort, built around 1774 to protect early settlers from Native American attacks. John and Valentine Cackley, brothers from Winchester, Virginia, and veterans of the American Revolution, came to the area around 1778.[615] John built the first mill, a log structure with one run of small stones, and Valentine stayed to run it when John returned east.[616]

The Cackley brothers were described as large, strong men and "good Indian fighters." In addition to running the mill, Valentine worked as a blacksmith. Court records from 1791 show William Taylor, "a poor infant," was assigned to learn the art of blacksmithing from Valentine Cackley at his mill.[617] (At this time, the legal term infant applied to any young person who had not attained the age of majority.) In rural communities, tax bases were small, with little resources to support the indigent,[618] so children from poverty-stricken homes were often assigned to indentures or apprenticeships, so that they might learn skills that would help them become productive adult members of the community.

In 1803, Valentine added a sawing apparatus to his mill and thus became the owner of the area's first sawmill. He died in March 1825,[619] and his heirs sold the property to Sampson Lockhart Matthews in 1834.[620] In 1850, Matthews's next-door neighbor was Richard McNeel, and several households of Cackleys lived nearby.[621]

Richard McNeel was a grandson of the area's first settler, pioneer John McNeel, who had arrived in the Greenbrier Valley in the 1760s.

He was at the battle of Point Pleasant, the only major engagement in Dunmore's War, on October 10, 1774, and served in the Eighth Virginia Regiment of the Continental Line.[622]

Isaac McNeel, Richard's nephew, intended to purchase and rebuild the Cackley Mill property around 1860. Some sources cite that date for the transaction, but the deed was not written until December 2, 1865.[623] It is possible the Civil War intervened and delayed the deed's preparation. McNeel completed construction in 1868.[624]

In keeping with available technology, Isaac chose a turbine to power the new mill. The millrace directed water into a "water box," evident on the outside of the mill at the second story in period photos. A gate on the millrace controlled the water flow into the box, which then regulated the amount of water that cascaded down onto the turbine.

As was typical, McNeel Mill served as a community hub and gathering place. A general store was built nearby, and Isaac was appointed postmaster of Mill Point in 1879.[625] The 1904 *West Virginia Gazeteer and business directory* lists Isaac McNeel as the owner of one of Mill Point's three flour mills, and Dr. H. W. McNeel as the village physician. A blacksmith, sawmill, shoemaker, and lawyer comprised the other businesses in the village.[626]

Bill McNeel, who is a cousin of the mill's current owners and Pocahontas County Historical Society treasurer, has files of correspondence and invoices pertaining to the mill, which show Isaac purchased equipment from The Wolf Company of Chambersburg, Pennsylvania, in 1905. The correspondence does not state exactly what Isaac acquired, but the company's letterhead lists Turbine Water Wheels among its products. Whatever Isaac bought cost him $387.

When Isaac died in February 1917, the mill went to his son Harvey Winters McNeel. Harvey owned the mill for only a few months before he ordered a new Fitz wheel. Bill McNeel's files include a proposal between Harvey Winters McNeel and the Fitz Water Wheel Company for a twenty-one-foot waterwheel, at the cost of $1,100, signed and accepted by Harvey on June 15, 1917.

Harvey may have decided to change from a turbine to a waterwheel due in part to the Fitz Water Wheel Company's advertisements, which claimed the company's Overshoot Wheel was more adaptable to conditions and more efficient than a turbine *(See Tuscarora Iron Works, page 109)*. A photo believed to be taken around 1910 may have been taken later and might show the wheel Harvey had installed in 1917.

In 1935, a flash flood washed out Stamping Creek and devastated the small community and surrounding area. A nearby house was dislodged from its foundation, and Cackley's Lower Mill and the blacksmith shop were washed completely away. Inside, the McNeel Mill, water rose to within inches of the buhrstones on the grinding platform. Even though the mill survived without serious damage, the flood swept away the millrace, and when the water receded, Stamping Creek no longer flowed near enough to the mill to provide an ample water supply, which hindered its productivity.[627]

Upon Harvey's death on November 1, 1948, his brother John Lanty McNeel became owner.

George M. Williams was the miller at that time. His obituary in *The Pocahontas Times*, dated March 11, 1948, states that Williams operated the mill until a week before his death on February 18.

After John Lanty died on October 22, 1955,[628] his son, Joseph Wilson McNeel, became the next owner. Following Joseph's death on August 31, 1982, the mill passed to Martha, Lanty, and Nora McNeel, nieces and nephew of Joseph.[629] Today the mill is the property of Sinking Springs Farms, Inc., which is owned by Lanty and Martha McNeel.[630]

The structure was used for grain storage until the 1980s. The Pocahontas County Historical Society made repairs to the mill in 1983.[631]

Afterward, it remained idle and might have languished if Matt Tate hadn't driven US Route 219 through Mill Point in 2006. A Massachusetts native who had studied mechanical engineering, Tate was working at the Mountain Institute at Spruce Knob when he first caught sight of the mill. He sought out owner Lanty McNeel and volunteered his spare time to repair the mill and make it operational again. As Tate's work progressed, members of the Pocahontas County Historical Society and members of the community hoped to have the mill running for the county's 200th anniversary celebration in 2021.

Tate lived in the McNeel house above the mill while he worked on the property and was able to restore the millrace and reconstruct the flume, so the mill can now be "run" for demonstration purposes.

Unfortunately, family commitments drew Tate back to his home state of Massachusetts before he could complete the restoration. So again, the future of the mill is in doubt.

In the early part of the twentieth century, the country road that ran past the McNeel Mill became part of US Route 219.
Author's collection

Despite recent efforts to make the mill operational,
its future remains uncertain.
Photo by Tracy Lawson

RANDOLPH COUNTY
Formed in 1787

46. DARDEN-ELKINS MILL

Randolph County
Address: 101 Railroad Avenue, Elkins, WV 26241
Coordinates: 38.9234585, -79.8511997
Year Built: 1902
Period of Significance: 1902-1954
Added to National Register of Historic Places in 2005

© Google Maps

The Darden-Elkins Mill is now home to two museums.
Photo by Tracy Lawson

Its proximity to the railroad tracks is not accidental. The original builder bought the lot next to the tracks to facilitate shipping product.
Photo by Tracy Lawson

The Darden-Elkins Mill stands as an example of the industrial growth in Randolph County and Elkins around the turn of the twentieth century. In 1901, the Elkins Milling Company purchased a lot on the railroad yard of the West Virginia Central and Pittsburg Railway Company for $1,000.[632]

The Elkins Mill operated as a merchant mill, producing flour processed from both spring and winter wheat. Its owners capitalized on the railroad's proximity, bringing in state-of-the-art technology to maximize output. Powered with a coal-fired steam boiler in 1902, when waterpower still dominated the industry, the mill's owners upgraded to electric power around 1910.[633]

The mill, of timber frame construction, stands three stories high, eight bays long and three bays wide, and boasts 10,500 square feet of interior space. The second floor is at railroad grade level on the west side.[634] The structure was originally four stories high, but the top story was removed after a 1937 fire damaged it beyond repair.[635] Logan Smith, the deputy director of Appalachian Forest National Heritage Area, said the building has suffered at least four fires.

Ralph Darden purchased the mill in 1919, and for years had a near-monopoly on the feed business in Randolph County. The Darden Mill also had an exclusive contract to supply feed for all the Great Atlantic and Pacific Tea Company, better known as A&P Grocery Stores, in the state of West Virginia.

Mr. Ralph Darden, a founding officer of the Elkins Milling Company and an investor in several other grain and milling-related companies in Randolph and Tucker counties, was a major employer in the region. He, along with Henry Gassaway Davis and Davis's son-in-law Stephen Elkins, were founders of the community which sprang into existence with the coming of the railroad.

Henry Gassaway Davis (1823–1916) was an early industrialist and self-made millionaire, with interests in lumber and railroads. He served in the US Senate from 1871–1883 and was the Democratic Party's nominee for Vice President of the United States in 1904. Davis's brother was US Congressman Thomas Beall Davis. The towns of Thomas, Davis, and Elkins were named for members of these influential families.[636]

Henry Gassaway Davis is both credited and criticized for his efforts to shape the state's industrial growth. Of humble origins, and with only an elementary school education, Davis began his career at the B&O Railroad at age nineteen, saving his money as he worked his way up from brakeman to station agent. He used his life savings to buy thousands of acres in what is now north and central West Virginia in the 1850s.

Recognizing politics could further his business interests, Davis used his time in the state legislature to push through a charter that allowed him to build a railroad to support transport of lumber and coal. He commenced building the West Virginia Central and Pittsburg Railway to connect West Virginia to eastern markets. By the late 1800s, his Davis Coal and Coke was one of the largest coal companies in the world.

In 1890, Davis and his son-in-law Stephen Elkins founded the city of Elkins as the location for railroad yards for the expanding WVC&P Railroad. During the boom days at the turn of the century, the city became a bustling hub of industrial activity since the railroad provided access to the surrounding countryside's coal and timber resources. The city soon sported many factories and hotels built to house the businessmen and politicians who frequented the mansions of Davis and Elkins to deal in the affairs of the state and nation.

The company towns under Davis's influence flourished in the first few decades of the twentieth century. They were among the first in their areas to get paved streets, electricity, and other modern amenities. In Elkins, Davis and Elkins College and Davis Memorial Hospital were funded by the Davis business empire. But Davis has been criticized for unethical political maneuverings that benefited his businesses, and for supporting the boom in timber, coal, and coke that caused harm to the region's environment.[637]

Elkins continued to grow and prosper through World War I and the 1920s, but the Great Depression spelled the end for many of the old industrial establishments. The railroad continued to service the region, with eighteen passenger trains arriving and departing from Elkins daily in the early 1930s.[638]

The Darden Company continued in operation through the Depression but, due to competition from the huge flour mills in the upper Midwest, eventually discontinued flour production and turned its efforts toward producing buckwheat, corn, and animal feed.

During World War II, the Darden Company sold the mill to Samuel D. and Minnie Girard, who leased it to Altman's Cash Feed Store. The Darden Company went bankrupt in 1946. Though its importance as an industrial center was waning, the city of Elkins emerged as a regional administrative center in the 1940s. The mill building continued to house feed stores and later went through a succession of owners and served as, among other things, a warehouse for used furniture and recycled construction materials.[639]

In the 1950s, regional transportation saw a shift from rail to automobile and delivery truck. After railroad passenger service ended in 1959, the rail yard shrank until operations ceased entirely in the 1990s.

Over the years, Davis and Elkins College attracted a growing number of artists and musicians to the area. Today, Elkins has a diverse economy and is known as a cultural, commercial, and tourism center.

In 1997, the Randolph County Development Authority purchased the Elkins rail yard and depot and dedicated the next decade to redeveloping the property to promote heritage tourism.

Today, scenic passenger trains take nearly 30,000 people a year on excursions out of Elkins and into the surrounding mountains. Elkins is also one of the leading tour bus destinations in the state, with three recognized National Register Historic Districts and many hotels, restaurants, and theaters.

The Randolph County Development Authority sold the Darden Mill building to interest groups and the county landmark commission for one dollar. It now houses two museums, and is owned by the Citizens for Historical Opportunity, Preservation, and Education (C-HOPE).[640]

The Appalachian Forest Discovery Center, which is run by the Appalachian Forest National Heritage Association, and staffed with some AmeriCorps volunteers, offers a look at the Appalachian Forest National Heritage Area's heritage. The Discovery Center acts as a welcome center for the AFNHA and provides information about other forest heritage sites in the region.

The West Virginia Railroad Museum, supported by the Preservation Alliance of West Virginia and AmeriCorps volunteers, is located on the second floor.[641] In addition to static exhibits, select pieces of equipment in the collection are restored and operated throughout the year to demonstrate steam, gasoline, and diesel technology.

For more information about the mill's exhibits and museum hours, visit afnha.org or call 304/636-6182.

36. DAY-VANDEVENDER MILL

Randolph County
Address: WV 32 and CR 32/9, Harman, WV 26270
Coordinates: 38.9327118, -79.5211371
Year Built: 1877
Period of Significance: 1877-1954
Added to the National Register of Historic Places in 1987

© Google Maps

The Old Mill - Photo by Tracy Lawson

The Old Mill has been a museum dedicated to preserving the art of milling, and displaying regional arts and crafts, since the 1960s.
Photo by Tracy Lawson

A 1980 newspaper article described the Old Mill at Harmon as a symbol of the resourcefulness of West Virginia's past residents and a model for preserving the area's history for future generations.[642] Since the 1960s, the last remaining operational water-powered grist mill in Randolph County has housed a museum dedicated to preserving the art of milling and displaying regional arts and crafts. Now, it's under the care of a new generation of budding artisans and volunteers.

Q&A Associates owns the mill and utilizes it as part of a residential treatment program. The organization's Cabin Mountain Living Center provides opportunities for individuals with autism spectrum disorder and other neuro-developmental disorders to help them achieve the highest levels of self-sufficiency possible. Individuals in this program sell handicrafts they make and operate the mill as a tourist attraction.

The mill reportedly dates to 1877, but my efforts to trace the deed records back to the original owner stalled out in 1892, when Solomon Cunningham and his wife, Mary, purchased the mill from Rachel B. Lawrence.[643]

Aaron Day purchased the "Lawrence Mill property" from James S. and Mary Cunningham in 1899.[644]

The following year, tragedy struck the Cunningham family when Solomon, James, James's wife, Mary, and their young daughter, Gertie, all died, presumably from an outbreak of infectious disease.[645,646]

Day, who had served in the Seventh West Virginia Infantry of the Union forces, filed a pension in 1888, indicating he was an invalid.[647] It may be that he purchased the mill for family members to run in his stead. In 1901, he transferred the mill property to his son David Miles Day, in exchange for Miles accepting responsibility to care for his father for the rest of his life, which was a common way for families to manage the end-of-life care for a relative. Aaron died in 1907,[648] and Miles and Mary Day sold the mill to Retta Warner in 1917.

In 1920, Fred Warner, Retta's husband, lists his occupation as a miller.[649] It may have been he who built the 1927 addition, which houses a large wood planer, on the north side of the mill. The Warners sold to Alva and Nora Lambert in 1928, and in 1930, Lambert reported he was running a feed and flour mill.[650]

The Lamberts sold to Frank Vandevender and his son Russell in 1933,[651] and in 1940, both Frank and Russell reported they were "working on their own account," which means they were self-employed.[652] The Vandevenders owned the mill until 1954.[653]

Many mills closed and fell into disrepair in the mid-twentieth century, but the Day-Vandevender Mill assumed a new role in the community, thanks to the Bucher family.

In 1946, Samuel Jacob and Margaret Mae Mininger Bucher, a young doctor and nurse, left the familiarity of their home community in southeastern Pennsylvania to move to Harman, WV.

At that time, during WWII, this area of WV was without a doctor and was considered a "national medical emergency" area. The Buchers, who were pacifists (choosing public service rather than military service), wanted to practice medicine in an area of need. So to Harman, WV, they came and stayed. They practiced medicine, raised a family, became pillars of their community, and thrived in the sheer beauty of the mountains and the Appalachian culture.

Dr. Bucher's medical work spanned 44 years (1946-1990). He delivered over 1,500 babies in those years. In the early years he made many house calls. For many years the "Mountain Clinic" provided in-patient rooms for obstetrical patients. While his primary clinic and office were located in Harman he also opened branch offices in Riverton and Davis.[654]

In addition to serving the medical needs of the community, Margaret was one of the founders of the Pioneer Memorial Library in Harman. In 1964, seeing the value of local crafts and wanting to preserve them, she opened The Old Mill to the public for tours. This water-powered grist mill served as an attractive venue for selling and supporting local crafts. She brought master craftspeople to The Old Mill to conduct weekend workshops. She learned to weave and promoted weaving classes.[655]

Samuel and Margaret's daughter Mary Beth Lind and her husband, Lester, filed the National Register of Historic Places form nominating the Day-Vandevender Mill for inclusion in 1986.[656]

The Buchers' heirs established the Bucher Family Fund in 2015 to support initiatives that promote community development, health, gardening, use of natural resources, alternate energy, historical preservation, and spirituality in Randolph, Tucker, Pendleton, and Barbour Counties.[657]

The mill's current role in healing is a fitting continuation of Samuel and Margaret Bucher's mission.

For information about The Old Mill's upcoming events, consult their Facebook page.

Chapter 3
Over the Mountains

HIGHLAND COUNTY, VIRGINIA
Formed from Bath and Pendleton Counties in 1847

Highland County is known as Virginia's Little Switzerland, due to its steep mountains and valleys. Its western border lies along the Eastern Continental Divide in the Allegheny Mountains, and its eastern border along the ridge line of Shenandoah Mountain. The county is bordered to the west by Pocahontas County and to the north by Pendleton County.[658]

The Blue Ridge Mountains presented a formidable barrier to early settlers, so most came up the valley across the Potomac River from Maryland and Pennsylvania, with the first arriving in the area around 1745.[659]

The new county was formed due to the great distance between the far reaches of present-day Highland County and the county seats in Bath and Pendleton.

At the creation of the new county, the land on which two mills profiled in this section stood became part of Highland County.[660]

29. BOTKIN-SIMMONS MILL

Highland County, VA
Directions: 8387 Cowpasture Road N., Headwaters, VA 24442
Coordinates: 38.4261660, -79.3699355
Year Built: c. 1860
Period of Significance: c. 1860-1962

© Google Maps

Due to its remote location the Botkin-Simmons Mill remained useful to nearby farmers in the years following World War II.
Photo by Elmer Napier

Around 1786, Thomas Jefferson stated that there was no community in the United States without access to a water mill. The picturesque Cowpasture River Valley in Highland County, Virginia, recalls an earlier time when water-powered mills contributed enormous value to life on the frontier and enabled the self-sufficiency that remains a prized characteristic of rural communities to the present day. Three miles south of the state line, in an area known as "The Divide," the South Fork River's name changes to the Cowpasture River.

By the mid-twentieth century, most water mills had outlived their usefulness, but with electric power not widely available in rural Highland County, Virginia, until around 1940, its small communities were powered by mules, draft animals, and water mills until the World War II era. Several ancient mills in the area were swept away by the 1985 flood, but the Simmons and Rexrode Mills survived *(See Rexrode Mill, page 311)*.

The Simmons Mill, also known as the Botkin-Simmons Mill and the Mill at Palo Alto, is so close to the Virginia-West Virginia state line that it is appropriate to include it in this book. As with the Rexrode Mill, the Simmons Mill stands on land that was once part of Pendleton County.

An Act of Assembly passed on March 19, 1847, established Highland County out of parts of Pendleton and Bath counties. The Act mentioned the new county line cut "through the lands of John Bodkin [records spell the name as both Bodkin and Botkin] below his dwelling house and to the top of Bull Pasture Mountain."[661] The Botkin land was at or near the present site of the Simmons farm and mill.

The Botkins were among the earliest settlers to the area.[662] In October 1765, Captain John Botkin (1740-1791), a veteran of the American Revolution, purchased one hundred acres on the Cowpasture River, part of a tract originally patented to George Wilson on December 15, 1758.[663]

Captain John's son John Botkin II (1770-1848), a veteran of the War of 1812, moved west to Ohio, but his grandson Joseph Botkin (1805-1886), stayed in the Cowpasture Valley. Some sources say it was he who started the mill in the 1850s,[664,665] while others say John and Addison Todd built the first mill on the site in the 1860s.[666]

The builders may have been John Todd Sr., a local millwright,[667] and his sons. Addison was eighteen in 1860, and John Jr., who was sixteen.[668]

It seems likely that if the Todds built the mill, the boys' father trained his young sons as they worked.

In 1866, Addison Todd married Marietta Puffenbarger, a granddaughter of Christian and Mary Mitchell Puffenbarger[669] *(See Mitchell Mill, page 251)*, who owned a mill in Sugar Grove. In 1870, Addison, Marietta, and their two-year-old daughter, Mary, lived next door to the Puffenbargers in Pendleton County.[670]

According to 1870 Census data, John H. Todd, a house carpenter, was living in Weston, in Lewis County.[671]

During the winter of 1873-1874, the Todd brothers, under the direction of John A. Botkin (1850-1922), demolished the original mill and build a larger one.[672] Addison and John would have been in their late twenties or early thirties then, and in their prime for such a task. Perhaps John Jr. returned to the area to work with his brother. The new mill housed the post office, and Botkin served as postmaster.

According to the 1880 Federal Census Non-Population Schedule for Industry in Highland County, John A. Botkin had invested a total of $2,500 in the business. He employed two men above the age of twenty for an average of eight hours a day from May to November and twelve hours a day from November to May.[673]

Botkin had paid out a total of $440 in wages over the preceding year, with $1.25 an average day's wage for a skilled hand and fifty cents for a regular hand.[674]

The mill had two run of stones and an overshot wheel and drew power from the South Fork River. Its maximum production capacity was thirty to forty bushels per day.[675]

The county prepared for a growth spurt around the turn of the twentieth century, when plans to build a railroad into Highland were discussed. But the railroad failed to materialize, and the promise of industrial growth faded. Highland remained an agrarian county.[676] With the slow pace of life unlikely to change, there was no need to upgrade the mill.

John A. Botkin's daughter Maggie married James Howard Simmons in November 1909, when he was around thirty-one years old, and she ten years younger.[677]

A few community notes mentioned Simmons in the *Highland Recorder* newspaper:

July 29, 1929: Harrison Malcolm has just completed a fine bank barn for J. H. Simmons.

March 4, 1938: Mr. James H. Simmons of Palo Alto has purchased an engine and saw mill.[678]

James and Maggie's son, Jared (1910-1991), ground buckwheat and corn for local farmers until the mill closed in 1962. Jared's son, Nelson, the fourth generation of the Botkin-Simmons clan to own the farm, maintains the mill building, though it is currently not operational.[679] Nelson recalled local farmers bringing grain to the mill on horseback when he was a boy, and he's an authority on buckwheat.

According to Nelson, buckwheat had to be planted in poor soil or it would grow too tall, and the stalks would fall over. It had to be harvested by hand with a cradle, as a mechanical binder was too rough and would knock the groats off the stalks. It was best cut in the morning when it was foggy and damp, but the groats must be very dry before they could be ground, or the flour would cake on the buhrs. He said nowadays, buckwheat groats are hulled before they are ground, and it doesn't taste as good.[680]

Nelson Simmons shows the toll box used to measure the miller's share of grain from each bushel brought to the mill for grinding.
Photo by Tracy Lawson

12. REXRODE MILL

Highland County, VA
Address: 3744 Blue Grass Valley Road, New Hampden, VA 24413
Coordinates: 38.4908736, -79.5652082
Year Built: 1816
Period of Significance: 1816- c. 1944

© Google Maps

Now a striking private residence, the Rexrode Mill is the product of a meticulous historic restoration. Photo by Tracy Lawson

Through various means, the mills in this book offer glimpses into the past. Millers and customers alike sometimes scrawled notes in pencil on doors, walls, and equipment, about everything from amounts owed for services rendered to party invitations. These notes echo the mills' roles as community gathering places and reveal a little about how people spent their time while they waited for their grain to be processed.

At the Rexrode Mill, individuals and families checked their weight on the mill's scale, which may have been the only reliable scale in the area. The dates on which men, women, and children wrote their names and weights on the bolting machine and flour box range from the 1880s to the 1940s.[681] Before the mill was renovated in 2015, members of the Highland County Historical Society disassembled both the bolting machine and the flour box to preserve these panels which were donated to the Society and are now stored at its museum in McDowell, Virginia.

The Rexrode Mill has dominated New Hampden's rural landscape since 1816, well before Highland County was formed in 1847. Because the Rexrode Mill once stood within Pendleton County's boundaries, it warrants inclusion in this book.

Located about five miles below the headwaters of the South Fork of the Potomac, in an area with rocky, mountainous terrain better suited to grazing cattle, the mill served the needs of local farmers who grew small amounts of grain for home use and animal feed.[682] It remained relevant in part because infrastructure and technology was slow to develop there. Highland County's portion of the only road that connects it to the Shenandoah Valley was unpaved until 1939. Two streams that crossed the road lacked bridges until the mid-1920s. The first electrical service, generated by a water-powered station, came to the area in 1930.[683]

Eventually, improved infrastructure and technological advances contributed to the mill's demise. Gasoline engines came into common use on farms in the 1930s, and small, all-in-one feed mills presented home-grinding options for farmers that had previously been unavailable.[684]

The late William D. Rexrode, an avid historian and genealogist, documented the history of the mill and the village of New Hampden. The results of his exhaustive research are on file at the Highland County

Historical Society in McDowell, Virginia, and provided the bulk of the mill's history in this profile. According to Rexroad's obituary in the *Hutchinson News*, "Family ties are everything."[685]

Bill Rexroad's ties to the mill go back to his 4x-great-grandfather, George Rexrode. The family name has changed spelling several times. George was one of nine children of Johann Zacharias Rexroth, who was born in Hesse around 1724.[686] He came to America before 1751 and brought his family to the Crabbottom Valley (later renamed Blue Grass) around 1774. Due to boundary changes, the land the Rexrodes settled on was, at different times, part of Augusta, Rockingham, Pendleton, and Highland Counties.[687]

John Rexrode (c.1766-1853)[688] another of Zacharias's sons, bought land in the Crabbottom Valley in January 1796.[689] In 1815, he petitioned the Pendleton County Court for permission to build a mill on his own property. As there were no objections, he proceeded and completed the mill in 1816. In 1825, the court responded to petitions and ordered a road built to the mill. When John died in 1853, the mill property passed to his widow, Margaret, and at her death the following year, their son Solomon became the mill owner.[690]

Wooden wheels typically lasted twenty years. In 1880, Solomon hired Andy Rankin to replace the wooden waterwheel with a turbine which would have enabled the mill to operate more efficiently.[691] Rankin is surely the Andrew J. Rankin who was the miller at McCoy's Mill, a few miles south of Franklin in neighboring Pendleton County[692] *(See McCoy Mill, page 245).*

Other machinery, like the Fitz Company smutting machine that remained in the mill decades after it closed, indicate Solomon was interested in keeping up with technological advances in milling.[693]

Solomon deeded the mill to his son William C. in April 1883 but retained life interest in it until his death in 1886.[694]

When a devastating flood in 1889 destroyed the mill dam and washed away the road above the mill, William C. had the dam replaced with one made of concrete.[695] Ten years later, he built a bridge where the road to the mill crosses the river.[696]

In 1916, the one hundredth anniversary of the mill's founding, William C. sold a half interest in the mill to his son Bob, who listed his occupation as miller on his World War I draft card.[697]

Bob bought the remaining interest in the mill in 1919 and continued to operate the mill through World War I and the Depression. He sold the mill to his younger brother Ray in 1936, but Ray, who may have been plagued by health problems, sold it back the following year.[698]

The mill ceased operation around 1944, and when Bob Rexrode died intestate in 1952, his heirs disagreed on how to divide his property. The court ordered the mill and other land to be sold and the proceeds divided among the heirs. After 136 years, the mill passed from the family's control.

Daniel W. Kiser (1920-1956),[699] a great-grandson of William Kiser (1786-1853), bought the mill for $9,800, on behalf of Albert Puffenbarger, a local farmer and merchant, with the property put in Kiser's name. It is uncertain whether Kiser and Puffenbarger intended to run the mill or if Kiser bought the property as an investment, but in January 1953, he sold the property to Puffenbarger for $10,800.[700] *(See Homan Mill, page 227)*

Kiser died in 1956, and when Puffenbarger died unexpectedly of a heart attack in 1959, he left the property to his children, Lillian and Harry. The mill remained in the Puffenbarger family for nearly a half century, during which most of the milling equipment was removed. For a time, the structure was used as a brood house for raising turkeys.[701]

Charles and Lou Ann Neely bought the mill in 2001. After it changed hands a few more times, the Highland County Historical Society took an active interest in the mill, hoping to purchase, restore, and open the mill as a historic site. A lack of funding resulted in the project being abandoned.

The mill measures thirty by thirty-five feet and rises to a height of over forty feet. Laid upon a limestone foundation, the mill is made entirely of wood, mostly oak, pine, and American chestnut, of mortise and tenon construction with wooden pegs. The existing siding was put on the building in 2019, and the metal roof was replaced as part of the 2015 renovation.

Old-timers in the area who visited the Rexrode Mill in the 1930s recall that the millrace was lined with heavy planks, a common practice to curtail erosion.[702]

Up near the roof peak, a catwalk provided access to the hoist used to raise the bags of grain into the upper stories.[703] At one time, wagons pulled up to the north side of the mill, where sacks were hauled up on the pulley rope into one of the three doors that opened on that side.[704]

In his history of the mill, Rexroad quoted Nancy Mullenax Hedges, who grew up in Blue Grass. She recalled stories that date to the 1850s of James Mullenax, her great-grandfather, coming home after a hard day's work doing construction at the Rexrode Mill.[705]

In 2013, New Hampden Investment LLC was formed as a joint venture and purchased the New Hampden Mill at auction.

Although the milling equipment had been removed decades before, the historic "bones" of the mill were still there, and plans were developed to convert the mill to a residence. The initial challenge was to stabilize the mill because it was precariously close to collapse, as the southwest corner of the limestone foundation had deteriorated to the point of failure. After almost a year of work stabilizing the structure, which included the pouring of a new western wall, work could begin on the mill itself. The goal was to carefully preserve the outside appearance of the mill and protect the structural components inside. Since the ultimate objective was to adapt the mill as a residence, it would be necessary to insulate the leaky, drafty, single-walled exterior.[706] The LLC developed a plan for adaptive reuse of the property with project architect Mark Paxton and submitted a proposal for rehabilitation to the Virginia Department of Historic Resources (DHR). The proposal was approved in 2014, but six months later, after much of the previously approved work had been completed, the DHR reversed its decision. The reason given for this change in determination was that by covering and/or altering the interior of the mill, the distinctive features and examples of craftsmanship would be lost. Without the DHR's approval, the LLC would lose the historic tax credits which were, through syndication, a major source of funding for the project. Lorraine White, the former director of the Highland County Historical Society, expressed concern that the DHR's reversal might affect future projects in the area. She worried people might hesitate to take on large renovation projects without the support of the historic tax credit program, and other historic structures might be lost.[707] Upon appeal, the DHR eventually reversed its decision, awarding historic tax credits for the qualified rehabilitation expenditures made during the renovation on the New Hampden Mill.

The renovation made the mill weathertight and allowed for the addition of partitions and rustic paneling like that which was found in the original structure.

The final interior design incorporates elements from the mill, such as conveyor augers and a wooden hopper mounted upside down and used as a light fixture. Kitchen cabinets and appliances stand side by side with the massive, hand-hewn support beams.

With the mill now adapted for use as a residence, it seems certain it will stand on the banks of the South Fork of the Potomac for many years to come.

The massive original beams, plus a drive shaft and gear, add character to the updated mill's kitchen. Photo by Tracy Lawson

A salvaged grain hopper is now a light fixture. Photo by Tracy Lawson

A screw augur enhances the rustic design.
Photo by Tracy Lawson

Historic Rehabilitation Tax Credits

Historic Rehabilitation Tax Credits can be used to offset Virginia income taxes. For every dollar of qualified rehabilitation expenditure that is made, twenty-five cents (or 25 percent) is awarded in tax credits which can be used over a ten-year period. These tax credits can also be syndicated if more credits have been earned than are likely to be used by the initial project participants. A similar federal historic tax credit, which is calculated at 20 percent of the same qualified rehabilitation expenditure amount, was not available since the mill was to have a noncommercial use.[708]

As of April 26, 2021, West Virginia has made its Historic Rehabilitation Tax Credit program permanent. But unlike Virginia, the bipartisan bill makes a 25 percent tax credit available only to those who rehabilitate historic, income-producing properties.[709]

Chapter 4
New River / Greenbrier Valley

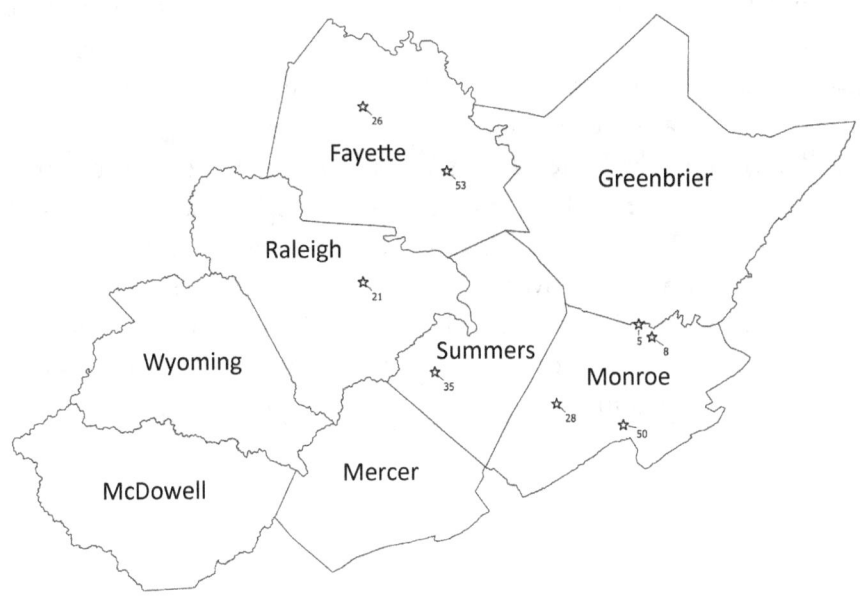

Southeastern West Virginia, made up of ridges and valleys along the state's border with Virginia, is known for whitewater rafting and kayaking. The New River winds fourteen miles through the thousand-foot-deep New River Gorge, dropping 240 feet in elevation and offering Class I to IV rapids. The relatively tame Upper New is suitable for lazy float trips, while the Lower New thunders through the gorge and under a 3,030-foot-long steel arch bridge. Thousands of acres of forest are protected by the New River Gorge National Park and Preserve, the Bechtel Summit National Scouting Reserve, and others. Concurrent with the construction of the bridge in 1974-77, the National Park Service established and began to develop the Preserve, which included part of the gorge and the narrow valley of the river to the south. The region includes the highlands around the New River far to the south, Fayette, Raleigh, Nicholas, and part of Summers Counties.[710]

The New River's erosion exposed several different rock formations. The fifty-two miles from Hinton to the New River Gorge Bridge offer a cross section of the earth's surface, exposing sedimentary rock layers totaling about 4,000 feet in thickness. Scientists estimate it took seven to ten million years for the layers of sand, mud, and rotting plants to accumulate and then compress and bond into sandstone, shale, and coal.

Here, measured in one lifetime, man has visually modified the gorge's features. The cut and fill of railroad construction and the coal mine tailings mark man's recent sculpturing.[711]

The Greenbrier Valley Region has long provided a rural retreat for residents of the mid-Atlantic states. Spas and resorts such as The Greenbrier, at White Sulphur Springs, have attracted visitors since their healing waters were discovered. Mineral springs and historical towns continue to attract vacationers and new residents. Popular ski resort Snowshoe Mountain is located within the Monongahela National Forest. Tourism and agriculture are the region's primary industries.[712]

FAYETTE COUNTY
Formed in 1831 from portions of Greenbrier, Kanawha, Nicholas, and Logan Counties

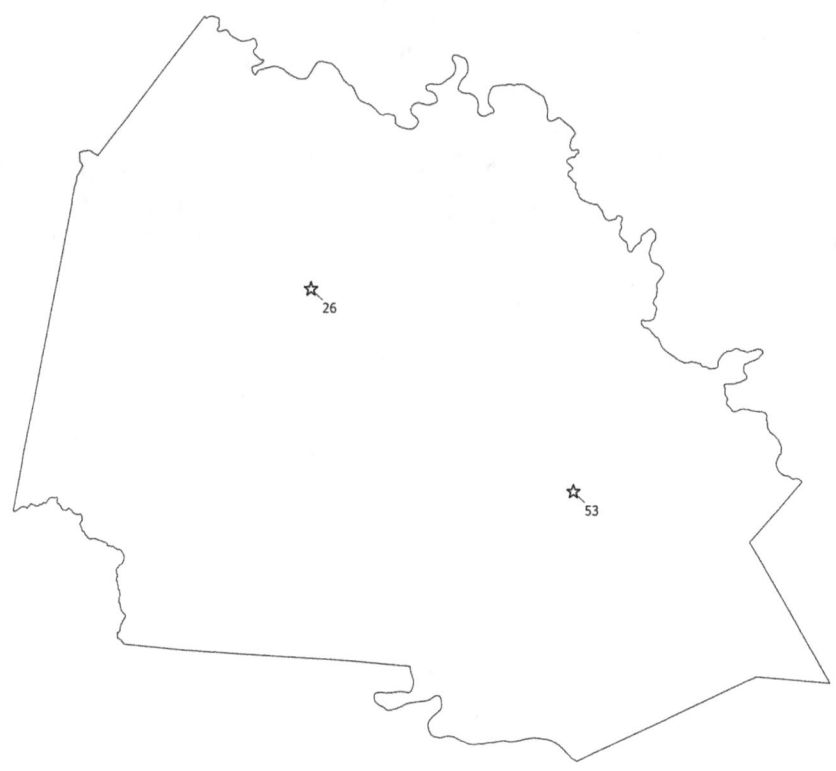

26. COTTON HILL MILL

Fayette County
Address: Beckwith Road (WV 16), Fayette County, WV 25840
Coordinates: 38.10068 -81.14927
Year Built: before 1854
Period of Significance: 1908-1960

© Google Maps

The Cotton Hill Mill and dam - Photo by Tracy Lawson

The mill pond was the area's first public swimming pool.
Photo by Tracy Lawson

The Virginian railway line, built between 1907 and 1909, connected southern West Virginia with the Chesapeake Bay ports at Hampton Roads, Virginia.[713] For the young man who became the owner of Cotton Hill Mill, the railroad helped forge a lasting and personal connection.

In the years following the Civil War, 90 percent of West Virginia's population lived on farms. In 1870, only eighty-five coal mines existed. That would change with the coming of the railroads. In 1869, industrialist Collis P. Huntington financed the Chesapeake and Ohio Railway. Crews laid rails west from White Sulphur Springs and east from the new railway town of Huntington on the Ohio River, until the railroad connected the Ohio River with the Atlantic Ocean in January 1873.[714,715]

Crews used the latest steam-driven machinery to sculpt the Great Bend Tunnel at Talcott in Summers County. This is thought to be the birthplace of the John Henry legend and folk song, in which a steel driver defeats a steam engine in a digging contest.[716]

In West Virginia, the Chesapeake & Ohio Railway served two purposes: importing miners and exporting coal.[717] Laurel Creek's station was a branch connection hub as well as a coal marshaling yard, where loaded railway cars were separated onto one of several tracks.[718]

The branches of the C&O made it possible to tap and transport this and other previously unreachable coal reserves in Raleigh, Fayette, and Wyoming Counties, paving the way for the rise of King Coal.[719]

Philip Fry, a well-to-do farmer, kept a boardinghouse for railroad workers above the Cotton Hill Mill on Laurel Creek. He installed a rope ladder to make it easier for them to climb up the steep embankment at the end of the day.[720] Among the workers was Oscar Preston Ball, a young telegraph operator from Summers County.

O. P., as he was known, and Philip Fry's eldest daughter, Emma, fell in love. When O. P. asked for her hand, Fry said, "What makes you think you can take care of my daughter?"

To prove he was up to the task, O. P. purchased land near Fry's, which included a log cabin and the primitive Cotton Hill Mill. He proceeded to build an empire on the banks of Laurel Creek that included a large family home, a telephone company, a hydroelectric plant, a gas station, and the area's first public swimming pool.[721]

The Cotton Hill Mill was one of two owned by the Warner family, neighbors who also had a dairy farm on the ridge above Laurel Creek. The Warner's sawmill, no longer standing, was about a half mile downstream. O. P. expanded all around the original mill building, until the original mill was a single room inside the structure. The mill used an Oliver Evans system of elevators.

The family homeplace also started small, and as O. P. and Emma's family grew to include five boys and three girls, the house grew to three stories to accommodate everyone.

David Ball, a grandson of O. P., recalls that his grandfather was a worker and a craftsman skilled in carpentry and stonework. Even in his later years, he would come home from a day's work at the railroad depot and go cut stone.

O. P. ran the mill himself until the late 1950s. When it was time to grind corn, he opened a gate to direct water from above the dam into a tunnel, and into a stone pit below the mill to power the Francis turbine. Francis turbines can achieve 95 percent efficiency and are ideal for generating electricity.[722]

Two large horizontal drive shafts with pulleys could be run off the turbine. O. P. had no backhoe, so he used the turbine to power a winch to drag rocks up from the creek bed to replace the old wooden dam and, later, to repair the mill's foundation.

A dynamo at the mill could generate 110 volts of power, which O. P. used to pump water to and provide electric power for the house.

He also kept a 6-volt generator to charge car batteries—either with the hydroelectric power generated by the turbine or the 1918 6hp IHC International 4-cycle hit-and-miss engine he kept at the mill, which sounded like guns firing.

O. P. ran the local telephone company for an undetermined time before and after World War II, until the company was bought out by Bell Telephone. One of David's cousins and her mother lived at O. P. and Emma's house during the years her father was in the military and recalled that the children had a telephone in their playhouse.

Once a week, O. P. and the boys would hook a chain to the gate in the center bottom of the dam and pull it out with a team of horses or a truck. When all the water flowed out of the pond, they would haul out trash, large branches, and sediment. The larger the volume of water in the pond, the longer he could run the mill.

The site of many baptisms, the pond also served as the community's first swimming pool. David's cousin Sally worked at the pool and still has the wooden till she once used to collect the 25 cent admission fees. They had bathhouses and swimming suits available for rent and boasted a diving board and a zip line, which was a popular attraction for local young people. In the mid-1940s, a 4-H camp was built nearby with a modern swimming pool.

O. P. replaced the wooden bridge over the creek in 1948 and, with his sons' help, built a big, curved stone bridge. His continuous improvements sometimes resulted in excitement, like the time he was adding a long porch to the second story of the house. The master bedroom was to open onto the porch. O. P. was down below when Emma opened the bedroom door that led outside, and accidentally stepped through a gap in the flooring and landed right beside O. P. David said the family often laughed while recalling O. P.'s astounded expression as he demanded, "Woman, what are you doing down here?"

David has a seemingly endless supply of fond memories of his youth, particularly time spent with his cousin T. J. Every day on his way home from work, O. P. would stop at the gas station by the bridge that led to the house, to have a word about the day's business with his son who ran the station. He would let David and T. J. take turns driving the car across the bridge—a big thrill for the young boys—and he always slyly left a bag of candy on the seat for them.

O. P. stocked the creek for trout season, and David recalls going out early and catching his limit before it was time to leave for school. He would take his string of trout to the mill and toss them into the water in the turbine pit to keep them fresh until after school when he could take them home.

The Cotton Hill Mill was so important to the community that when Route 16 was put in, the government did a study of the road's possible adverse effects on the mill and its power plant.

After O. P.'s death in 1957, Emma Ball sold off much of the mill's machinery, including the dynamo. A friend of David's bought a dynamo three years ago, and remarkably, it was the exact machine that had come out of the mill years before.

Julie Hattier and Eric Clarke, who purchased the mill in 2014, are on the hunt for appropriate inner workings. They recently purchased a Queen of the South, which is a portable French buhrstone cornmill and corn crusher.

Manufactured by the Isaac Straub Company from Cincinnati beginning in 1844, the Queen of the South was the mainstay of their product line. In 1863, the company became Simpson & Gault, with Isaac Straub staying on as designer. In 1910, the company name changed to Orville Simpson Co., and in 1974 it changed to ROTEX Inc., after the company's line of sifters.[723]

The Queen of the South is unique in its configuration. Unlike most buhrstone mills, the bottom stone is the runner, while the top stone remains stationary.[724]

One of the buhrstones in the mill is dated 1854 and was reportedly cut from stone taken from the River Seine.[725]

Queen of the South portable mill
Photo courtesy of Julie Hattier and Eric Clarke

53. GLADE CREEK GRIST MILL

Fayette County
Address: Park Forest 802, Danese, WV 25831
Coordinates: 37.9797626, -80.9468481
Year Built: 1976
Period of Significance: 1976-present

© Google Maps

Glade Creek Grist Mill at Babcock State Park is the state's most photographed mill. Photo by Elmer Napier

The mill's entrance - Photo by Tracy Lawson

Glade Creek Grist Mill is easily the most recognizable and most photographed mill in the state. Nestled in a picturesque setting in Babcock State Park, it stands as a working monument to West Virginia's industrial past and the hundreds of mills that once dotted the state. Anyone planning a visit to nearby New River Gorge, designated the sixty-third U.S. National Park in 2021,[726] should include Babcock State Park on their itinerary.

Glade Creek Grist Mill was built in 1976 using parts from three ruined West Virginia mills: Spring Run Grist Mill in Petersburg, Grant County; Stoney Creek Grist Mill in Campbellstown, Pocahontas County; and Roaring Creek Mill in Seneca, Pendleton County. The popular attraction draws thousands of visitors each year from as far away as Europe and Asia.[727]

The main shaft and wheel assembly were salvaged from Spring Run Grist Mill, which was built in the 1850s. The wheel's wooden buckets were replaced with metal before it was installed at Glade Creek. The mill gets its basic structure from the Stoney Creek Mill and the mill deck and workings from Roaring Creek, both of which date to the 1890s.[728]

The walking path along Glade Creek offers different points from which to view and photograph the mill, as well as the aqueduct system, which includes a hundred-yard-long underground culvert to channel water from the dam on Glade Creek into the wooden sluice above the wheel.

The mill stands near the site of Cooper's Mill (not the Summers County mill profiled in this book) that operated there long before the area became a state park. That mill, which stood on the present site of the administration building parking lot, was destroyed by fire in the 1920s. The cause of the fire is unknown, but it has been said it was started on purpose to get rid of the drinking and gambling crowd that were using the abandoned mill as their hangout.[729]

After the Fitz Water Wheel Company closed *(See Tuscarora Iron Works, page 109)*, some wheels were sold to other companies that produced and sold mill products. Because these secondary companies had only the wheels and lacked the Fitz plans for the water tanks, sluice gates, and spouts, their substitutions didn't always measure up to the scientific principles worked out by Fitz.[730]

The Glade Creek Grist Mill is a prime example. When you see it in person, take note of the wooden sluice's placement. Though it appears appropriate to the period, it incorrectly delivers the water past the vertical center of the wheel instead of ten degrees behind, as recommended by Fitz. As a result, the water pours over the wheel, most of it missing the buckets entirely.[731]

Even with this engineering flaw, the mill is a must-see and the perfect way to witness the milling process firsthand, so be sure to plan your visit for when the mill is open to the public and giving demonstrations.

When we visited in November 2020, a costumed interpreter ground cornmeal as he explained the steps in the milling process. Of particular interest was a machine I hadn't seen before called the Miller's Piano, a bolter mounted high on the wall with three descending chutes that separated and graded the flour from fine to coarse.

The miller's piano
Photo by Tracy Lawson

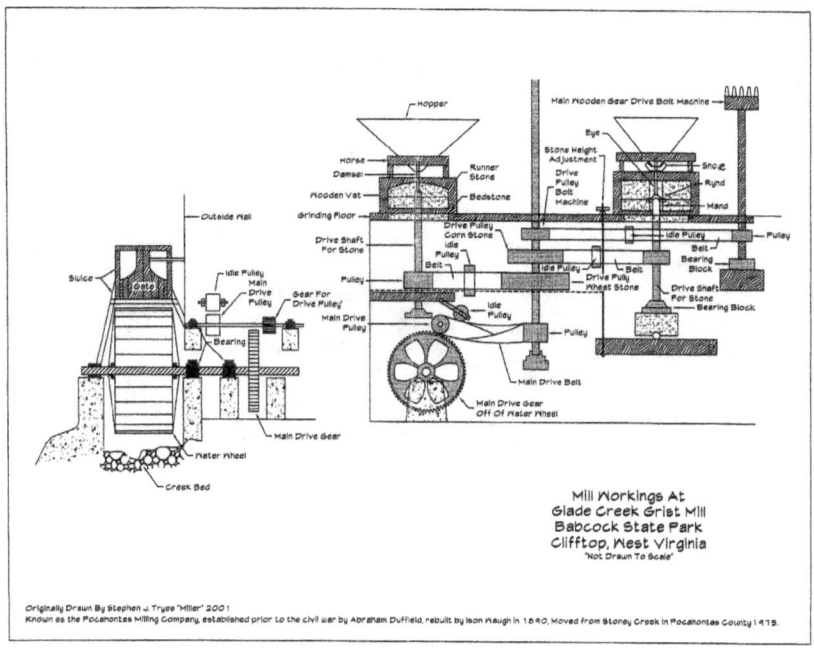

The inner workings of the Glade Creek Mill, drawn By Stephen J. Tyree, were once part of the Pocahontas Milling Company and were moved to the site in 1975. Tyree, who began working at the Glade Creek Mill in 1976 while a college student, learned the craft of milling by doing.

MONROE COUNTY
Formed from Greenbrier County in 1799

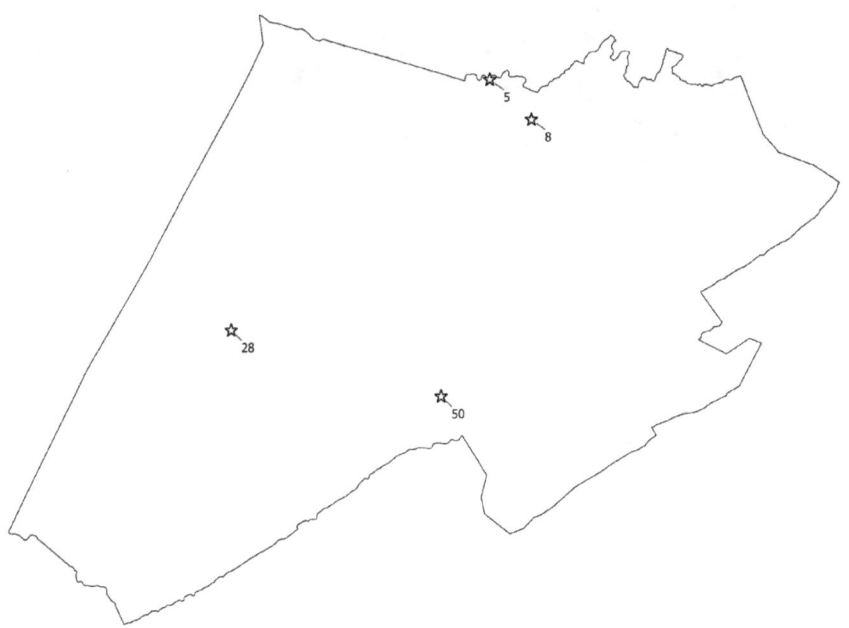

28. COOK'S OLD MILL

Monroe County
Address: 5255 Greenville Road, Greenville, WV 24945
Coordinates: 37.5453423, -80.6868073
Built: 1857
Period of Significance: 1796-1964
Added to the National Register of Historic Places in 1989

© Google Maps

The Cook's Old Mill complex - Photo by Tracy Lawson

The forge at Cook's Old Mill - Photo by Tracy Lawson

Cook's Old Mill was built on the limestone block foundation of an earlier mill constructed in approximately 1796. The two-and-a-half-story frame building has hand-hewn post-and-beam construction, with massive timbers pegged at their mortise and tenon joints, and a metal roof.[732]

The first mill on the site was close to a fort built by Valentine Cook Sr. in the early 1770s. There is also evidence that Cook owned a powder mill, as saltpeter for gunpowder was manufactured in the area from the time of the American Revolution until the close of the Civil War.[733]

Valentine was known by his Dutch nickname "Felty" or "Felty Koch" in many courthouse records. (Felten is the Dutch spelling for Valentine, and Koch means Cook.) There is a creek near here called Felty's Run and a gravestone in the Methodist cemetery in Greenville labeled "F. Cook."[734]

Valentine Cook Sr. was born in about 1730 near London, England. When he was six years old, his father died. His mother, whose name is undetermined, is believed to have married a second time to a Mr. Sly. The family moved to Amsterdam, Holland, where Valentine was educated.

In about 1750, the family immigrated to America and settled in York County, Pennsylvania. Valentine Cook married Susannah Baughman, daughter of Jacob Baughman and Margarita Schwizler, who were natives of Switzerland. By 1763, Cook was a resident of Rockingham County, Virginia, and in 1773 moved to Greenbrier County, where he settled on Indian Creek, a tributary of New River.[735]

There he erected Cook's Fort, the larger of several forts in what is now Monroe County. Cook's Fort stood about midway in the Indian Creek Bottom, on the south side of the stream, and encompassed an oblong space of an acre and a half. In the building of the palisade, the settlers dug a four-foot-deep trench. A double row of logs was planted inside, set in a vertical position and projecting about ten feet above the general level of the ground. The double rows left no crevices for bullets to pass. Within the stockade were cabins, the palisade forming one of the walls, and the cabin roof serving as a parapet from which to shoot. Valentine Cook served as a private in the building and defended the fort on his land during Dunmore's War (1774) and probably also during the American Revolution.[736] Three hundred people found refuge in Cook's Fort for the entire summer of 1778, during Indian hostilities spurred by the execution of Cornstalk.[737] A leader of the Shawnee, Cornstalk was on a diplomatic mission to Ft. Randolph in 1777 when an American militiaman was killed by natives in the fort's vicinity. In retaliation, soldiers executed Cornstalk. His murder enraged Shawnees and deprived them of an important voice of moderation.[738]

Valentine Cook is a recognized patriot who supported the cause of American independence by providing food and supplies for the army.[739] His death in 1797 "ended a trail blazed with history, and a life blessed with great service to his country and to his fellow residents of Indian Creek."[740]

* * *

Today, the three-and-a-half-acre Cook's Old Mill site includes the mill and millpond, tailrace, and stream, as well as a log house dating to 1843 that was moved to the site in 1990, and a forge building built in the 1980s to house a blacksmith business.[741] Members of the Cook family owned the mill for its first century of existence.

A 2017 study used tree-ring analysis to date the beams in the mill to 1868 and confirms old Cook family letters that the mill was burned by northern troops during the Civil War.[742] After the war, Jacob A. and Riley Cook, grandsons of the original owner, contracted with James Humphreys to build a new "Mill House and Mill" on the same site. The mill was powered by a waterwheel.[743]

Within three years, Jacob A. Cook fell into debt. He owed his brother Riley $2,560, and when he was unable to pay off his debt, Riley bought the mill and forty acres. In 1868, Riley Cook entered a partnership with Hinton, Barley & Co. The company installed two Leffel turbines, one of which still powers the mill. In 1872, William Barley sued Riley Cook, opening a series of lawsuits which involved the other parties and were not resolved until 1889. The partners apparently forfeited the mill in 1876, and their shares were sold to Anderson McNeer and Richard T. McNeer in a public sale.[744]

The 1891-1892 *West Virginia Gazetteer and business directory* lists McNeer's Flour Mill in Greenville.[745]

By 1894, the McNeers sold the "Centreville Mills," which by then included a gristmill, sawmill, and dwelling house, to E. L. Dunn. A few years later, the mill, now known as Greenville Roller Mills, changed hands again, beginning a string of sales until finally, Aaron V. Canterbury and his wife sold the Greenville Mill, minus the milling equipment, to the BiRite Furniture Company, owned by Harold "Ernie" LaBelle, in 1964.[746]

Valentine Cook faced threats on the frontier, but it was Ernie LaBelle who disappeared in 1972, a suspected victim of foul play. In 1975, the skull of a murder victim was discovered in Wyoming County, though it was not linked to Ernie LaBelle through DNA testing until 2006.

When Ernie's brother, John "Dave" LaBelle sold the mill to Jim and Nan Wells in 1987, the building's days as anything other than a mill came to an end. The Wellses undertook major repairs to the millpond, dam, foundation, and roof. They purchased milling equipment from defunct mills in the area and bought up other adjoining land, so that when Fred and Barbara Ziegler purchased the property in 2002, it came with six acres.[747] The Wellses built the forge building and moved the log house to the site, and, with help of grants from the West Virginia Department of Culture and History, saved the mill for posterity.[748]

Though the mill is on private property, the Zieglers welcome visitors to the site during daylight hours. The picturesque setting is great for photos. The Zieglers live across the road in the yellow miller's house and may be reached at frednbarbara@frontier.net.

Artists and artisans interested in workspace in the blacksmith's forge or the mill should make their wishes known.

5. GROMER-NICKELL'S UPPER-RODGERS MILL

Monroe County
Address: 926 Rogers Mill Road, Ronceverte, WV 24970
Coordinates: 37.6915183, -80.4876306
Year Built: 1785
Period of Significance: 1785-1946

© Google Maps

The Gromer-Nickell's Upper-Rodgers Mill predates the formation of Monroe County. Photo by Tracy Lawson

The Gromer-Nickell's Upper-Rodgers Mill
Photo by Tracy Lawson

The Allegheny Front, an escarpment that spans southern Pennsylvania, western Maryland, and eastern West Virginia, forms the boundary between the Ridge and Valley Appalachians to the east and the Appalachian Plateau to the west.[749] The Front enters Monroe County as a series of six ridges. The three to the west terminate on Second Creek, so named because it was the second creek system on the western side of the Eastern Continental Divide. Monroe is the only county in West Virginia that sends it waters partly to the Atlantic and partly to the Gulf of Mexico.[750]

Monroe County was formed from Greenbrier County in 1799 and named for James Monroe, who was then governor of Virginia. Most area settlers were either German and Scotch-Irish who had come west from Pennsylvania, or of English extraction, from eastern Virginia. Settlers gained title by paying the Greenbrier Land Company's surveyor ten dollars for each hundred acres surveyed. Frontier surveying and land acquisition in the eighteenth century was far from an exact business. Some settlers went around the land companies and claimed their acreage by "tomahawk rights," notching trees along their perceived land boundary with a tomahawk or ax.[751]

Frederick Gromer an early landowner in the area, built the mill about 1785. The three-story structure stands on a stone foundation, has a log facade on the side facing the road, and weathered board siding on the other three sides and the gable dormer. The mill is a three-by-two bay, with six-over-six windowpanes. It was powered by a wooden, undershot wheel, and had wooden gears and shafts.[752] The gristmill could grind about twenty bushels of corn or wheat in a day. An attached dormer-style shed, added later, was where lumber was fed into the up-and-down saw blade,[753] which could turn out 400-500 feet of lumber a day, sawed to uneven thicknesses.[754]

It is unclear from available records whether Gromer's powder mill, in operation around 1788, was housed in the extant building on the site or in a separate structure, but it seems likely it was housed away from the grist and sawmill. A story gleaned from published records and supported by interviews with local historians goes like this: A woman and a boy went to Gromer's powder mill on an errand, entered carrying a lighted candle, and ignited the mill's explosive contents. The boy was killed, and the woman died a few days later.[755] Robert Patton, who succeeded Gromer in the powder mill enterprise, was killed along with one of his workers in another explosion in 1808.[756]

Thomas Nickell, another settler, received a patent for 500 acres adjacent to Frederick Cromer [sic] in 1788.[757] Gromer acquired 218 acres adjacent to Thomas Nickell's land in 1793, and in 1796, he paid tax in Greenbrier County on two "white tithes" and seven horses. A tithe, or tax, was levied at that time on each male member of a household over the age of sixteen.[758]

The first miller's house may have been built as early as 1775.[759] It was located across the creek from the mill, in present-day Greenbrier County.[760] There is a traditional ford between the house and mill. The second miller's house, built in the Victorian style around 1890, is located across the road on the mill's other side.

Thomas Nickell's son James Albert Nickell bought the mill when the Gromer family pulled up stakes and moved west to Kentucky.[761]

John Nickell Sr. settled in Moffatt's Branch, Augusta County, Virginia, around 1745. Like many Irish immigrants, he came to the American colonies to escape heavy taxes and discrimination in his home country.[762] He married Barbara McCombe, and their six sons served in the militia during the American Revolution. They were in the Battle of Point Pleasant in 1774, waged between the colonial militia and Shawnee natives under Cornstalk. One of the early battles of the Revolution, the colonial victory led to the Ohio country opening to white settlement[763] (*For more on the Shawnee leader, Cornstalk, see Cook's Old Mill, page 339*).

John Sr. willed his eldest son, John Jr., the greater part of his plantation in Augusta County, and his other children settled on the Greenbrier River.[764]

Around 1800, Frederick Gromer sold the mill to Thomas Nickell's son James Albert, who added the up-and-down sawmill.[765] He also built another mill on the property around 1814,[766] also located on Second Creek, about three miles downstream from the Gromer Mill.[767]

James Albert married his first cousin Barbara Nickell, a daughter of his uncle Isaac Nickell. James Madison Nickell (1813-1886), James Albert and Barbara's son, inherited the land and mills from his father. Some sources say he added yet another mill to the property on the upper end of the farm.[768] According to the Monroe County Historical Society, the old Gromer Mill was known as "Nickell's Upper Mill."[769]

James Madison Nickell, the second of three generations of Nickells to own the Gromer Mill, was elected Justice of the Peace in 1856 and 1860 and was a captain in the Monroe County Home Guard during the Civil War. A small settlement developed close to the Nickell property, with two general stores, a carding mill, blacksmith, tannery, cigar factory, and post office. He is remembered as a slave owner who refused to sell off individual members of families and began a school to educate all the children, both black and white, who were his responsibility.[770]

James Madison Nickell's son Charles Coray Nickell inherited the property in 1886 and continued operating the farm and mills. It may have been he who built the second miller's house. Charles sold the upper mill to a J. Humphreys in 1900 and deeded the other to a relative.[771]

The 1904-1905 *West Virginia Gazetteer* lists C. C. Nickell as the owner of the flour mill.[772]

The J. Humphreys mentioned in historical records was James W. Humphreys, a son of James Humphreys, a millwright.[773] He lived in Peterstown, thirty-five miles from Second Creek, in 1860.[774] By 1870, Humphreys and his family had relocated to Second Creek, where he again reported his occupation as millwright. His son James W. was working as a mill hand.[775]

In his will, dated 1883, he makes the provision that his wife could sell his "interest in the Laurel Creek Land at any time if needed to keep up the mills and farm, or for the benefit of [his]heirs."[776]

James W. Humphreys married Mary Susan Byrd in 1872. Mary was a sister of Luther Byrd, who married James W.'s sister Agnes Jane. Luther Byrd, a neighbor of James Madison Nickell's, was a "worker in grist mill" in 1880.[777] I was unable to establish a family connection between Luther Byrd and James William Byrd, the Pendleton County millwright *(See McCoy Mill, page 245).*

It was likely James W. Humphreys who sold the mill to James Madison Rodgers around 1900. The Rodgerses, the final family in this mill's story, would own and operate it for nearly half a century.

James Madison Rodgers was a son of Daniel Rodgers and a grandson of Michael and Catherine Rodgers, Irish immigrants who settled in the Irish Corner community in Greenbrier County before the American Revolution. Deed records show that pioneer Michael Rodgers acquired 123 acres on Second Creek from Samuel Carrell in 1797.[778]

In the early 1900s, James Madison Rodgers purchased the mill from James Humphreys. He made repairs and reconditioned the mill[779] while planning for his family's future. His son Homer D. Rodgers, the mill's final owner, married Bertha Byrd, the daughter of Luther and Agnes Byrd, in 1908, and formed an alliance between the two milling families.

Homer D. Rodgers, a third-generation miller, listed that as his occupation in 1920,[780] but in 1930[781] and 1940[782] he stated he was "farming." He could have been milling part-time and considered farming his primary occupation for the census record.

The mill drew its power from the waters of Second Creek until 1946, when its remote location, which contributed to a decline in business, caused it to close for good.[783] Today, Rodgers Mill Road pays tribute to the mill's importance to the community.

* * *

In November 2020, Elmer and I set out to view both the Rodgers and the Nickell Mills. I piloted us deeper and deeper into the rural interior of Monroe County along the hilly, one-lane road until I had to ask if we had gone too far.

Elmer insisted he'd been out this way a few years before and had taken photos of both mills. It was just a bit further. On we went.

We arrived at Rodgers Mill first. Though it was nearly hidden in the underbrush, the 1890 miller's house across the road, with its Victorian details and tall front columns, was easy to spot.

I parked, and Elmer and I bushwhacked our way back to the mill. The sawmill shed's metal roof sagged under downed branches and debris, and the wooden waterwheel had fallen away from the driveshaft and into the wheel pit. The structure's dilapidated condition was more of a deterrent to entry than the "Keep Out" and "No Trespassing" signs tacked on the door. I would not have set foot inside even if invited, but I could admire the structure. Frederick Gromer's handiwork had survived over 230 years.

Back in the car, we headed over the ridge toward the Nickell Mill site. We passed James Madison Nickell's brick plantation house, which I recognized from its description on the National Register of Historic Places Nomination Form. When we reached the spot where Elmer expected to find the Nickell Mill, there was nothing but the remnants of a stone foundation in a relatively clear spot at the bottom of a hill.

Disappointed, we drove away. On our way back to the main road we came upon a pickup truck. The driver pulled to the side so we could pass and rolled down his window. In response to our inquiry about the mill, he stated with certainty that Barnwood Builders had torn down the mill and used the reclaimed boards in projects in nearby White Sulphur Springs. The original Rodgers Mill miller's house had apparently met the same end.[784]

Later, in response to my inquiry, Barnwood Builders' representative stated they hadn't torn down any mills in Monroe County. Regardless, my search for the story of the Nickell Mill's demise reached a dead end.

50. MCCLUNG MILL

Monroe County
Address: 8688 Zenith Road, Zenith, WV 24983
Coordinates: 37.5035583, -80.5270992
Year Built: before 1926
Period of Significance: c. 1870-1970

© Google Maps

McClung Mill, long vacant, is a landmark in the tiny village of Zenith.
Photo by Tracy Lawson

The McClung Mill is a one-and-a-half-story frame structure with its twenty-four-foot, metal, overshot wheel.[785] Due in part to its location, tucked away on a rural road near the tiny hamlet of Zenith, West Virginia, this mill remained in operation, serving the isolated community, until around 1970.[786]

According to information on file at the Monroe County Historical Society, Will Crosier, who built the first store in Zenith, had John Ballard, a carpenter from nearby Gap Mills, construct a gristmill and an up-and-down sawmill built shortly after.[787] The property passed to an A. B. Beamer in 1887. The inner workings of the current mill were moved from Craig County, WV, in the early twentieth century and rebuilt upon an earlier mill's foundation.[788] The mill stands on a cinderblock foundation, which shows it was renovated or modified in the late nineteenth century, when cinderblock first became available.[789]

On my final research journey to West Virginia, I stopped at the Monroe County Courthouse, hoping to unravel the family connections that led to the McClungs' ownership of the mill. I could find no early records that proved Will Crosier owned a store in Zenith, nor details of how the mill property may have passed from the Crosiers' ownership to that of Thomas Jefferson Miller, so I started again with the latter as my focus. A 1911 deed referred to the mill parcel as "T. J. Miller's land," which was conveyed to M. E. Talbott from Miller's heirs after his death in 1905.

The heirs' surnames in the deed established a familial connection between the Crosiers, the Millers, the Talbotts, and the Beamers.

Mrs. R. S. Beamer, née Romanza Silstine Miller, was a daughter of T. J. Miller[790] and the widow of Rev. Augustus Ballantyne Beamer.[791] Beamer, who was a native of Monroe County, graduated from the United Presbyterian Theological Seminary in Allegheny, Pennsylvania, and was licensed to preach in 1855. He returned to serve at the Associate Reformed Presbyterian Church in New Lebanon in Monroe County.[792,793]

In 1860, he reported his occupation as AR Presbyter M.[794] In 1870, he reported he was working as a millhand,[795] probably for his father-in-law. He was appointed postmaster of Zenith in 1886,[796] and in 1900 was working as a minister.[797] He died in 1903.[798]

The 1891-92 *West Virginia Gazetteer* shows James E. Miller running the flour mill in Zenith, a hamlet with twenty residents.[799] James was a son of Archibald Miller, who lived near T. J. Miller in 1870 and may have been T. J.'s younger brother or a cousin.[800] He lived next door to T. J. Miller in 1900. Martyn Miller lived next door to Augustus and Romanza Miller Beamer.[801]

The 1900-01 *Gazetteer* listing for Zenith shows A. B. Beamer was the postmaster, Martyn Miller was running the mill, T. J. Miller was the blacksmith, and A. V. Shires operated the general store.[802]

In 1904, J. E. Miller was running the gristmill again, and A. V. Shires had taken his son into the general store business.[803]

The Miller family stayed involved in mill operations. In 1892-1893 James E. Miller ran the flour mill in Zenith. Martyn Miller was running the gristmill in 1900-1901, and J. E. Miller was back in charge in 1904-1905.[804]

In 1910, it was James E. Miller who lived next door to then-widowed Romanza Beamer.[805]

In 1911, after T. J. Miller's death, the property passed to M. E. Talbott, née Malinda Elizabeth Miller, another of T. J. Miller's daughters, and her husband, George Talbott, a merchant.

Dr. Greg Ware, the mill's current owner, was able to fill in more of the mill's history. His grandfather, Herman Omer McClung, came from Fayette County to work at a sawmill on Turkey Creek, on the other side of the little mountain the mill faces. He met Ware's grandmother, Sadie Anna Miller, who was a granddaughter of T. J. Miller, and the couple married in March 1917. Herman and Sadie purchased the mill property from Romanza Miller Beamer in 1923.[806] According to Ware, McClung had millworks from another mill moved to the site, carried by railroad to Waitville and then brought over Peters Mountain by horse and wagon.[807]

In 1940, McClung reported his occupation as millwright.[808]

Greg Ware also mentioned his mother's first cousin Herbert Shires, who lived in Zenith his whole life, in the house attached to the general store that faces the mill. His father, Clarence,[809] the son of A. V. from the Gazetteer listings, died in 1952,[810] when Herbert was about thirteen years old, and the store closed. He helped Herman McClung operate the mill until it closed and was leased by the historical society.

Finally, I found the first mention of the McClung Mill in a lease agreement dated April 23, 1970. The McClungs leased the mill property to the Monroe County Historical Society, which had the right to restore and run the mill. The Historical Society could then use it for demonstrations and as a place to manufacture and sell arts and crafts to the public. The twenty-year lease was renewable for an additional twenty years if the parties so desired.[811]

Greg Ware recalled that Jack Kilburn was the miller and lived on the property during the time it was leased by the Monroe County Historical Society.

Herman McClung died in 1978, and in 1989, after Sadie McClung's death, their heirs entered into an agreement of joint tenants with the right of survivorship. Kathleen McClung Ferrell and her husband, Robert, and Mary Ann McClung Ware and her husband, Kenneth Ware, were the joint tenants of the fifty-seven and three-quarters acres from their parents' estate. The other two siblings, Omer McClung and Lucille Dickson, conveyed title to the Ferrells and the Wares.[812]

Mary Ann McClung Ware was the last surviving sibling. Since her death, her son, Dr. Greg Ware of Watkinsville, Georgia, has owned the mill.[813]

The mill seems to elicit happy childhood memories for individuals like Robyn Huffman, who commented on a blog post in May 2021: "My grandmother ran that store in Zenith and lived in the house next to it. I used to go to the mill, across the street to the spring house for water, to Ray's ponds, and we got milk from McClung's farm up the hill in the mid-1960s to early 1970s."[814]

8. REED'S MILL

Monroe County
Address: 1331 Second Creek Road, Sinks Grove, WV 24976
Coordinates: 37.6674509, -80.4561644
Year Built: 1791
Period of Significance: 1791-2021; still in operation
Added to the National Register of Historic Places in 1993

© Google Maps

Reed's Mill - Photo by Tracy Lawson

Reed's Mill has been in operation since 1791.
Photo courtesy of Daniel Walker for West Virginia Public Radio

In 1716, Alexander Spottswood, the Colonial Governor of Virginia, sent a party of explorers on an expedition across the Blue Ridge, seeking a route to the Pacific Ocean. They followed the James River system to the present site of Covington, Virginia, then up Dunlap Creek (First Creek), across the Great Eastern Continental Divide, from the Sweet Springs Valley to the Gap Mills Valley, and down into the Second Creek system, so named because it was the second creek system on the western side of the Eastern Continental Divide. In early days, Gap Mills was known as Moss Gap or Moss Hole.[815]

Several main springs from Peters Mountain feed Second Creek's headwaters. The creek's steady drop in elevation, from 2,400 feet above sea level to 1,700 where it empties into the Greenbrier River, made it a power source for industry. As many as two dozen mills lined Second Creek's thirty miles: sawmills, woolen mills, gun powder mills, ironwork mills, and gristmills. The earliest, a saw, grist, and powder mill, presently called Rodgers Mill, was built by Frederick Gromer in 1785[816] *(See Gromer-Nickell's Upper-Rodgers Mill, page 345).*

Reed's Mill, one of the earliest built along Second Creek, tapped its power for two centuries. These days, it runs on a gasoline engine. The building's older section dates to 1791 and is mortise and tenon construction with wooden pegs, traditionally called "tree nails,"[817] set atop a raised stone basement. The newer, three-story section with a basement and covered loading dock was added in 1948.

Archibald McDowell, the mill's original owner, was a private in John Stuart's company from Greenbrier County during Dunsmore's War in 1774. He and his wife, Catharine, came to Second Creek before 1780. Owen Frederic Morton reported in *The History of Monroe County West Virginia* that McDowell's mill is still on the same site as the Beamer Mill.[818] The roster of owners includes Morgan, VanStavern, Beamer, and Boggs. Another mill, run by Augustyne [sic] Beamer, was located twenty miles away in Zenith, West Virginia *(See McClung Mill, page 353).*

When Archibald McDowell died in 1813, his personal property appraised at $1,192.70. In his will, he left his plantation house and mills to his wife, Catharine,[819] who died in 1844. Her heirs sold the mill out of the family—but as with many rural mills, it eventually came back.

* * *

Andrew E. Reed and his son Isaac ran the Hollywood Woolen Mill. Isaac married Margaret Ann McDowell, a great-granddaughter of Archibald and Catharine, in 1877.[820]

The first Reed to own Reed's Mill was Will Reed in 1914. Aubrey Reed has the distinction of operating the mill the longest. He worked there for over seventy years, and likely learned the trade from his relatives from the time he was a small boy.

The mill was at the center of a vibrant rural community with prosperous farms that benefited from the rich bottomland around Second Creek. The millhouse, currently owned by Joe Reed, housed the Second Creek Post Office until 2010. The Holesapple Store building is located nearby.

In an interview, Aubrey once said the worst drought year he remembered was 1932, when it hardly rained from May until October, yet Second Creek continued to flow.

His nephew Larry Mustain, who grew up across the street from the mill, stepped in to help Aubrey run it in 1989 and took over operations in 1992. He and his son operate the mill sporadically, producing cornmeal and two varieties of high-quality buckwheat flour. They use a portable stone grinder, but his dream is to keep the mill running again in the old-fashioned way. Turbines still power the mill, but at this writing, they were temporarily relying on a gasoline engine. Every fifteen years or so, it is necessary to clean out the silt buildup from the millrace.

The equipment in Reed's Mill tells the story of mill technology's evolution. Two run of buhrstones that hark to the mill's earliest days share space with a 1920s Midget Marvel, a self-contained flour-milling machine. Mustain still has the original instruction manual for the Marvel and for the Fitz Water Turbine, both over a century old.[821]

Bloody Butcher, the strain of corn used to produce Reed's Mill's signature cornmeal, was developed commercially in Virginia by around 1845, and some say it was a part of Native American commerce long before then.[822] Its seeds produce ears with a mix of red, yellow, and tan-orange kernels. Recently, local crops of Bloody Butcher have been devastated by deer, geese, and turkeys. The local wildlife prefers the heirloom corn, as do most of the customers who come to Reed's Mill. The corn's popularity is not just because of its history, but also its appearance. The white cornmeal has bright red flecks sprinkled throughout, like a butcher's apron, and the hull gives the meal a unique, gritty texture.

Mustain would prefer not to switch to genetically modified corn, but it's hard to find an affordable source of Bloody Butcher, or other heirloom corn, grown outside of West Virginia. In recent years, he located a nearly identical corn at Spring Creek farm in Craigsville and buys 1,200 pounds yearly to grind.[823]

Like other rural mills, Reed's houses a sideline broom-making shop. Its nineteenth-century equipment, once owned and used by Everett Hogsett,[824] cleans seeds off the broomcorn, cuts it to a uniform length, wraps it to the handle, and soaks, clamps, and stitches the broom.[825]

In 2018, the Preservation Alliance of West Virginia listed Reed's Mill as one of the top endangered properties in West Virginia. This designation highlights the risk of losing the property, to attract attention from the public and encourage others to help restore the building. Recently, Mustain applied for grant funding to address some maintenance issues. Powder-post beetles have invaded the ancient wood, and there's a large amount of silt buildup in the millpond.[826]

* * *

You'd never guess that a mere fifteen miles from Reed's Mill's bucolic setting, a state-of-the-art bunker lay underground, ready to protect our nation's elected officials in the event of a nuclear attack. The bunker remained secret from the tense days of the Cuban Missile Crisis to after the fall of the Soviet Union.

The secret remained buried—literally—for thirty years. Today, it's known as The Bunker, but its official name was the US Government Relocation Facility, also dubbed "Project Greek Island" while it was under construction from 1958-1961.

During the height of the Cold War, President Dwight D. Eisenhower and Congressional leaders wanted a safe place where the US government could continue to function in the event of a national emergency. Eisenhower had recuperated at The Greenbrier Hotel during World War II, and often visited the area. His affection for the resort, where he golfed, coupled with its secluded location in the Allegheny Mountains and relative proximity to Washington, DC, made The Greenbrier a perfect fit.

The two-story bunker was built 720 feet into the hillside under the West Virginia Wing of The Greenbrier. When finished, it could house up to 1,100 people—all the members of the Senate and House of Representatives, as well as key staff—with a self-sustaining infrastructure and enough provisions for up to sixty days.

Forsyth Associates, a group of government employees who blended seamlessly into The Greenbrier's landscape, masqueraded as television and telephone repairmen. Locals who had worked on the construction crews were unaware of its true purpose.

After the collapse of the Soviet Union in late 1991, *Washington Post* reporter Ted Gup wrote an article revealing the bunker's existence. Once the facility was compromised, it was no longer useful to the government, and the lease with The Greenbrier was terminated three years later.

Everyone I'd interviewed while researching this book was eager to share stories, and Mustain was no exception. He said that President Eisenhower, while on site at the Greenbrier Hotel, wanted stone-ground yellow cornmeal to have cornbread made and sent his driver to Reed's to buy some. Aubrey said he was grinding white corn, not yellow, that day. The driver asked if Aubrey could switch over to yellow corn, but Aubrey refused—not even for the President of the United States! The driver returned the next day and procured the desired yellow cornmeal.[827] Larry says his mother added her own quip to the story, claiming Aubrey would have stopped the mill and ground the yellow corn quick enough if Eisenhower had been a Democrat.

Reed's Mill is open most Saturdays, and other days if a group or tour bus calls ahead.

To schedule a visit call Larry Mustain at 304-772-5665.[828]

All seeds carry a genetic blueprint. In nature, every time a flower's pollen blows in on the wind, or is carried by insects, or finds some way to make it to another flower, the pollen and the flower come together to create seeds. This process is called open pollination and is the most random way of mixing genes up to create seeds.

Humans realized long ago that manual pollination and other techniques to breed plants improve the odds of getting a desired trait like a bigger apple or a sweeter berry. It's a similar, but more controlled, version of what happens in nature.

Over time, a plant's genetics can be stabilized by selectively breeding similar plants with each other until they reliably create the desired result. If a plant's genetics remain relatively stable over a period, the variety becomes known as heirloom. https://planthardware.com/heirloom-vs-hybrid-vs-openpollinated/

RALEIGH COUNTY
Formed in 1850 from Fayette County

21. BECKLEY MILL RUINS

Raleigh County
Address: County Route 9-7, Beaver, WV 25813
Coordinates: 37.7734949, -81.1502882
Year Built: 1838
Period of Significance: 1838- c. 1915
Added to National Register of Historic Places in 2017

© Google Maps

A hiking trail now leads to the Beckley Mill ruins.
Photo by David Sibray

Beckley Mill ruins - Photo by David Sibray

Alfred Beckley's dream was to build a town, and a mill was the first step in that direction. Remnants of that old gristmill, which Beckley Common Councilman Tom Sopher called the "crown jewel of Piney Creek,"[829] were recently at the center of a plan to boost the city's local economy.

Historian David Sibray described the mill's origins:

Before Alfred Beckley arrived in the wilderness of western Virginia to settle the lands left to him by his father, John James Beckley, he wrote to his maternal cousins, William and Clarkson Prince, who had already settled on nearby Beaver Creek, requesting that they establish a well-located gristmill, to be operational upon his arrival in 1835. The location they chose was just downstream of one of the few significant falls on Piney Creek, the only stream in the area that sustained an appreciable year-round flow. Their ambitious cousin's plan to develop a viable settlement in the wilderness would depend on a reliable mill.[830]

One of the few written descriptions of the mill was penned by Rutherford B. Hayes, the nation's 19th president, who visited the site in January of 1862 while a colonel in the Union army.

"Found it a most romantic spot," Hayes wrote in his diary. The mill, then operated by John Beckley, son of the town's founder, came equipped with "a cabin by a roaring torrent in a glen separated from all the world," where the younger Beckley lived with his "pretty wife and daughter," the future president wrote. "I shall long remember that quiet little home."[831]

With the advance of railroads into the region, the need for a local mill became less pressing, and eventually the Beckley Mill fell out of use. Access to the site was blocked by a refuse dump operated by the city. By the 1950s, the mill had fallen into ruin.

In the late 1980s, the Raleigh County Historic Landmarks Commission took interest in the mill ruins and added the site to its register of historic places, but the area was neglected until 2012, when historians began a campaign to rescue and preserve the site in a way that could benefit the community and promote tourism. Grant money was used to finance an archaeological dig, which gave the project more credibility.

The mill was placed on the National Register of Historic Places on May 1, 2017,[832] thanks to the efforts of Beckley Historical Society president and Beckley Common Councilman Tom Sopher, Teresa Sopher and the Piney Creek Watershed Association, Susan Landis and the Beckley Area Foundation, the Carter Family Foundation, Tom Lemke, Scott Worley and the Historic Landmarks Commission, Friends of the Library, Piney Creek Trail Committee, former mayor Emmett Pugh, historian David Sibray, archaeologist David Fuerst, Dan Pizzoni and Jeff Smith of the West Virginia Division of Culture and History,[833] and others.

Remnants of the locally cut sandstone walls that supported and contained the mill are still visible along Piney Creek, a short distance from Beckley's municipal water treatment plant. Although an active CSX track operates on a railbed across Piney Creek from the mill site, the lack of easy access to the mill helped allow the structure to slip from public memory and helped preserve the site from vandals.[834]

Now, the old wagon road that led to the mill has become part of a series of pedestrian trails that lead to the mill ruins and a streamside park that provides public access for fishing.[835]

The trail to the mill ruins is about a fifteen-minute walk and is steep in places.

SUMMERS COUNTY
Formed in 1871 from Fayette, Greenbrier, Mercer, and Monroe Counties

35. COOPER'S MILL

Summers County
Address: Bluestone River Road (CR 27/3), Jumping Branch, WV 25969
Coordinates: 37.606099, -80.978249
Year Built: 1869
Period of Significance: 1869-1950
Added to the National Register of Historic Places in 2001

© Google Maps

Cooper's Mill, one of the most remote in this book, will be accessed by hiking trails in the planned Summers County Community Forest.
Photo by Elmer Napier

The last remaining mill in Summers County is nestled in the stream-cut highlands that drain into the Bluestone River, where the terrain is rugged and steep. It served its community from the post–Civil War era until a few years after the end of World War II.

In 2020, the Summers County Commission bought a 10.25-acre tract which includes the mill and blacksmith shop. A second tract of approximately 275 acres, which includes 128 acres on the same side of the Little Bluestone River and 146 acres on the other side of the river, is being purchased by the West Virginia Land Trust. Combined, the nearly 300 acres will become a community forest, with walking trails and a trailhead located near the road. Jack Wills, one of the family members who have worked hard over the last decade to preserve the mill and adjacent blacksmith shop, hopes the site will be used as an exhibit and for demonstrations of old-time milling.

Cooper's Mill is the only one in this book I did not view in person. I tried. Oh, how I tried! I drove up and down Ellison Ridge Road several times before I doubled back to the convenience store on the main road and asked if anyone knew where to find the mill. Every person in the shop had an opinion, and several pulled out their phones to get more information. I set out again with fortified resolve, but after several more passes, I finally had to admit defeat. Elmer told me later, "Oh, well it's about half a mile off the main road." He, dauntless, had hiked out to the mill on one of his previous driving trips to take photos.

Jack Wills confirmed the old road Elmer used to access the mill: "The county road does leave Route 27 (Ellison Ridge Road) just before you cross the third bridge and continues along the left descending bank of Little Bluestone to the mill, and, in fact, all the way to the Bluestone River; however, maintenance ceased after the Bluestone Dam was finished in the late 1940s. The road is now overgrown and impassible by vehicles. One can, in fact, walk directly to the mill along the road."[836]

Cooper's Mill remained active longer than most of the mills in this book and owes its survival to its remote location and the surrounding area's need for a local mill. Though it's been idle since 1950, the mill is so far off the beaten path that it has been immune to vandals and is virtually pristine.

* * *

Robert "Miller Bob" Lilly built the original mill of notched logs in 1869. Its working parts may have been salvaged from the Levi Neeley Mill, which was built on the Bluestone River around 1840.[837] Lilly used a simple setup that is found in mills predating Oliver Evans's innovations, which made me wonder if he was familiar with other mills that dated to the eighteenth century.

In 1883, Miller Bob sold the mill to Josiah Cooper, who renamed it Cooper's Mill. The mill has remained in the Cooper family ever since. Josiah ran the mill and later sold it to his son Thomas Moody Cooper, who was known to play the fiddle for his customers while they waited for their grain to be processed.[838]

Tom rebuilt the mill in the 1930s, at a time when many rural mills were shutting down for good. The diminutive structure, just eighteen feet long by sixteen feet wide, was originally built of logs notched at the corners.[839] Tom dismantled the original superstructure down to the last five log courses and built a two-story frame structure with chestnut board-and-batten siding and a gable roof above the lowest level, which houses the driveshaft and gears.

During the renovation Tom replaced the original wooden wheel with an overshot Fitz Wheel that measures fourteen feet in diameter and three feet wide. The rest of the equipment in the mill is original.

Tom operated the mill until just before his death in 1945, and his son Elisha B. Cooper ran the mill occasionally until 1950, when he sold it to Owen Wills, Tom Cooper's oldest grandson. The mill has been idle since then, but after Owen's death in 1997, several Cooper family members banded together to see it restored to working condition.[840]

A wide, shelflike waterfall burbles a few feet upstream from the mill. When the mill was operating, an earthen millrace channeled water from a dam about a quarter mile upstream, with a wooden trough directing it the last fifty feet or so to the waterwheel.[841]

When customers brought grain sacks to the mill, the miller dumped them into hoppers on the second floor. From the lower level, the miller adjusted the gap between the millstones to the customer's wishes and then opened a series of gates outside in the millrace to set the wheels turning. Gravity drew the grain from the hoppers to the stones, and centrifugal force carried the ground flour or meal over the edge of the millstones and into the collection area below, where it was sacked. There the process ended.

Now that the mill and the surrounding land is earmarked for a recreation area, the Cooper descendants' dream of offering old-time milling demonstrations to school groups and holding traditional music events on the property will come to fruition. Events held there will serve to preserve the area's cultural heritage.[842]

Friends of Cooper's Mill has produced two short videos about the mill, which can be viewed on YouTube.

The falls near Cooper's Mill (date unknown)
Image courtesy of West Virginia & Regional History Center
Used with permission

Chapter 5
Mountain Lakes

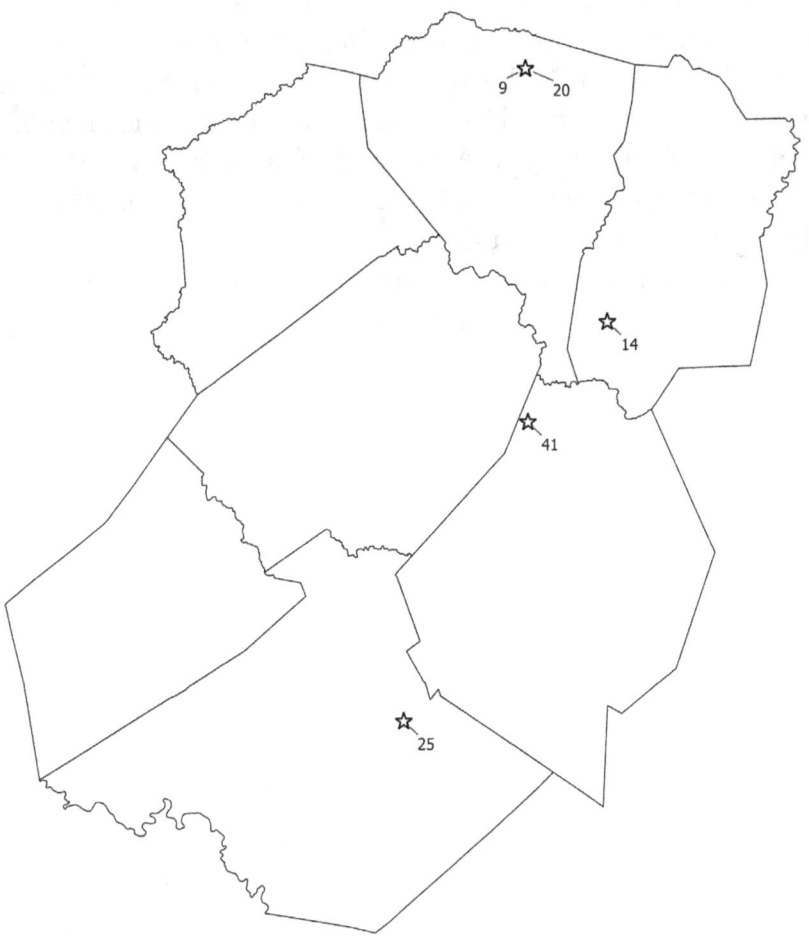

The Mountain Lakes Region, the central-most cluster of counties, is historically the most isolated region in the state, with the smallest population. Major coal and lumbering companies operated in the region.[843]

Around the turn of the twentieth century, the railroad spurred economic growth. The lumber industry responded, expanding rapidly, and the Cherry River Boom and Lumber Company built one of the world's largest sawmills at Richwood. Other industries followed, including a paper mill, handle and hub factories, a tannery, and what was then the world's largest clothespin factory. Coal mining drove an economic surge into the twentieth century until the industry softened in the 1970s. Currently, Fayette and Nicholas Counties are part of the 4C Economic Development Authority, which fosters regional economic growth. The completion of the four-lane Appalachian Corridor L (US Route 19) through Nicholas County in the 1990s brought heavy north-south traffic and prosperity to roadside businesses.[844]

The Mountain Lakes Region boasts some of the state's most famous, and most scenic, rivers, lakes, and streams.[845]

LEWIS COUNTY
Formed from Harrison County in 1816

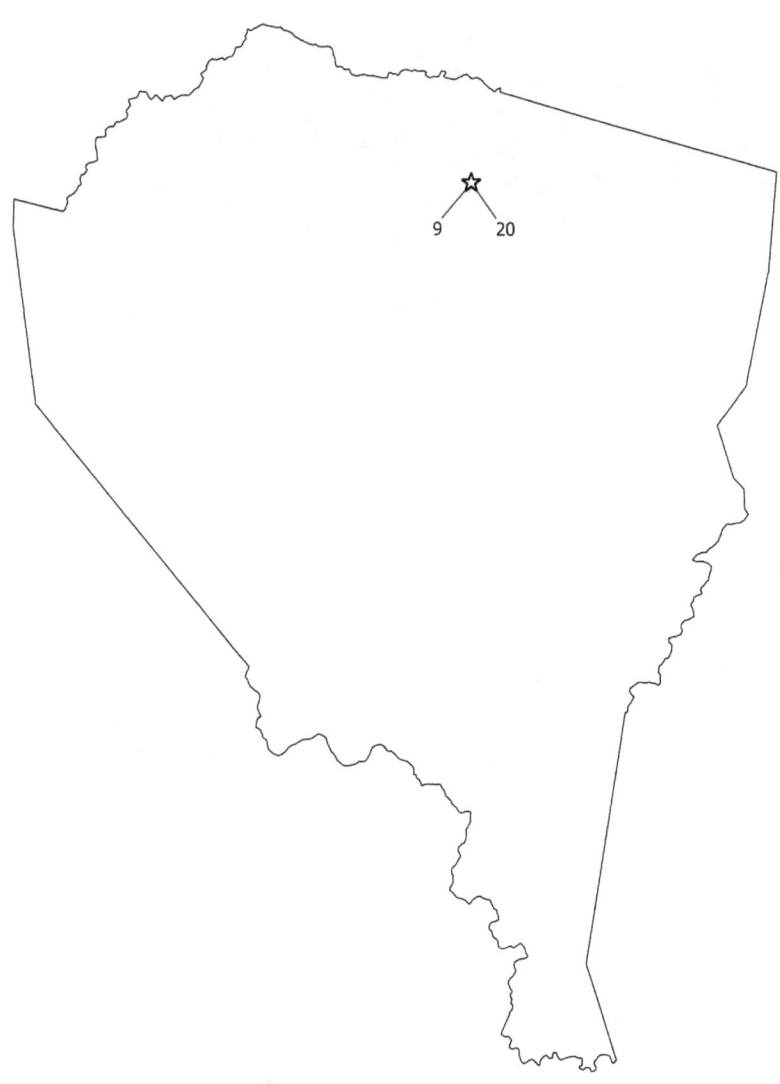

9. BLAKER'S MILL

Lewis County
Address: 160 Jacksons Mill Road, Weston, WV 26452
Coordinates: 39.1007133, -80.4711715
Year Built: 1794
Period of Significance: 1794-1962
Added to the National Register of Historic Places in 2005 as part of the Jackson's Mill 4-H Camp Historic District

© Google Maps

Blaker's Mill was moved from Greenbrier County to Jackson's Mill Historic Area.
Photo by Tracy Lawson

Blaker's Mill once ground cornmeal, flour, and buckwheat every day but Monday, according to the sign on the old Dutch door.[846] The mill has found new life as part of a living history museum at Jackson's Mill, 150 miles north of its original location.

Jacob and Mary Niswander Hockman, the first German family to settle in Greenbrier County, built their mill in 1794 at the confluence of the Muddy Creek and Mill Creek. Hockman operated the mill until his death in 1842, when he willed it to Susan, the youngest of his three daughters.[847] Susan married George Lewis in 1831, and the couple eventually had ten children. In 1850, their next-door neighbor, George Thomas, who listed his profession as miller, may have been hired to run the Hockman Mill.[848] In 1860, one of George and Susan's sons, Harvey, was the miller.[849]

Various sources indicate that the family later hired John A. Blaker of Loudoun County, Virginia, to run the mill. In Census records, John listed his occupation as "carpenter," so it is possible he was hired in that capacity. John and Elizabeth Susan Lewis, George and Susan's daughter, married in 1866.

Harvey does not seem to have continued in the profession long after the Civil War. In 1870, John Pollack, a neighbor, listed his occupation as "grist miller,"[850] and in 1880, a neighbor, Z. Taylor May, was a miller.[851] The Blakers had eight children, of which four—James, Susie Alice, Ida Florence, and Mamie Frances—remained unmarried. Together, the four siblings ran the mill, a mail order business selling wheat, buckwheat, cornmeal, and other specialty flours, a general store, and the community's post office. James was an excellent carpenter and built a shop at the side of the mill. He harnessed waterpower to operate his woodworking tools.[852]

James was the last surviving of his siblings, and after his death in May 1962, his nephew Robert Hockman Blaker Jr. inherited the mill. He later donated it to the state so that it could be preserved and enjoyed by future generations. Funds were raised to have the mill disassembled and brought to Jackson's Mill 4-H Camp, where each numbered board and stone was put back together with the help of AmeriCorps and local volunteers who came from cities, villages, hills, and hollows all over the state. Many worked a few days, several worked a few weeks or months, and a handful worked for years to complete the reconstruction of the relocated mill as it was originally built—with hand tools.[853]

To help stabilize the building, the numbered stones were split in two and reassembled around a cinderblock section, so that one half of each original stone is visible from the outside, the other on the inside.[854]

After a few successful trial runs, the mill opened for demonstrations at its new location in 1993. Since then, it has been a popular attraction at the Farmstead.

When Blaker's Mill is in operation, about a thousand gallons of water pass over the wheel per minute. One of its three sets of millstones is freshwater quartz that is pieced together, and two are hewn from single pieces of granite. Whole wheat flour and cornmeal, ground in the mill, is for sale in the general store.

Dean Harden, a longtime employee of Jackson's Mill, was our tour guide when we visited. At the time, he was in the process of retiring and relocating to Florida, and it was a treat to hear the history of both Blaker's and Jackson's Mills from the man who oversaw the team that restored Blaker's Mill and got it running again, as he said, "with a combination of luck and skill."[855]

Each individual brick and board was numbered before the mill was dismantled and moved. Photo by Tracy Lawson

20. JACKSON'S MILL

Lewis County
Address: 160 Jacksons Mill Road, Weston, WV 26452
Coordinates: 39.1008881, -80.4712226
Year Built: 1837
Period of Significance: c. 1786-1904
Added to the National Register of Historic Places in 1972

© Google Maps

The Jackson family owned a mill at this approximate location by 1800. The current structure replaced an earlier mill that was destroyed by fire.
Photo by Tracy Lawson

Jackson's Mill is the centerpiece of the historical site and museum at the Jackson's Mill Center for Lifelong Learning and 4-H Camp. The facility, which sits on 500 acres, has a campground with cottages donated by and named for several West Virginia counties, a large dining hall that is a replica of Mount Vernon, and an outdoor amphitheater.[856] It also serves as a special campus for West Virginia University and the WVU Extension Service.[857]

Colonel Edward Blake Jackson, a veteran of the American Revolution, built the original mill. He was born in 1759 near Moorefield in what is now Hardy County, at a time when hostilities between the French and native Americans prompted settlers to build a string of forts for protection *(See Old Fields Mill, page 195).*

Harrison County records from December 20, 1786, indicate that Jackson was granted liberty to build a mill, which he located on his land three miles north of Weston on the east bank of the West Fork of the Monongahela River.

Randolph County was formed from a large swath of Harrison County and small parts of eight others in October 1787,[858] and Jackson took an active part in local government. The minutes of the first Randolph County Court contain a recommendation to appoint Edward Jackson surveyor of the county. He was appointed a county justice on May 29, 1787, commissioned a Captain of Militia in May 1790, Commissioner of Revenue in 1791, and sheriff in 1792.[859]

An Act of the Virginia Assembly dated January 20, 1800, declared the Monongahela publicly navigable as far as Edward Jackson's Mill on the West Fork.[860] That mill was located directly across the stream from Jackson's Mill's present location. Due to erosion of the bank, the mill was moved to the opposite bank some time prior to 1830 by Cummins Jackson, Edward's son, who had come into possession of his father's farm and mill after Edward's death in 1828.[861]

In 1830, Cummins and his mother, Elizabeth Jackson,[862] took in his orphaned niece and nephew, Julia Ann and Thomas Jonathan Jackson. Young Thomas attended school when he could, but mostly he helped in the mill and on his uncle's 1,500-acre farm, tending sheep and helping harvest wheat and corn. Motivated to learn, he would often sit up late with a book, and he taught one of his uncle's slaves to read, in defiance of the laws of the time.⁸⁶³

The original mill was destroyed by fire in 1837, and soon after, Cummins built a new gristmill, which also housed a general store and served as a community hub where people gathered to exchange news and talk politics.

Cummins built a dam six feet high and 150 feet long to direct the river's power to two horizontal tub wheels submerged under the mill. He also built a separate sawmill that supplied much of the lumber for the town of Weston.

As a young man, Thomas became a schoolmaster and, in 1842, won an appointment to West Point. After graduation, he served as an instructor at the Virginia Military Institute.

Cummins Jackson left Jackson's Mill in 1847 and went to California in search of gold. He died there in 1849.

Thomas Jackson and his sister, Laura, remained close throughout their lives until, like so many families, they found themselves on opposite sides of the Civil War. Laura opened her house in Beverly, West Virginia, to Union troops as a hospital. Thomas joined the Confederacy, advanced to the rank of general, and earned the nickname Stonewall at the First Battle of Bull Run. He was wounded in a friendly-fire incident in the Battle of Chancellorsville in 1863.⁸⁶⁴ As he lay wounded, General Lee sent a message: "Give General Jackson my affectionate regards, and say to him; he has lost his left arm, but I have lost my right." Jackson died eight days later of complications from the injury.⁸⁶⁵

Jackson's Mill and the rest of Cummins Jackson's property was held in heirship until 1868 when his sister, Catherine Jackson White, purchased the property.⁸⁶⁶ Upon her death, the farm was sold, but members of the Jackson family appear to have stayed involved with the mill.

The 1882-83 *West Virginia Gazetteer and business directory* listing for the village of Jane Lew shows that the Jackson family was active in local commerce. B. Jackson and J. W. Jackson both ran general stores; Edward Jackson, a grandson of Col. Edward Blake Jackson,⁸⁶⁷ ran the flour mill; and Isaac Jackson was the railroad agent.⁸⁶⁸ In 1891-92, none of these individuals were engaged in business there, but J. G. Jackson ran the general store, and V. B. Flesher ran the flour mill.[869] In 1900, it was F. B. Flesher who was in charge of the flour and sawmill, and in 1904,[870] partners Flesher & Jackson were operating the mill.[871]

The Monongahela Power Company acquired the mill in 1915, and in 1924 donated the property to the state of West Virginia as a meeting place for the youth enrolled in the 4-H program.[872]

Jackson's Mill is a three-story structure, 41feet long by 36 feet 8 inches wide. The weatherboarded frame structure is maintained by the West Virginia State 4-H Camp personnel under the operation of the West Virginia University Extension Service. When the state acquired the mill, it required repair. Though the building retains a significant amount of the original woodwork and equipment, some of the siding was replaced and has been regularly painted and maintained since that time. In 1956 the roof was replaced with hand-cut shingles made in West Virginia and is regularly weatherized and stained green. The West Virginia University Extension operates a museum inside the mill, which attracts thousands of visitors during the summer months.[873]

On the main floor, visitors can see the cogs and blade of a simple sash sawmill, which is not original to the building. An original feed hopper and millstone from the gristmill can be viewed on the second floor.

Blaker's Mill, a water-powered gristmill constructed in 1794 near Alderson in Greenbrier County, was disassembled, each board, stone, and piece of equipment numbered, and relocated to the property in the 1980s. It stands within sight of Jackson's Mill *(See Blaker's Mill, page 381)*.

There are twenty-three contributing buildings at Jackson's Mill, most of which, like Blaker's Mill, were moved to the site. When you visit, be sure to examine the dozens of millstones lining the camp's walking paths, all cut in unique patterns form various types of stone.

Dean Harden, our tour guide, ran the History on the Road program through WVU Extension. He was active in both the Midwest Open-Air Museums Coordinating Council and the Association for Living History, Farm, and Agricultural Museums. At WVU at Jackson's Mill, demonstrations can include grist milling, weaving, spinning, basketmaking, candle dipping, woodworking, blacksmithing, paper marbling, and other heritage arts that were a part of frontier life. These

LEWIS COUNTY 389

activities are set against a historic backdrop of authentic eighteenth- and nineteenth-century buildings. Tours and programs can run from a few hours to all day. Classes in various heritage arts can also be arranged. Check www.jacksonsmill.wvu.edu or call 304-406-7023 for current information about programming.

This undated image shows the mill fell into an extreme state of disrepair before it was restored and protected.
Image courtesy of West Virginia & Regional History Center
Used with permission

An up-and-down saw blade and log carriage on display inside Jackson's Mill. Photo by Tracy Lawson

NICHOLAS COUNTY
Formed in 1818

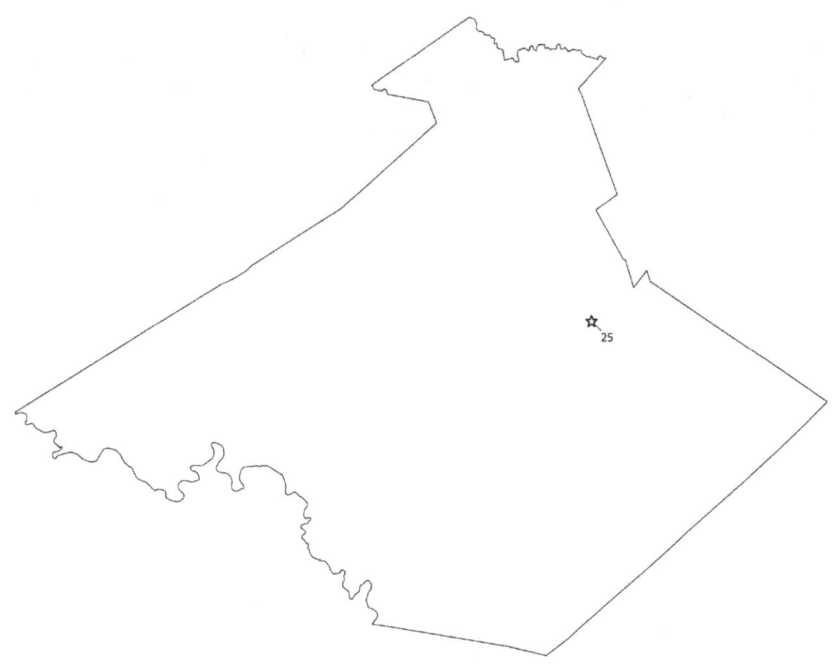

25. BEAVER MILL

Nicholas County
Address: East Webster Road and Beaver Hills Road, Craigsville, WV 26205
Coordinates: 38.3268023, -80.6684646
Year Built: 1852
Period of Significance: 1852-1932
Added to the National Register of Historic Places in 2001

© Google Maps

Beaver Mill may become the centerpiece of a picnic area with walking trails.
Photo by Tracy Lawson

Beaver Mill, an intact example of mid-nineteenth-century Oliver Evans plan, is the sole remaining mill in the county and is under the care of the Nicholas County Landmark Commission.

Beaver Mill is only a few miles from Craigsville, but it feels as though you're much farther away from civilization as you drive through the rolling hills and farmland on County Road 5, Old Beaver Road.

Beaver Mill was constructed around 1852, and ground wheat, corn, and buckwheat. The two-story frame structure is sided with clapboards painted red. It is of modest size—twenty-five feet wide by thirty feet long, with two bays and a single window in the gable.

A raised stone foundation forms the north wall of the tailrace, where, it is believed, turbines were once located.

Inside, the grinding floor is raised about eighteen inches above the first floor of the building and is supported by a Hurst frame.

The two sets of French buhrstones, housed within round wooden boxes, are plastered in the seams and held together with iron hoops around their perimeters. This is typical, as the stones were often used as ship's ballast, and once the ships reached their destination, they were sold as sections for millstones. One set of stones would have been used to grind wheat, the other for corn and buckwheat.[874] On the second floor, the bolters and separators remain in place. With the exceptions of the roof and some siding, everything is believed to be original.[875]

The historic village of Beaver Mill was located on an early road between Summersville and Greenbrier County in the southeast part of Nicholas County. Though that little community has faded into memory, it was important to Nicholas County's early history. Its post office predated the one in nearby Craigsville, and in the mid-1800s the town boasted two blacksmith shops, a schoolhouse, a general store, a church, and several residences.[876]

The village's location, determined by the presence of waterpower from Beaver Creek, was on a tract of land originally owned by John McClung.

Any mention of this region bears a mention of the McClung family, and not least among them was William McClung, an early pioneer and land speculator who is believed to be the first white settler in Greenbrier County. He first scouted the area in the 1760s and returned a few years later to take "tomahawk entry" to about 10,000 acres, a frontier method of claiming land by notching trees bounding the area with a tomahawk or ax.[877]

With the arrival of several of his brothers, McClung formed a family community in the area near Rupert, and as time went on, their land holdings spread north into Nicholas County.

In partnership with General Andrew Moore and Alexander Welch, William McClung patented a tract of land containing between 43,000 and100,000 acres, depending on the source, between the Meadow and Gauley Rivers.[878]

William and Abigail McClung's son Joseph was the first white child born in the area. William McClung fathered fifteen children with two wives and, in his old age, gave hundred-acre parcels of land to his grandchildren as birthday gifts.

In 1852, Kyle Bright, who married John's niece Elizabeth McClung, acquired part of that tract and built the mill. Later that year, Bright acquired another portion of land from McClung's heirs.

Bright sold the mill in 1872 to William Cofer, who is believed to have installed the bolters and separator that are still in place on the second floor.[879] He, in turn, sold the property to George Henry Alderson in 1889.

The 1891-1892 *West Virginia State Gazetteer and business directory* lists local businessmen, including "George Henry Alderson, flour mill, William Cofer, carpenter, and J. K. Cutlip, flour mill."[880]

George Henry Clay Alderson hailed from another prominent family, for whom the town of Alderson in Greenbrier County was named. His father, Col. George Alderson, was toll collector for the James River and Kanawha Turnpike (now the Midland Trail) and kept a stage stand at Lookout, Fayette County. When the statesman Henry Clay was a guest at the Alderson's inn in 1844, George reportedly asked Clay what to name their new baby boy. Clay replied, "Name him for the two greatest men in the United States—yourself and myself."[881]

George Henry Clay Alderson grew up to fight in the Virginia cavalry during the Civil War and later became a prominent farmer and businessman in Nicholas County.

He sold the mill property to William H. Woods in 1896, and thought the mill ceased operations after the village post office and general store were destroyed by fire in 1932, it remained in the Woods family until 1983.

The Nicholas County Historic Landmark Commission now owns Beaver Mill. Bob Johnson, the president of the commission, reported that significant foundation work had been done on the mill in 2018 to restore a corner column and replace rotting sills, using traditional methods. Once this critical stabilization of the mill was complete and brought the mill back to plumb, portions of the drop siding must also be restored.

The commission may never have the resources to get the mill running again but hope to offer the mill as a fixed-display museum with occasional tours. A walking trail and family picnic area on the surrounding grounds have been proposed.

UPSHUR COUNTY
Formed in 1851 from Randolph, Barbour, and Lewis Counties

UPSHUR COUNTY   399

14. FIDLER'S MILL

Upshur County
Address: 6612 Heaston Ridge Road, Rock Cave, WV 26234
Coordinates: 38.7996292, -80.3467945
Date built: 1821
Period of significance: 1821-1949
Added to the National Register of Historic Places in 1997

© Google Maps

Like many rural mills, Fidler's Mill was a community gathering place.
Photo by Alex Rubenstein

Fidler's Mill, a rural grain and carding mill on the banks of the Little Kanawha River, started small, with expansions in 1844 and 1916. It grew on its foundation over time and retains its original equipment, including two run of buhrstones on the main floor, chutes with glass view holes, hoppers, and belts. It is an excellent example of a rural nineteenth-century mill.

In 1847, William Fidler emigrated to Upshur County from Fluvanna County, Virginia, and within a year purchased a 200-acre farm which included a mill built by Daniel Peck in 1821. Within a few years, Fidler enlarged the mill using the labor of his enslaved workers, who reportedly also helped operate the mill.[882] A wooden millrace diverted water from the Little Kanawha to power the twenty-foot overshot wheel and a sawmill that stood a short distance upstream.

The carding machines on the second floor were used seasonally, after sheep shearing. The machinery would "pick the wool into a fluff, whirl it into rolls about two feet long and about a half inch thick. It was then ready for the spinning wheel."[883]

After William's death in 1865, his son William Martin Fidler took over the operation and ran the mill with his son Valerius.[884] By 1900, Valerius had moved to Braxton County and was working as a wagonmaker.[885]

His family sold the mill to E. G. Wilson, who added an upper floor, bringing it to its present configuration. When Wilson ran into financial difficulties several years later, he sold the mill to Hudson V. Fidler, another of William Martin Fidler's sons. Hudson listed his occupation as "miller" in the 1920 Federal Census and ran the mill with his son Russell's help.[886]

Like many rural mills, Fidler's Mill was also a community gathering place that sponsored an annual Halloween dance. Russell kept a barber chair in front of the mill and often cut customers' hair while they waited for their grain to be processed.[887]

When a flood washed out the mill dam on the Little Kanawha in 1942, operations ceased for a few years. After World War II, the family bought a Hammermill machine to provide cornmeal for local families.

Hudson Fidler divided the interest in the mill between his sons, but by 1967 Russell was the sole owner. Russell ceased operating the mill at an unknown date before his death in 1985. The NRHP Nomination Form states that the mill's period of significance ended in 1949.

The Grafton Coal Company bought the mill in 1978 and donated the property to the Southern Upshur County Business Association, which maintains the mill and has offered tours on weekends. Contact them through the Fidler's Mill Facebook page to inquire about available tours.

The mill site is lovely, unspoiled, and easy to access. If you're moderately adventurous, you can take the short path down to the river and get great photos from out on the rocks.

WEBSTER COUNTY
Formed in 1860 from Randolph, Braxton, and Nicholas Counties

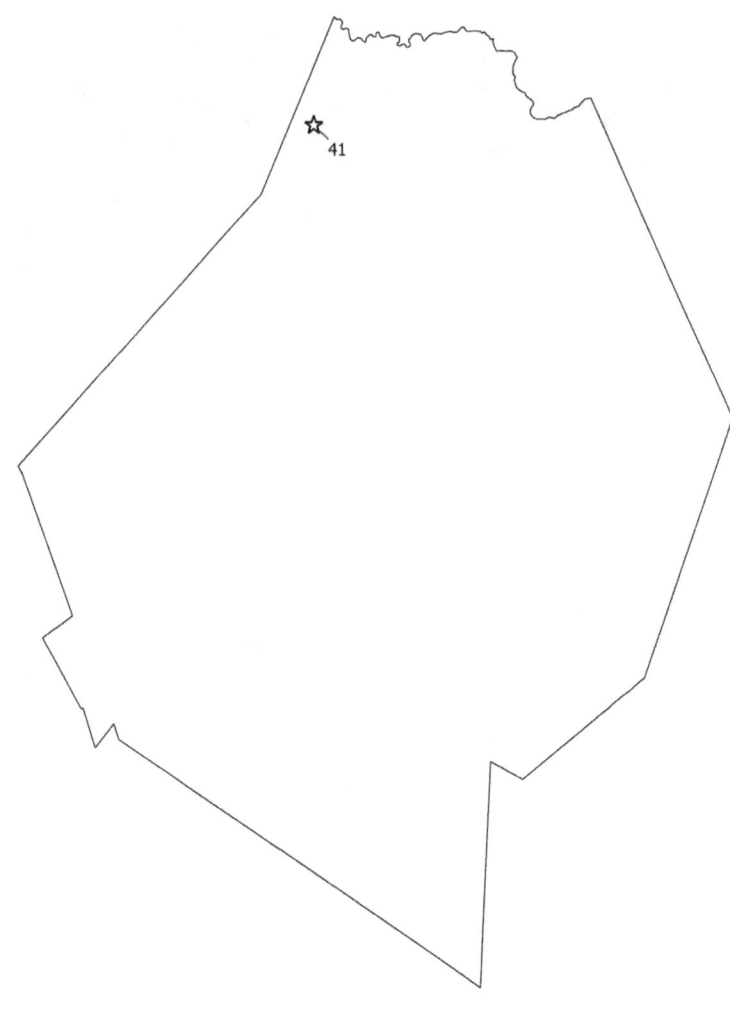

41. MOLLOHAN MILL

Webster County
Address: 1447 Poling Road, Hacker Valley, WV 26222
Coordinates: 38.6817758, -80.4718938
Year Built: 1894
Period of Significance: 1894-1953
Added to National Register of Historic Places in 1982

© Google Maps

Mollohan Mill's last miller was Winnie Mollohan, who operated the mill after the death of her husband. Their daughter, Beth, is the current owner. Photo by Tracy Lawson

Mollohan Mill is the only one in the state that retains one of its original wooden turbines. Photo by Alex Rubenstein

The drive to this mill is an off-the-edge-of-the-map experience. You'll wend your way past remote farms and will most likely lose your internet connection. It's best to take a hard copy of a map with you and keep an eye out for the towns of Cleveland, Jerry Run, and Replete. You'll also pass under some truly spectacular hanging rocks, so be sure to enjoy this experience! Mollohan Mill is best viewed from across the river near the sign that announces its presence.

In times past, gristmills were as important as gas stations are today. Nearly every family went to mill several times a year.[888]

Mollohan Mill, an unaltered example of mid- to late nineteenth century construction and technology, is a two-story, gable-roofed structure with hewn post-and-beam timber construction and pegged mortise-tenon joints. The building measures 38 feet x 23 feet, and the exterior is covered with unpainted sawn clapboards and a corrugated metal roof. It has two run of buhrstones. This is the only mill in the state with one of its original wooden turbines. It was built on the site of an earlier Mollohan mill.[889]

The mill's remote location serves as a reminder of how generations of Mollohans have lived close to nature and its perils. George Mollohan Sr., an Irish immigrant who settled in the area,[890] disappeared without a trace about 1815 while traveling from the home of his son James to visit another son who lived sixteen miles away.

About ten days after his departure, a settler from Little Kanawha came through Birch River and James inquired about his father. He was told that his father not arrived at his intended destination, and George's son had sent word by the settler, asking his father to come for a visit. The settler had not passed George on the path. A search for the old gentleman yielded only his gloves, which were placed in a forked branch of a bush, and his horse, which was found grazing in the bottomlands nearby.[891]

About the time of George's disappearance, his son James and James's wife, Martha, called "Mattie," purchased land on the Back Fork of the Holly River in what was then Randolph County. It had an excellent mill seat, and James built the log mill and dam which served the community until it was washed away in the great flood of 1861. James did not rebuild.[892]

Webster County, Virginia, was formed on January 10, 1860, from parts of Randolph, Nicholas, and Braxton Counties. Bernard Mollohan, a son of George D. Mollohan and a grandson of James and Mattie, was elected Surveyor of Lands for the county in May of that year and surveyed the original county boundary.[893]

When Bernard took the job, there was very little land left to be surveyed in Webster County. In the years that followed, most of his duties involved surveying land that was being sold for delinquent taxes as the country struggled to recover from the war years. Speculators bought up thousands of acres of land in West Virginia.[894]

During the Civil War, emotions ran high in border counties like Webster, and bushwhacker raids were common. Every household in Webster County was under siege at one time or another, and the presence of the guerillas drove the respectable families out of the isolation of the hills and into more populated areas.[895]

As many women had been swindled out of their husband's lands, savvy landowners placed the property in the wife's name so she and her children could not be put off the land if her husband predeceased her. In keeping with this wisdom, the deed to the Mollohan farm was in the name of Bernard's wife, Mary Strong Mollohan.[896]

Though the Mollohans protected their right to their land, they could not stop the war from bringing devastation to their family. Crops were destroyed, family members lost—some in combat, others dead of disease.[897] Bernard and Mary lost their two young daughters to diphtheria in the fall of 1865, just months after the war's end.

Perhaps there was solace in work, for Bernard took on several projects in the postwar years. In 1866, Webster County contracted with Bernard to construct a frame building to serve as the county courthouse for the sum of 1,700 dollars.

Bernard Mollohan constructed more than one mill. It is said that one of his mills, on the back fork of the Elk River, was constructed prior to 1874. Mollohan swapped land with Benjamin Conrad, a childhood friend, and moved to Mt. Pleasant, where he assumed the duties of postmaster. Conrad took over the mill business and became postmaster for the village known as Webster Court House. In later years, the mill

Bernard had built and then swapped to Conrad continued as a thriving business. When it became necessary to change the name of the Mt. Pleasant post office, Bernard supposedly selected the name Replete because the area of Brown's Mountain was replete with flowers and trees.[898]

In the 1880s and 1890s, the lumber business in West Virginia was in full swing, and Bernard surveyed for the lumber companies that were buying large tracts of land.[899] Bernard and his younger brother, Harrison, likely made repairs to Fidler's Mill in neighboring Upshur County[900] before building their own mill.

Bernard stayed busy as the county surveyor for Webster County and, in 1882, resurveyed the county line between Webster and Nicholas Counties to settle a boundary dispute. His great-granddaughter Marie "Beth" Mollohan, author of *By the Banks of the Holly: Notes and Letters from the Desk of Bernard Mollohan*, noted that as her great-grandfather traveled between Brown's Mountain and Addison, he passed the Left Fork of the Holly River, where the old James Mollohan mill site had been vacant since before the War Between the States.[901]

When Bernard was asked to survey 800 acres left to his uncle Charles Mollohan by his grandfather, James, Bernard made note of the piece he wanted, and when he returned with the finished plats, he purchased the mill site from the executor of the estate.

In 1894, Bernard and Harrison spent the better part of a year clearing the land and building the Mollohan Mill that stands on the banks of the Holly River. Once the mill was open for business, Bernard built a house nearby.

While Bernard continued as the county surveyor, Harrison served as justice of the peace in neighboring Braxton County, assisted Bernard as a surveyor, and operated his own mill.

Bernard died of typhoid fever on October 19, 1899.[902] After his father's death, George Bernard Mollohan ran the mill, which was then taken over by Elmer A. Mollohan, Bernard's grandson, who operated the mill until it closed in 1951. Although Elmer's wife, Winnie, would have hastened to add that *she* was the last miller to operate the Mollohan Mill!

The gristmill stayed in operation from 1895 until around 1951, when a flood washed away the mill dam, and in the years that followed, the turbines and the forebay fell into disrepair. In 1984, with a grant from the West Virginia Department of Culture and History, the mill dam, forebay, and turbines were reconstructed and repaired. The forebay directs the flow of water from the river under the mill and past the turbines, which are believed to be the last remaining wooden turbines in the United States.

Beth Mollohan, Elmer and Winnie's daughter and the mill's current owner, has no current plans for additional restoration. Though the mill could be made operational, government regulations regarding flour and meal production are too prohibitive to make it worthwhile.

Chapter 6
Mountaineer Country

Many of the leaders who established the state of West Virginia came from the Northern Panhandle. Wheeling was the state capital from 1863 to 1870, and from 1875 to 1885. Early settlers derived their livelihood from agriculture, but abundant reserves of coal, iron ore, petroleum and natural gas, timber, clay, and glass sand encouraged industrial development, and the proximity of the National Road, the Ohio River, and railroads to transport goods.

In 1758, Tobias Decker and a party of fifty settlers established first white community in Monongalia County, where Deckers Creek enters the Monongahela River at the present site of Morgantown. With the establishment of Monongalia Academy in 1814 and the Morgantown Female Collegiate Institute in 1831, Morgantown became known as an educational center. A second school for females, Woodburn Female Seminary, followed in 1858. When West Virginia was formed in 1863, the legislature made plans to establish a federal land grant college under the terms of the Morrill Act. Several towns expressed interest in having the college, but Morgantown officials backed up their request by pledging the established buildings and resources to the new institution. West Virginia Agricultural College was established on February 7, 1867, and the following year, the name was changed to West Virginia University.[903]

MONONGALIA COUNTY
Formed in 1776

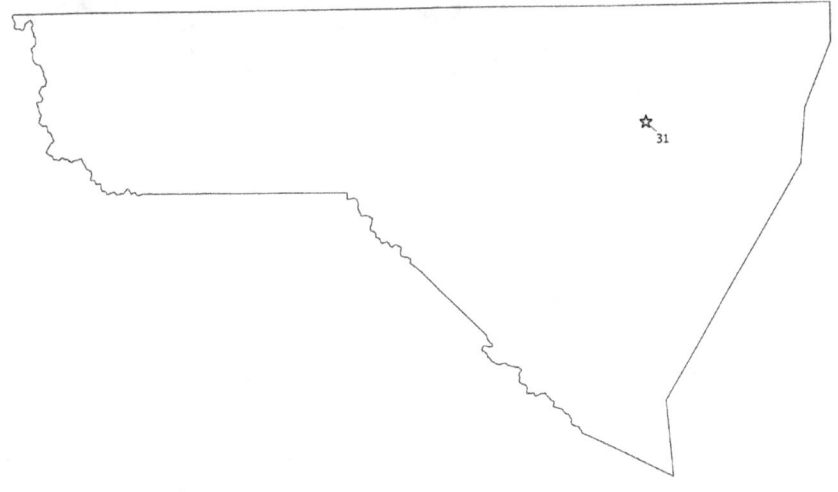

31. EASTON ROLLER MILL

Monongalia County
Address: 54 Easton Mill Road, Morgantown, WV 26508
Coordinates: 39.650324, -79.912539
Year Built: 1867
Period of Significance: 1867-1940
Added to the National Register of Historic Places in 1976

© Google Maps

The Monongalia Historical Society maintains the Easton Roller Mill as a museum. Photo courtesy of Richard Walters

Easton Roller Mill, an excellent example of Victorian design, is about the same age as the state of West Virginia. Photo by Elmer Napier

Once one of forty-five mills in the Morgantown area, today Easton Roller Mill stands alone as the last in the county. It is an excellent example of a later-stage technology mill, with Victorian-era exterior detail and modern steam power and roller mills supplemented by a run of buhrstones and a corn crusher.

A still-functioning part of West Virginia's industrial history, Easton Roller Mill exemplifies the period of transition from small custom mills typical during the early part of the nineteenth century to factories full of modern equipment. It is about the same age as the state of West Virginia.

In 1859, Henry Koontz of Frostburg, Maryland, purchased a 600-acre farm near Easton, a small community three miles east of Morgantown. In 1864, he hired Henry Mack, a Philadelphia carpenter, to build a mill.[904] The original mill measured approximately 30 feet x 32 feet and was later expanded to its current length of fifty-six feet. It is a two-and-a-half-story frame structure with poplar board-and-batten siding and a raised stone basement. The boiler room that once stood at the rear of the building was torn down and the boiler sold for scrap during World War II. The mill's ornamental cornice brackets give it a distinct Victorian flair, but inside it's all about utility, and today it retains a range of equipment from its earliest days forward, including stone buhrs, roller mills, and the prime mover, a forty-horsepower Bodney and Lane steam engine patented in 1874.

Easton Mill ground wheat, corn, rye, and flax with buhrstones driven by a steam engine, in a mix of old techniques and new technology. Most mills in West Virginia during this period used water, but the water supply in nearby creeks was insufficient to power the mill with a waterwheel. Coal, however, was easily available to run a steam engine. There is no evidence of other power sources that could have run the mill.[905]

Koontz sold out around 1876 and moved west to Clark County, Ohio, where he and his family are found in Census records in 1880,[906] 1900,[907] and 1910.[908]

William Anderson, who had also come to the area from Maryland, bought the mill and ran it with his brother, Tom, who was the proprietor of the general store and postmaster for Easton.[909] The Andersons reportedly brought Jemima Capito, an enslaved widow with two sons, with them when they moved to Easton, but freed them around 1850. The Capitos were the first free black family in the area and worked for the Andersons for wages.[910]

While many rural mills could carry on business well enough without installing a costly roller system or switching to a steam or gasoline engine, the Easton Mill's location—near the state's flagship university in a large, diversified population center—made its owners more likely to respond to national trends like the demand for white "patent" flour. The various owners of the Easton Mill apparently tried to keep up with the times, and by 1883 it was described as a "large steam mill" with a capacity of 120 bushels a day.[911]

But even with the most up-to-date machinery, milling was an uncertain business, and the Easton Mill saw a rapid turnover of owners in the 1880s. The Andersons quarreled over the mill. When the tensions resulted in a lawsuit, they were compelled to sell, and Eldridge Weaver, an area farmer,[912] purchased the property for $3,170 in 1884.[913]

M. P. Wells was listed as the operator of the Easton Mill in the 1882-83 *West Virginia Gazeteer and business directory*.[914] Based on what we know of the circumstances that led the Andersons to sell, Mr. Wells may have been running the mill on an interim basis until the Andersons' lawsuit was settled.

Eldridge Weaver had financial difficulties of his own and declared bankruptcy in 1884, the same year he purchased the mill.

Isaac Morris bought the property at auction,[915] and ten years later, in 1894, he became one of the first millers in the area to upgrade to a roller mill system.[916] He purchased equipment from the Nordyke and Marmon Company of Indianapolis[917] that used a three-step reduction method to produce the desirable fine, white flour. He had one set of buhrstones removed and kept the other for processing cornmeal. From this time forward, the mill was known as Easton Roller Mill.[918]

Roller mill systems required more power than buhrstones, and many millers met that demand by upgrading their wooden waterwheels to either a steel wheel, such as those manufactured by Fitz in Martinsburg, West Virginia, or changed them out for a turbine, such as those manufactured by the Leffel company of Springfield, Ohio.

Many companies that produced mill equipment, whether it be roller mills, steam engines, or steel waterwheels, sent trained factory representatives to install the new equipment and a miller to instruct the owner on its operation.[919]

William C. Ley, the last of the mill's owner/operators, purchased the business in 1910. He kept the mill in perfect working order and ran it around the clock, grinding flour during the day and feed at night.[920]

In 1920, Federal Census records show Fred Pickenpaugh, a 23-year-old miller, living in the Ley's home as a boarder.[921] By the time the census taker came around in 1930, William Ley was still the proprietor of the mill, and Fred had married the Ley's daughter, Estella, and found work as a chauffeur at a feed mill store.[922] It's uncertain if he meant he was a delivery driver for the mill or if he had a second job as a chauffeur.

Hard times brought on by the Great Depression forced Ley to shut down operations in 1930.[923]

Until the Great Depression, the Easton Roller Mill had stayed abreast of new technology and remained relevant to the surrounding community. Ley and his partner, Frank Walls,[924] repaired the line shafts, pulleys, and the roller mills in 1939[925] and tried to reopen the business, but they found little demand for wheat grinding. Local farmers no longer produced grain, and most people bought their flour at the grocery store. Ley retired, and after his wife died in 1940, he lived with Fred and Estella, who owned a retail feed store.[926] They inherited the mill when Ley died in 1941 and donated it to the Monongalia Historical Society in 1978. The organization has preserved it as a museum.

In June 2020, Richard Walters, one of the volunteers at the mill, met my daughter Keri, her then-boyfriend Alex, and me there and gave us a tour. "Careful of your heads," he said as he led the way to the basement. "OSHA standards don't apply here."

The mill sits on a laid stone foundation, with a short retaining wall recently built around it to protect it from rising floodwater. The original boiler, which had been housed in a building behind the mill, was sold for scrap during World War II, when the mill was not operating, and the boiler room/shed torn down. The mill and its machinery are largely the same as they were in 1894, except for the steam engine.[927] Today, the mill is demonstrated with a compressed air system simulating steam-powered operation.

The millstones and roller mills are located on the first floor. On the second floor, you'll find sifting equipment, including five sieve scalpers which separated the bran from the raw flour.

A scouring machine, which cleaned the grain before it was sent through the roller mill, is located on the third floor.[928]

Though public tours and activities were suspended during the Covid crisis, the Society hopes to recruit new volunteers and resume teaching new generations about Monongalia County's milling history. Contact the Monongalia Historical Society website, monongaliahistoricalsociety.org, to inquire about tours and events taking place at the mill and other Society activities.

PRESTON COUNTY
Formed from Monongalia County in 1818

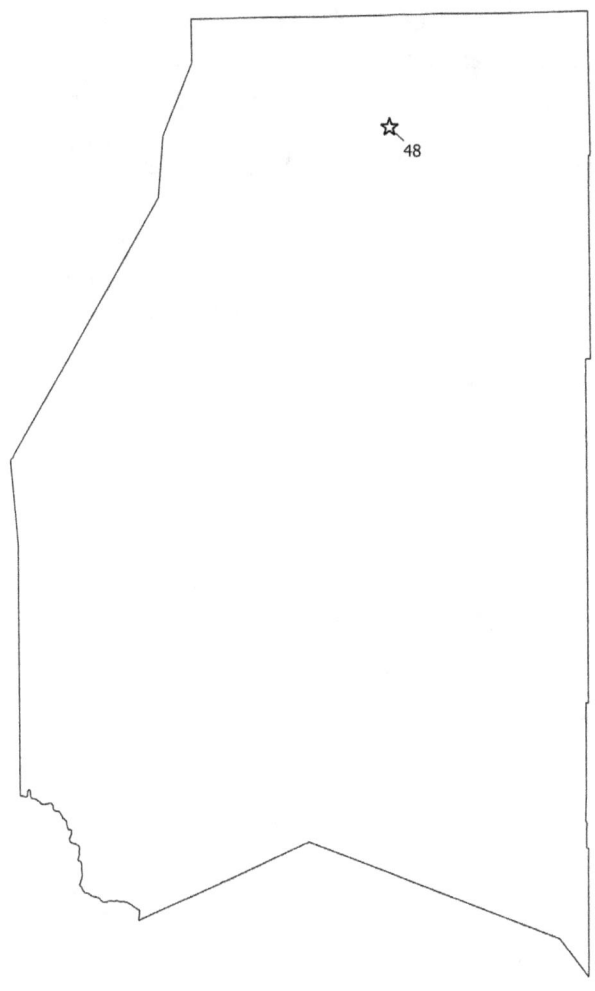

48. HAZELTON MILL

Preston County
Address: 38 Maryland Line Road, Bruceton Mills, WV 26525
Coordinates: 39.6602820, -79.6277465
Year Built: 1914
Period of Significance: c. 1784-2012

© Google Maps

Until 2012, the Hazelton Mill ground the meal for the area's famed Buckwheat Festival. Photo by Tracy Lawson

Hazelton Mill - Photo by Elmer Napier

"[1882] is the centennial year of Mill Run . . . and it proposes to celebrate the occasion by changing its name to Hazelton, in honor of... Samuel Hazlett, who built the first flouring mill here."[929]

The first mill on the site of the Hazelton Milling Company was built in the late 1700s, on the banks of Mill Run. In an 1801 petition filed in Monongalia County, Samuel Hazlett was among approximately twenty area men who requisitioned a mill road.

"April Court 1801, We, your humble petitioners, pray that you will grant to us a mill road leading from John Willet's to the Maryland line beginning and running as followeth: from John Willett's to Samuel Willet's, thence to Hazlet's Mills..."[930]

Local historian Janice Cole Sisler sent me a copy of "Hazelton Memories," which states:

About 1784 a man named Hagerman erected a 'corn cracker,' as the rude corn mills of that day were called. This is believed to be the first mill ever built in the eastern end of the county... Hagerman's mill stood on the opposite bank from the present flouring mill, and a short distance below it. Soon after its erection the stream began to be called Hagerman's Mill Run, and when the property passed to other hands Hagerman's name was dropped, and it was henceforth known as Mill Run.

About the beginning of the 1800s Samuel Hazlett bought the property, and in 1818 he erected a new mill and installed two run of Alleghany grinding stones. Before this time all the best land in the vicinity had been taken up and settled by immigrants from eastern Virginia, Pennsylvania, Maryland, New Jersey, and elsewhere, and... Hazlett did a thriving business. About 1825 he sold the mill to his brother-in-law Peter Fike and moved to Maryland.[931]

Fike started a carding mill about 1835, and his son, Harrison Fike, acted as superintendent. About 1848, a store and then a post office, were established in the vicinity. Fike continued to run the mill until 1850, when he had it torn down and another built on the same foundation. The mill remained in the Fike family until around 1867, when it was sold to J. B. Nicola. Saw and planing mills were put up in 1873 and 1874.[932]

In the 1891-1892 *West Virginia Gazetteer*, William D. Arthur was the postmaster and ran the general store and the flour mill.[933]

The Evans family, the mill's final owners, came into possession of it around the turn of the twentieth century. John Daniel Evans reported his occupation as miller on the 1900 Census[934] and was listed as running a flour mill in Hazelton in the 1904 *West Virginia Gazetteer*.[935] The saw and carding operations were phased out. Evans built the current mill, the third on the site, of wormy chestnut in 1914.

His son Joseph Dayton Evans took over operations by 1930[936] and switched from waterpower to diesel engines in the 1950s, while retaining the 1857 set of buhrstones for grinding. Dayton's son John G. Evans ran the Hazelton Mill until his death in 2012 and was known for his buckwheat flour. "After more than seven decades of living and working around the family mill, John [Evans] knows when the cacophony of slapping, whirling, grinding, and chugging indicates a healthy state of things just beyond the door of his office. The sounds of the machinery, belts, stones, blowers, and gears laboring against buckwheat are as familiar to his ears as the voice of his wife, who, according to John, makes his buckwheat cakes the way he likes them: thin and brown."937

As the nation emerged from the Great Depression in the late 1930s, many rural areas found recovery slow and tedious. Preston County farmers grew buckwheat as an insurance crop because of its short growing season and hoped it might help spur economic growth. Buckwheat became the focus of an end-of-harvest celebration for farmers in 1938, which included horse racing and a farmers' auction.

At subsequent festivals, attendees enjoyed frivolities like sack races, hog calling and husband calling, nail driving for women, eating contests, tugs of war, and rolling pin throwing—and of course, plenty of buckwheat cakes and sausage dinners, sold for thirty-five cents in the church basement.938 Those simple gatherings matured into the Preston County Buckwheat Festival, now hosted by the Kingwood Fire Department and named one of the Top 20 Events in the Southeast for 2019 by the Southeast Tourism Society. The festival has been canceled just twice in its history—during the World War II years of 1943-1945, and during the Covid crisis in 2020. Buckwheat is a fruit, rather than a grain, closely related to rhubarb and sorrel. It was first sown in Preston County in 1859, when a June frost killed the grain crops. Buckwheat can be planted as late as July for an October harvest.939 It was originally called "beech wheat" because the buckwheat germ, or groat, is in a triangular shape, like a beech nut.940 Buckwheat grows best in thin, stony soil. If a stalk gets too tall, the weight of the fruit can tip it over.

In today's market, people with gluten sensitivity use buckwheat, which is naturally gluten-free, as a substitute. Buckwheat hulls can be used in pillows instead of down and other stuffing.

At the Preston County Buckwheat Festival, young people enter livestock they have raised over the past year to be judged and sold at auction. Exhibits and contests for baked and canned goods showcase the bounty of the county's farms, and visitors from near and far enjoy carnival rides, a parade, a car show, and craft exhibits.941 High school students vie for the titles of King Buckwheat and Queen Ceres, the queen so named for the Roman goddess of the harvest.

Hazelton Mill was the last mill in the state dedicated exclusively to milling buckwheat. In September and October, its busiest months, Hazelton Mill once operated twelve to fourteen hours a day.[942]

Since 2012, Stanton Mill at 125 Casselman Road in Grantsville, MD, has processed buckwheat for the festival.

Chapter 7
Northern Panhandle

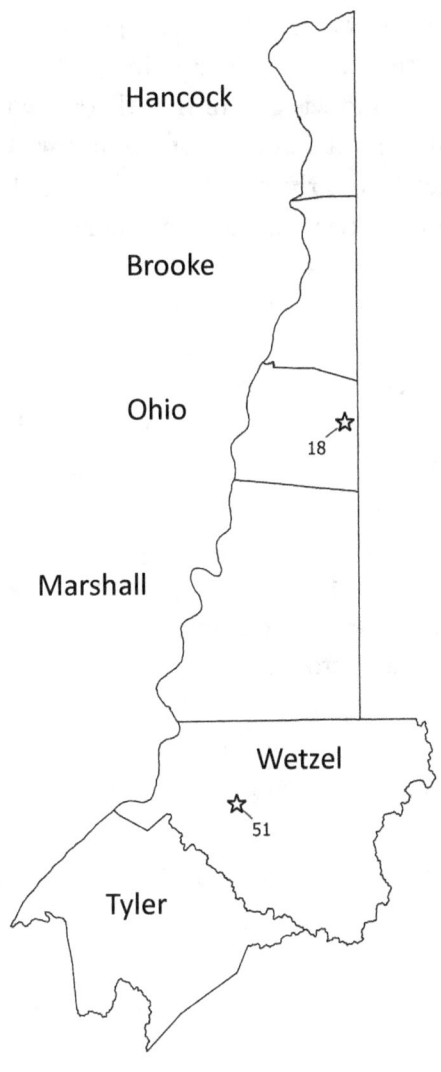

In 1779, when Pennsylvania and Virginia established the Mason-Dixon Line as their mutual boundary, it was to extend due west five degrees and then straight north to the Ohio River. This began to shape the Northern Panhandle. In 1784, Virginia ceded all its territory north and west of the Ohio River to the United States, making it Virginia's western boundary. The long sliver of territory in the panhandle, extending sixty-four miles to an apex at Chester, became the northernmost part of West Virginia when the state was created in 1863.

The Northern Panhandle is part of the Allegheny Plateau and slopes westward from a maximum elevation of about 1,400 feet down to the Ohio River. At Chester, the river is about 660 feet above sea level, and about 620 feet at New Martinsville near the panhandle's base. The plateau drains to the Ohio by creeks that include Grave, Wheeling, Kings, Harmon, Buffalo, Fish, and Cross. The Ohio River and its flood plain are the most conspicuous physical features.

Before railroads, people traveled by flatboat, keelboat, and steamboat, with a busy port at Wheeling. In the modern era, Ohio River navigation is maintained by a system of modern locks and dams.

Grave Creek Mound at Moundsville, the largest of its kind in the country, is the panhandle's most important prehistoric feature. The mound was built in the Adena period, probably between 400 and 200 BC. By the time of white colonization, the Indians who had followed their mound-building ancestors were sparse and mainly members of the Delaware tribe.[943]

The Northern Panhandle produces glass, pottery, iron and steel, chemicals, petroleum and natural gas, and coal.

OHIO COUNTY
Formed in 1776

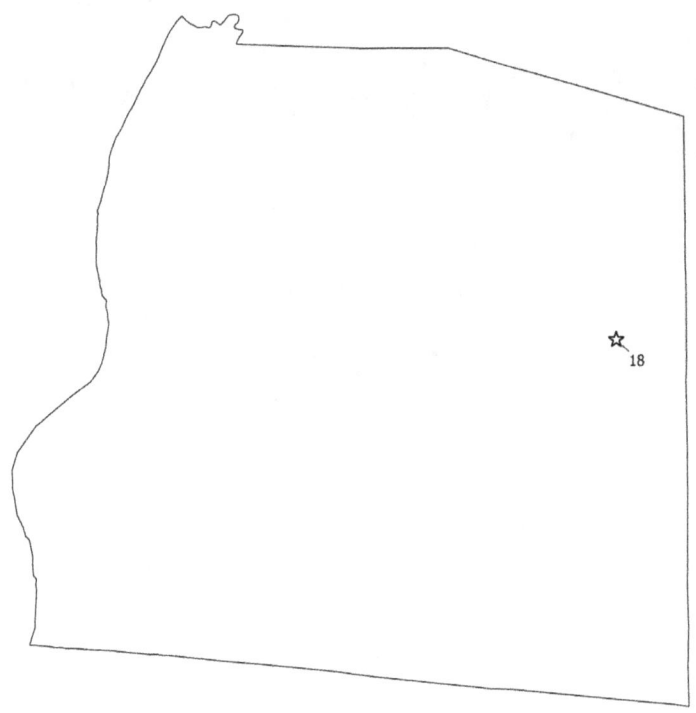

18. REED'S MILL

Ohio County
Address: 13203 National Road, Valley Grove, WV 26060
Coordinates: 40.1048952, -80.5463787
Year built: 1834
Period of Significance: 1834-1955
Added to the National Register of Historic Places in 1993 as part of the National Road Corridor from Mt. Echo to Triadelphia

© Google Maps

Reed's Mill, located on the once-bustling National Road, has been called a time capsule of early twentieth-century industry. Photo by Elmer Napier

Reed's Mill is the last of three known gristmills that once stood along the sixteen-mile span of the National Road in Ohio County, West Virginia.

The mill resembles popular barn construction with large, hand-hewn square beams covered with wood siding. On its National Register of Historic Places Nomination Form, Katherine M. Jourdan and Laura J. Pfeifer of the West Virginia Division of Culture and History note that the early construction, combined with the milling equipment installed around 1908 that remains inside, make the mill a "time capsule of early twentieth century industry."[944]

Deeds from 1852 to 1887 use the corner of an S-bridge on the National Road as one of the property markers. Daniel Shepherd, the eldest son of Capt. Thomas Shepherd *(See Shepherd's Mill, page 143)* lived in Wheeling after the American Revolution and built the distinct S-bridges along the National Road from the Pennsylvania line to Wheeling.[945]

William Roberts purchased 150 acres in Ohio County in 1798. In the early part of the nineteenth century, the route for the Cumberland Road, also known as the National Road, the nation's first federally funded highway, was planned to pass near his land. It was completed as far as Wheeling in 1818, and when Roberts built his mill around 1834, he was poised to take advantage of the road's constant, heavy traffic and sell sacks of flour directly to passing travelers. He could also ship quantities to distant markets that had, until recently, been in accessible.

When Roberts died around 1850, his will specified that his farm be sold and the proceeds be divided among his heirs.[946]

William Bushfield, who purchased the mill in 1868, installed a boiler and ran the mill with steam power. According to the 1880 Federal Census, both he and his twenty-nine-year-old son, William Blair Bushfield, worked as millers.[947] The waterwheel, standing idle on the south side of the building, was destroyed when the Little Wheeling Creek overflowed its banks in 1884.

After William Bushfield died in 1887, Robert Reed bought the mill at auction. William Blair Bushfield moved west along the National Road, and subsequent census data places him in Cambridge in 1900,[948]

Zanesville in 1910,[949] and finally Columbus in 1920,[950] where he worked as a carpenter.

Reed, a Pennsylvania native who had served in that state's militia in 1861 and its light artillery in 1864, ran the mill with his son, Carson. They installed a Griscom and McFeely[951] roller mill and elevator system.

The Griscom and McFeely Company of Philadelphia was profiled in the June 1898 edition of *The Roller Mill*. The article named Walter Griscom as the "efficient office man," while Thomas McFeely proved himself "a most successfully missionary [for the business] on the road, where he is as much at home as a bird on the wing." The article described a system installed in another mill in Pennsylvania as "a complete spring and winter wheat Oscillator Mill, using one thirty-inch and one twenty-seven-inch turbine waterwheel, Butler roller mills, oscillators, Philadelphia purifiers and reels, and a wheat steamer."[952]

As of the filing of the NRHP forms in 1990, the system installed at Reed's Mill between 1902-1906 was intact, and at the time of the mill's closing in the 1950s, was run by a one-cylinder gasoline engine.

Carson Reed died in 1953, and his widow, Irene, sold the mill in 1955. William and Delores Laderer III, the owners at the time the NRHP form was filed, had purchased it and the adjacent 1906 house at auction in 1984.

Reed's Mill, though in a decaying state, is a strong example of a private business that developed along the National Road in the first half of the nineteenth century. Later modified to make use of new technology that increased its efficiency, the mill maintained its value to its rural community long after commercial mills and bakeries made flour and bread available on store shelves and most American households owned cars.

If you're driving out the National Road in search of Reed's Mill, it's easier to see the farmhouse next to the mill. The mill sits close to the road, but it can be hard to spot because the road curves, and trees and brush camouflage the unpaved road that leads to the mill.

WETZEL COUNTY
Formed in 1846

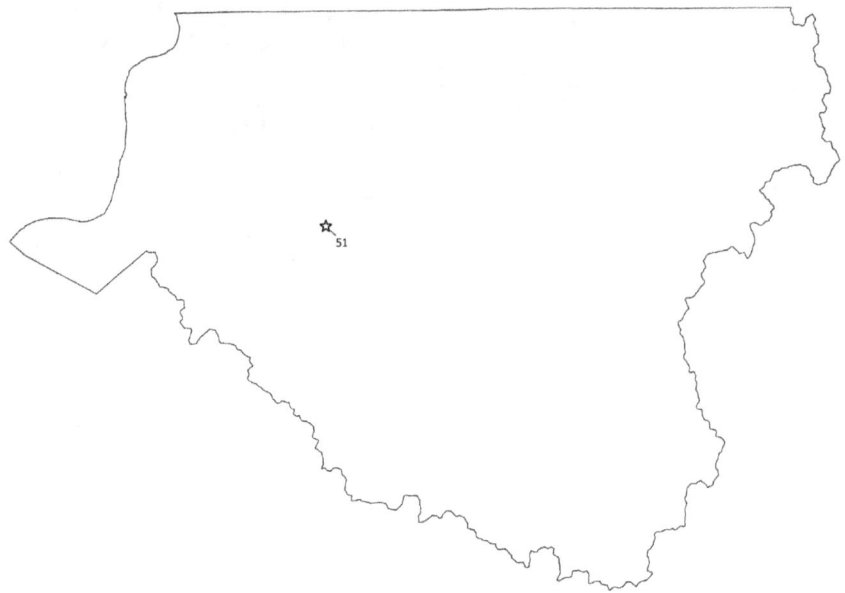

51. HOWELL'S MILL

Wetzel County
Address: (1930 Mill) 11456 Mountaineer Highway, New Martinsville, WV 26155
Coordinates: 39.6133305, -80.7322903
Address: (2006 Mill) 30 Carpenter Ridge, New Martinsville, WV 26155
Coordinates: 39.620169, -80.722329
Year Built: 1930, 2006
Period of Significance: 1930-present

© Google Maps

© Google Maps

Howells Mill, has been operated by three generations of the Howell family, is now open only sporadically. Photo by Elmer Napier

The sign outside the mill pays homage to its millers Winfield, Winfred, and Ardell Howell. Photo by Tracy Lawson

Ardell's brother Benny continues the family tradition in the second Howells Mill location, just up the road. Photo by Elmer Napier

The sign in front of the original Howell's Grist Mill pays homage to Granddad Winfield and Dad Winfred, and announces that the mill, which produces "old time cornmeal" is now operated by Ardell Howell.

The mill, situated close to the road on Mountaineer Highway (WV-7) near New Martinsville, is recognizable by the old-time Mail Pouch Tobacco ad painted on the front. Though it was closed when we arrived, we pulled over nearby to take photos. Dan Howell happened by on his tractor and introduced himself as a grandson of Winfred and part owner of the mill. Dan told us his uncle Ardell didn't run the mill regularly, but his dad, Benny, who lived just up the road a mile, had a gasoline-powered buhrstone mill.

At Benny's, we met the dogs first, but soon his wife, Aleatha, came outside, and when we told her Dan had sent us, she welcomed us and called for her husband.

Benny's granddad and uncle set up the mill around 1930, which makes the two Howell mills the most recently established, privately owned mills profiled in this book. The mill's run of buhrstones, purchased from Hall's Mill, which closed in 1916, are powered by a 1912 gasoline engine. Benny's father, Winfred, took over in 1962. Since Winfred's death in 2005, Ardell took charge of the mill, though he doesn't do much grinding these days.

Inside Benny's garage, a 1919 Whitten engine powers a 1940s vintage set of vertical buhrstones. The engine is hooked up to a reservoir, and the water keeps the engine cool even if it runs all day.

He purchases the wheat and yellow and white corn he grinds and sells the flour and meal at a local farmers market.

When I asked if he happened to have any on hand to sell, he opened a deep freeze with a flourish. We bought a sack of each, and Mrs. Howell shared with us the recipes she hands out to customers at the farmers' market. (see Appendix)

Out front, the millstones that lean against Benny's garage are just for show. He found one down the road in the brush and pulled it out with his tractor. He bought the other two, and is pretty sure they're relics from Hall's Mill, which he says also used to be the post office for the area.

Benny uses a gasoline engine to power his portable mill and sells the product at farmers markets. Photo by Tracy Lawson

Benny Howell displays millstones found discarded in the nearby woods. Photo by Tracy Lawson

Benny Howell's mill is found in a picturesque rural setting. Photo by Tracy Lawson

Conclusion

In the classic children's book *Wagon Wheels: A Story of the National Road*, the peddler Amos Fair speaks to some new settlers:

"Here's a town just beginning, like a beansprout pushing up when the ground gets warm enough for planting! Mostly, a part of the country gets settled and after that somebody starts to think of a mill. But you're doing it the other way; you'll build a grist mill and that will bring people to this section. Then there'll be a store and a tavern and a blacksmith shop and a church and school and all. Same things happens when you start with a ferry on a river. A town begins, where there wasn't anything but wild country...You can talk about wars and exploring and inventions all you want to, but right here is where I get excited!"953

In America, the rise of the independent mill began at the end of the colonial period and carried into the early twentieth century. I hope this guide has helped you gain a deeper appreciation for the skill and ingenuity that went into building and operating these mills, as well as the miller's vital role in West Virginia's history and development.

Appendix - Recipes

I interviewed dozens of mill owners and their families for this book, and two shared recipes, which I am pleased to include below. Alethea Howell shares her recipes for wheat bread, brown bread, cornbread, and mush with customers who buy Howell's Mill products at farmer's markets. Danny Lutz, owner of Feagans Mill, thought the Washington family's recipe for walnut ketchup would be of interest. But be forewarned—if you attempt the walnut ketchup, wear protective gear to avoid staining your hands and arms!

Mrs. Aleatha Howell's Wheat Bread

1 cup lukewarm water
3 tbsp. molasses
2 tbsp. butter
1½ cups wheat flour
1½ cups white flour
1 tsp. salt
¾ tsp. ginger
1 package quick dry yeast

Mix well and let rise. Bake at 350 for 30-35 minutes. Makes one large loaf

Brown Bread

4 cups wheat flour
2 cups white flour
2 cups brown sugar
½ cup white sugar
3 cups buttermilk or sour milk
2 tsp. salt
2 tsp. baking soda
2 eggs (lightly beaten)
1 cup raisins (optional)
½ cup chopped pecans
NO yeast

Mix well and bake at 350 for 50-60 minutes. Will be brown on top. Makes 2 loaves

Amish Buttery Corn Bread

2/3 cup butter
1 cup granulated sugar
3 eggs
1 2/3 cups milk
1 2/3 cups flour
1 cup corn meal
4 ½ tsp. baking powder
1 tsp. salt

Preheat oven to 400 F. In mixing bowl, cream the butter and sugar. Combine eggs and milk. Separately, combine flour, cornmeal, baking powder, and salt.

Add dry ingredients to butter and sugar mixture.

Pour into greased 9"x 13" baking pan. Bake for 30 to 35 minutes until golden brown on top and until toothpick inserted near center comes out clean. Cut in squares and serve warm. 12 servings.

Cornmeal Mush

In large heavy saucepan, combine 3 cups water and 1 tsp. salt. Bring to a boil.

In a small bowl, combine 1 cup water and a cup of cornmeal. Stir well and gradually add to boiling water, stirring constantly. Cook for 20-25 minutes, until it thickens.

Serve with sugar and milk while hot or, if you prefer, make fried mush.

Pour hot mixture into loaf pan and chill overnight. Cut in slices and roll in flour, fry in skillet until golden brown on both sides. Serve with syrup.

The Washington Family's Walnut Ketchup, by Hank Shaw
Courtesy of Daniel Lutz

Prep Time: 20 minutes
Cook Time: 45 minutes

I used unripe black walnuts for this recipe, but any unripe walnut will do. Ideally, they should be young enough to jam a knife all the way through, but you can use older nuts where the inner shell of the nut itself is still forming.

Walnut ketchup is not as thick as tomato ketchup. It's more like a Worcestershire sauce, but it tastes more like A.1. Use as a marinade or splash it on any red meat—beef, venison, duck, goose, hare, etc.

Makes 6 cups.

Ingredients:
About 50 green walnuts
3 tbsp. kosher salt
1 12-oz. bottle malt vinegar
2 oz. anchovies, well rinsed
1 large onion, chopped

1 cup red wine or port
1 tsp. ground nutmeg
2 tsp. ground black pepper
1 tsp. cayenne
¼ cup chopped or grated horseradish
A one-inch piece of ginger, unpeeled and sliced thin
½ tsp. xanthan gum (optional)

Instructions:

Crush, chop, crack, or grind walnuts. This is messy and the liquid will stain. Wear gloves and a long-sleeved shirt you don't mind getting stained. Chop with a stainless-steel knife on a dark cutting board to minimize the staining.

Put the walnuts in a large glass or other nonreactive container and just barely cover with vinegars. If you prefer, you can use a mix of malt and cider vinegar. Put the lid on the container and let sit at room temperature for 8 days.

Move the walnuts and vinegar into a large, nonreactive pot and add the remaining ingredients. Boil gently for 45 minutes, then strain through a fine-mesh sieve to separate the solids. You can wait until the sauce cools and then whip it in the blender with the xanthan gum. This will keep the fine solids suspended in the ketchup and give you a sauce with more body.

Bottle the sauce and keep it in a cool, dark place indefinitely.

451

Notes

Introduction

1. Ken Drenten, *Waterwheelin': A Travelers Guide to Ohio Mills: Where to find history, culture, education, food, entertainment, & fun at 28 Ohio mills.* (Zanesville, OH: Published by the author, 2013), 4.
2. Elizabeth V. Biggs and C. Nelson Hoy, "Waterpowered Mills of the Cowpasture River Valley," http://www.berriedalefarms.com/Essays.html.
3. Herman Steen, *Flour Milling in the United States*, (Minneapolis, MN: T.S. Denison and Company, Inc., 1963), 426.

Section One
I. A History of Milling

4. D. W. Garber, *Waterwheels and Millstones: A History of Ohio Gristmills and Milling, Historic Ohio Buildings Series Volume 2.* (Columbus, OH: The Ohio Historical Society, 1970), 3.
5. Jeremy Cherfas, "Paleo People Were Making Flour 32,000 Years Ago," https://www.npr.org/sections/thesalt/2015/09/14/440292003/paleo-people-were-making-flour-32-000-years-ago.
6. Lina Zeldovich, "14,000-Year-Old Piece of Bread Rewrites the History of Baking and Farming," https://www.npr.org/sections/thesalt/2018/07/24/631583427/14-000-year-old-piece-of-bread-rewrites-the-history-of-baking-and-farming.
7. Zeldovich, "14,000-Year-Old Piece of Bread Rewrites the History of Baking and Farming."
8. Trevor Neve, "The History and Uses of the Mortar and Pestle," https://cambridgeenviro.com/blogs/news/the-history-and-uses-of-the-mortar-and-pestle.

9. Wikipedia online, "Quern-Stones," https://en.wikipedia.org/wiki/Quern-stone.
10. Rafael Frankel, "The Olynthus Mill, Its Origin, and Diffusion: Typology and Distribution," https://www.ajaonline.org/article/1354.
11. "The Rise and Fall of Ancient Bread," https://www.chicagotribune.com/news/ct-xpm-1986-02-09-8601100787-story.html.
12. Jill Barth, "The Secret Life of Yeasts: Spontaneous Fermentation in Wine," forbes.com/sites/jillbarth/2019/07/26/the-secret-life-of-yeasts-spontaneous-fermentation-in-wine/?sh=39bddc7619b3.
13. Hungry Monster online, "The Timeline of Bread," http://www.hungrymonster.com/food-facts/food_facts.php?p=Breads&fid=4997.
14. Terry S. Reynolds, *Stronger Than a Hundred Men: A History of the Vertical Water Wheel*, (Baltimore and London: Johns Hopkins University Press, 1983), 32-33.
15. Reynolds, *Stronger Than a Hundred Men*, 33.
16. Hungry Monster, "The Timeline of Bread."
17. Grain Maker online, "A Brief History of Milling," https://grainmaker.com/a-brief-history-of-milling/.
18. Reynolds, *Stronger Than a Hundred Men*, 24.
19. Victor Labate, "Roman Mills," https://www.ancient.eu/article/907/roman-mills/.
20. Reynolds, *Stronger Than a Hundred Men*, 19.
21. Eric Sloane, "The Mills of Early America," https://www.americanheritage.com/mills-early-america.
22. Labate, "Roman Mills."
23. Ancient Civilizations textbook online, "The Fall of the Roman Empire," //www.ushistory.org/civ/6f.a.
24. Thomas K. Ford with the assistance of Horace J. Sheely. *The Miller in Eighteenth-Century Virginia: An account of Mills & the Craft of Milling, as well as a Description of the Windmill near the Palace in Williamsburg*, (Williamsburg, VA: Published by Colonial Williamsburg, 1978), 4, https://www.gutenberg.org/files/58036/58036-h/58036-h.htm.

25. Khan Academy, "Serfdom in Europe," https://www.khanacademy.org/humanities/world-history/medieval-times/european-middle-ages-and-serfdom/a/serfdom-in-europe.
26. Wiktionary, "thirlage," https://en.wiktionary.org/wiki/thirlage.
27. Enid Gauldie, *The Scottish Country Miller, 1700–1900: A History of Water-Powered Meal Milling in Scotland*. (Edinburgh: John Donald Publishers; distributed by Humanities Press, Atlantic Highlands, N.J. 1981).

II. Milling in Colonial Virginia

28. Theodore R. Hazen, "The Automation of Flour Milling in America, Part 1," https://www.angelfire.com/journal/millrestoration/learn.html.
29. Ford, *The Miller in Eighteenth Century Virginia*, 18.
30. Ford, *The Miller in Eighteenth Century Virginia*, 16.
31. Ibid.
32. Garber, *Waterwheels and Millstones*, op. cit., p. 7.
33. Thomas Miller and Hu Maxwell, West Virginia Archives and History, "Social and Industrial Life in Early Settlements," acchttp://www.wvculture.org/HISTORY/settlement/settlementlife.html.
34. Ford, *The Miller in Eighteenth Century Virginia*, 16.
35. Jack Wills, "Gristmills," https://www.wvencyclopedia.org/articles/67.
36. Garber, *Waterwheels and Millstones*, 7.
37. Garber, *Waterwheels and Millstones*, 9.
38. Margaret Middleton Rivers Eastman and Edward Fitzsimons Good, *Hidden History of Old Charleston*. (Charleston, SC: History Press, 2010), 35.
39. Ibid.
40. DNA Consultants online, "Virginia Surnames and Families with Possible Jewish (and Muslim) Roots," https://dnaconsultants.com/virginia-surnames-families-possible-jewish-muslim-roots/.

41. Arthur G. Peterson, Ph.D., "Flour and Grist Milling in Virginia: A Brief History," *The Virginia Magazine of History and Biography*, Vol. XLIII, April 1935, No. 2, 98.
42. Ford, *The Miller in Eighteenth Century Virginia*, 12.
43. Eastman, *Hidden History of Old Charleston*, 35.
44. Deidre Nansen McCloskey, "The Industrial Revolution," http://deirdremccloskey.com/index.html.
45. Robert F. Smith, "Manufacturing Independence: Industrial Innovation in the American Revolution," https://en.wikipedia.org/wiki/Technological_and_industrial_history_of_the_United_States.
46. Virginia Places, "The Fairfax Grant," http://www.virginiaplaces.org/settleland/fairfaxgrant.html.
47. Roberta R. Munske and Wilmer L. Kerns, eds., *Hampshire County West Virginia 1754-2004*, (Romney, WV: Published by the Hampshire County 250th Anniversary Committee, 2004), 50.
48. Munske and Kerns, eds., *Hampshire County West Virginia*, 2.
49. The West Virginia Encyclopedia, "History of West Virginia," http://www.wvencyclopedia.org/articles/414.
50. Michael Theis, *The Shepherdstown Chronicle*, "Group Wowed by Shepherd's Mill Tour," https://www.shepherdstownchronicle.com/news/2009/10/23/group-wowed-by-shepherd-mill-tour/.
51. Wills, "Gristmills."
52. Garber, *Waterwheels and Millstones*, 4.
53. Joseph D. Parriott, WV GenWeb online, "Marshall County's Water Powered Grist Mills," https://www.wvgenweb.org/marshall/gristmill.htm.
54. Peterson, "Flour and Grist Milling in Virginia: A Brief History," 106.
55. Ford, *The Miller in Eighteenth Century Virginia*, 26.
56. Garber, *Waterwheels and Millstones*, 24.
57. Garber, *Waterwheels and Millstones*, 75.
58. Tracy Lawson, *Pride of the Valley: Sifting through the History of the Mount Healthy Mill (Newark, OH: McDonald & Woodward Publishing Co., 2017)*, 163.

59. Medieval Technology and American History, "The grist milling process," https://www.engr.psu.edu/mtah/articles/grist_milling_process.htm.
60. Ford, *The Miller in Eighteenth Century Virginia*, 26.
61. National Register of Historic Places (NRHP) Inventory Nomination Form, "Beaver Mill," Section 7, 3.
62. Garber, *Waterwheels and Millstones*, 25.
63. Peterson, "Flour and Grist Milling in Virginia: A Brief History," 99.
64. Ford, *The Miller in Eighteenth Century Virginia*, 15.
65. Hazen, "The Automation of Flour Milling in America Part 2."
66. Ford, *The Miller in Eighteenth Century Virginia*, 15.
67. Wikipedia, "Grist Mill," https://en.wikipedia.org/wiki/Gristmill#Early_history.
68. Peterson, "Flour and Grist Milling in Virginia," 103.
69. Petersen, "Flour and Grist Milling in Virginia," 105.
70. Evans, *The Young Millwright and Miller's Guide: Section 2, The Young Millwright's Guide*, 25-26.
71. Robert Vitale, Waterwheel Factory, "Why Metal Over a Wooden Waterwheel: History of the Fitz Water Wheel Company," http://www.waterwheelfactory.com/fitz.html.
72. Behrens, Rudy, *Backwoods Home Magazine*, "Design calculations for overshot waterwheels," https://www.backwoodshome.com/design-calculations-for-overshot-waterwheels/.
73. Charles D. Hockensmith, *The Millstone Industry: A Summary of Research on Quarries and Producers in the United States, Europe and Elsewhere, with a foreword by Alain Belmont*. (Jefferson, NC: McFarland & Company, Publishers, 2009), 113.
74. Hockensmith, *The Millstone Industry*, 114.
75. Hockensmith, *The Millstone Industry*, 11.
76. Ford, *The Miller in Eighteenth Century Virginia*, 14.
77. Garber, *Waterwheels and Millstones*, 84.
78. Garber, *Waterwheels and Millstones*, 54.
79. Tracy Lawson, *Fips, Bots, Doggeries, and More: Explorations of Henry Rogers' 1838 Journal of Travel from Southwestern Ohio to New*

York City, (Newark, OH: McDonald & Woodward Publishing Company, 2012), 34.
80. Reynolds, *The Millstone Industry*, xi.
81. Reynolds, *The Millstone Industry*, 42.
82. Reynolds, *The Millstone Industry*, 46.
83. Medieval Technology and American History, "The Grist Milling Process."
84. The Depot Lodge, "Tinglers Mill," https://www.depotlodge.com/tinglers-mill.
85. Ford, *The Miller in Eighteenth Century Virginia*, 26.
86. Garber, *Waterwheels and Millstones*, 25.
87. Medieval Technology and American History, "The Grist Milling Process."
88. Reynolds, *The Milling Industry*, 109.
89. Reynolds, *The Milling Industry*, 100.
90. WV Encyclopedia, "Gristmills."
91. Tide Mill Institute, "Water Mills and Wheels," https://www.tidemillinstitute.org/grist-mills/.
92. Garber, *Waterwheels and Millstones*, 89.
93. Garber, *Waterwheels and Millstones*, 91.
94. Thomas Kemp Cartmell, *Shenandoah Valley Pioneers and Their Descendants: A History of Frederick County, Virginia from its Formation in 1738 to 1908*, (Berkeley County, WV: Eddy Press, 1909), 69.
95. The History of Loudoun County, "Early 19th-Century Milling and Wheat Farming," https://www.loudounhistory.org/history/agriculture-mills-and-wheat/.
96. Encyclopedia of North Carolina, "Gristmills," https://www.ncpedia.org/gristmills.
97. Reynolds, *The Millstone Industry*, 192.
98. Reynolds, *The Millstone Industry*, 115.
99. Steen, *Flour Milling in the United States*, 426.

III. Innovations in Milling Makes Flour Cheaper, More Portable, and Less Nutritious

100. Kansas Farm Bureau, "Wheat Fun Fact Sheet."
101. The History of Loudoun County, "Early 19th Century Milling and Wheat Farming."
102. Old Stone Mill National Historic Site of Canada, "Sorting the Flour Using the Bolter."
103. Resilience, "The History and Processes of Milling," www.resilience.org/stories/2011-01-25/history-and-processes-milling.
104. Resilience, "The History and Processes of Milling."
105. Old Stone Mill National Historic Site of Canada, "Sorting the Flour Using the Bolter," http://www.deltamill.org/flour/sorting.html.

IV. Historic Preservation

106. New Hampshire Division of Historical Resources, "Benefits and Restrictions to Listing a Property on the National Register," www.nh.gov/nhdhr/programs/nr_benefits.htm.

Section Two
Chapter 1 – Eastern Panhandle

107. National Register of Historic Places Inventory Nomination Form, "Historic Resources of Berkeley County, West Virginia," Section 7.
108. West Virginia Encyclopedia, "Eastern Panhandle," http://www.wvencyclopedia.org/articles/1991.
109. Berkeley County Historical Society, "History of Berkeley County, WV," https://www.historicberkeley.org/county-history/.
110. NRHP Form, "Historic Resources of Berkeley County, West Virginia," Continuation Sheet 7, 2.
111. West Virginia Encyclopedia, "Eastern Panhandle."

112. Berkeley County Historical Society, "History of Berkeley County, WV."
113. West Virginia American History and Genealogy Project, "Early Land Grants and Settlers of West Virginia," https://wvahgp.genealogyvillage.com/early-land-grants-and-settlers-of-west-virginia.html.
114. National Register of Historic Places (NRHP) Inventory Nomination Form, "Lick Run Plantation," Section 8, 1.
115. Find a Grave, "Peter Light," https://www.findagrave.com/memorial/54169679/peter-light.
116. Clarke County Historical Association, "West Virginia-Berkeley Co. Mills," https://clarkecounty.pastperfectonline.com/photo/F1E3A6CB-8259-49A6-AB71-973427384262.
117. Marjorie Lundegard, "Bedinger Roller Mill in Berkeley County, West Virginia," *Old Mill News*, August 2010, p. 7.
118. Ancestry, "Bittinger and Bedinger Families," https://www.ancestry.com/mediaui-viewer/tree/28110672/person/12770327973/media/22acdab7-aa69-47c3-8f2d-c883cc94f840?_phsrc=bMR4362&_phstart=successSource.
119. Bedinger Family History and Genealogy, "Henry Bedinger (4)," http://www.bedinger.org/henry-bedinger-4.html.
120. Ancestry, "Bittinger and Bedinger Families."
121. Bedinger Family History and Genealogy, "Henry Bedinger (4)."
122. NRHP Form, "Lick Run Plantation," Section 8.
123. Bedinger Family History and Genealogy online, "Henry Bedinger (4)."
124. Clarke County Historical Association online, "West Virginia-Berkeley Co. Mills."
125. Jefferson County, West Virginia Will Book 10, 330-331.
126. Walter Ailes, former owner of Lick Run Plantation, in discussion with the author, June 2020.
127. R. L. Polk, *West Virginia Gazetteer and business directory 1882-1883*, (Wheeling, WV: R. L. Polk & Co., 1882), p. 54.
128. R. L. Polk, *West Virginia Gazetteer and business directory for 1904-1905, Vol 1*, (Wheeling, WV: R.L. Polk & Co., 1904), 86.

NOTES   461

129. Joe Germino, email message to author, August 19, 2021.
130. Historical Architectural and Engineering Record (HAER) Form WV-29, "Bunker Hill Mill (Cline and Chapman Roller Mill) Bunker Hill vicinity," 2.
131. HAER Form WV-29, 2.
132. Berkeley County GenWeb, "Berkeley County, West Virginia Boyd Biographies," http://sites.rootsweb.com/~wvberkel/boydbios.html.
133. Washington Heritage Trail, "Bunker Hill Mill," https://washingtonheritagetrail.com/bc_23.html.
134. Washington Heritage Trail, "Bunker Hill Mill."
135. HAER Form WV-29, 3.
136. United States Census Special Schedules of Manufacturers, Numbers 7 and 8, Flour and Grist Mills, Berkeley County, West Virginia, West Virginia Archives, Charleston, WV.
137. HAER Form WV-29, 3.
138. HAER Form WV-29, 4.
139. Polk, *West Virginia Gazetteer and business directory for 1891-92*, 90.
140. Polk, *West Virginia Gazetteer and business directory for 1904-05*, 137.
141. HAER Form WV-29, 6.
142. HAER Form WV-29, 6.
143. HAER Form WV-29, 6.
144. Mill Pictures, "Bunker Hill Mill/Giles Mill/Cline Mill/Chapman Roller Mill," https://www.millpictures.com/mills.php?millid=1587.
145. Mill Pictures, "Bunker Hill Mill/Giles Mill," 5.
146. HAER Form WV-29, 7-10.
147. Mill Pictures, "Janney Mill/J. H. Miller & Sons, Berkeley Co. West Virginia," https://www.millpictures.com/mills.php?millid=4021.
148. U.S. National Park Service, "The Baltimore and Ohio Railroad Martinsburg Shops," https://www.nps.gov/places/the-baltimore-and-ohio-railroad-martinsburg-shops.htm.
149. West Virginia GenWeb Archives, "Berkeley County, West Virginia, Biography of Aquilla Janney," http://files.usgwarchives.net/wv/berkeley/bios/janney.txt.

150. James Morton Callahan, *The History of West Virginia, Old and New* (Chicago and New York: The American Historical Society, Inc. Vol. III, 1923), 393-394.
151. United States Federal Census Year: *1860;* Census Place: *Berkeley, Virginia;* Archive Collection Number: *T1132;* Roll: *8;* Page: *43;* Line: *1;* Schedule Type: *Industry.*
152. Polk, *West Virginia Gazetteer and business directory for 1882-1883,* 246.
153. National Register of Historic Places (NRHP) Inventory Nomination Form, "The Baltimore and Ohio Railroad and Related Industries Historic District," Item Number 7, 5.
154. Paul Kesselring, *Gas Engine Magazine,* "Janney Mfg. Company," https://www.gasenginemagazine.com/gas-engines/janney-mfg-company/.
155. Samuel B. Evans, ed. *History of Wapello County, Iowa: And Representative Citizens,* (Chicago: Biographical Publishing Company, 1901), 659.
156. Kesselring, "Janney Mfg. Company."
157. Ibid.
158. National Register of Historic Places (NRHP) Inventory Nomination Form, "Tuscarora Creek Historical District," Item 7, 3.
159. Ancestry, Probate Loose Papers, 1772-1885; Author: *West Virginia. County Court (Berkeley County)* Probate Place: *Berkeley, West Virginia, M-R.* https://www.ancestry.com/imageviewer/collections/9087/images/007616659_01130?pId=23797.
160. Wilmer P. Kerns, Ph. D., *The West Virginia Advocate,* "Historic Mills of Old Frederick County, Va.," February 15, 1989.
161. United States Federal Census Year: *1850;* Census Place: *District 9, Berkeley, Virginia;* Roll: *936;* Page: *309b.*
162. United States Federal Census Year: *1860;* Census Place: *Berkeley, Virginia;* Page: *766.*
163. United States Federal Census Year: *1870;* Census Place: *Hedgesville, Berkeley, West Virginia;* Roll: *M593_1684;* Page: *212B.*
164. Polk, *West Virginia Gazetteer and business directory for 1882-1883,* 190.

165. Polk, *West Virginia Gazetteer and business directory for 1891-1892*, 197.
166. R. L. Polk, West Virginia Gazetteer and business directory for 1900-1901, (Philadelphia, PA: R. L. Polk & Co., 1900), 242.
167. Polk, *West Virginia Gazetteer and business directory for 1904-1905*, Vol. 1, 359.
168. United States Federal Census Year: *1900*; Census Place: *Hedgesville, Berkeley, West Virginia*; Page: *3*; Enumeration District: *0013*; FHL microfilm: *1241755*.
169. Ancestry, Wills; Author: *West Virginia. County Court* (Berkeley County); Probate Place: Berkeley County, West Virginia, Vol. 25-26, 1910-1926.
170. NRHP Form, "Tuscarora Creek Historical District," Section 8.
171. Karen Rice, owner of Patterson Mill, in discussion with author, August 2020.
172. Frederick County, VA Deed Book 5, 209.
173. Iberian Publishing Company, "Berkeley County Virginia," http://genealogyresources.org/Berkeley.html#:~:text=Berkeley%20County%20Virginia%20Berkeley%20County%20was%20formed%20in,with%20boundaires%20contiguous%20with%20that%20of%20the%20county.
174. Berkeley County, VA Will Book 1, 253.
175. Os Batans online, "What is a fulling mill?" https://osbatans.gal/?page_id=20&lang=en.
176. NRHP Form, "Tuscarora Creek Historic District," Continuation Sheet 7, 4.
177. Berkeley County, VA Deed Book 13, 451.
178. Berkeley County, VA Deed Book 15, 639.
179. Berkeley County, VA Deed Book 36, 405.
180. Ancestry online, "John Jonas Janney," https://www.ancestry.com/family-tree/person/tree/114609447/person/132240127289/facts.
181. Berkeley County, WV Deed Book 65, 539.
182. Ibid.
183. United States Federal Census Year: *1870*; Census Place: *Hedgesville, Berkeley, West Virginia*; Roll: *M593_1684*; Page: *213A*.

184. Berkeley County, WV Deed Book 66, 408.
185. Berkeley County, WV Deed Book 67, 274.
186. United States Federal Census *1870*.
187. Ancestry, National Archives and Records Administration (NARA); Washington, D.C.; *Consolidated Lists of Civil War Draft Registration Records (Provost Marshal General's Bureau; Consolidated Enrollment Lists, 1863-1865);* Record Group: 110, https://www.ancestry.com/imageviewer/collections/1666/images/32178_620305173_0196-00074?pId=2057726.
188. Berkeley County, WV Deed Book 117, 41.
189. National Register of Historic Places (NRHP) Inventory Nomination Form "Spring Mills Historic District, Berkeley County, WV," Section 7, 1.
190. NRHP Form, "Historic Resources of Berkeley County, West Virginia," Continuation Sheet 7, 3.
191. *Martinsburg Gazette*, January 2, 1839.
192. NRHP Form, "Spring Mills Historic District," Section 8, 2.
193. United States Federal Census Year: *1860*; Census Place: *Berkeley, Virginia*; Archive Collection Number: *T1132*; Roll: *8*; Page: *45*; Line: *12*; Schedule Type: *Industry*.
194. NRHP Form, "Spring Mills Historic District," Section 8, 3.
195. Archie P. McDonald, ed. *Make Me a Map of the Valley: The Civil War Journal of Stonewall Jackson's Topographer* [Jededia Hotchkiss] (Dallas: Sothern Methodist University Press, 1973), 80.
196. NRHP Form, "Spring Mills Historic District," Section 8, 3.
197. Historical Marker Database, "Hammond House Headquarters and Hospital," https://www.hmdb.org/m.asp?m=154839.
198. NRHP Form, "Spring Mills Historic District," Section 8, 3.
199. NRHP Form, "Spring Mills Historic District," Section 8, 4.
200. Theresa's Haunted History of the Tri-State, "Hammond Mansion and Grist Mill," 2021; https://theresashauntedhistoryofthetri-state.blogspot.com/2011/03/hammond-mansion-and-grist-mill.html.
201. Only in Your State, "Stay Away From West Virginia's Most Haunted Road, Route 901, Or You May Be Sorry," https://www.onlyinyourstate.com/west-virginia/ghost-street-wv/.

202. NRHP Form, "Historic Resources of Berkeley County, West Virginia," Section 7, 1.
203. NRHP Form, "Baltimore and Ohio Railroad and Related Industries Historic District," Continuation Sheet 7, 4.
204. NRHP Form, "Baltimore and Ohio Railroad and Related Industries Historic District," Continuation Sheet 7, 4.
205. Reynolds, *Stronger Than a Hundred Men*, 165.
206. *Fitz Steel Overshoot Wheel Bulletin No. 70*, (Hanover, PA: The Fitz Water Wheel Company, 1928), 23.
207. Robert Vitale, Water Wheel Factory online, "History of the Fitz Water Wheel Company," http://www.waterwheelfactory.com/fitz.html.
208. Vitale, "History of the Fitz Water Wheel Company."
209. "Virginia Historic Property Form Continuation Sheet, "Beeler's/Clipp's Mill Property," 7.
210. United States Federal Census Year: *1860;* Census Place: *Berkeley, Virginia;* Archive Collection Number: *T1132;* Roll: *8;* Page: *45;* Line: *1;* Schedule Type: *Industry.*
211. Vitale, "History of the Fitz Water Wheel Company."
212. *Fitz Steel Overshoot Wheel Bulletin, No. 70,* 6.
213. Vitale, "History of the Fitz Water Wheel Company."
214. *Illustrated Handbook of James Leffel's Improved Turbine Water Wheel for 1883 and 1884.* (Springfield, OH: Leffel Newsprint, 1883), 21.
215. *Fitz Steel Overshoot Wheel Bulletin No. 70,* 15.
216. *Fitz Steel Overshoot Wheel Bulletin No. 70,* 24.
217. Vitale, "History of the Fitz Water Wheel Company."
218. Theodore R. Hazen, "A History of the Fitz Water Wheel Company," https://www.angelfire.com/journal/millrestoration/excel.html.
219. Hazen, "A History of the Fitz Water Wheel Company."
220. Vitale, "History of the Fitz Water Wheel Company."
221. United States Federal Census Year: *1900;* Census Place: *Martinsburg Ward 1, Berkeley, West Virginia;* Page: *17;* Enumeration District: *0015;* FHL microfilm: *1241755.*

222. United States Federal Census Year: *1900;* Census Place: Martinsburg Ward 3, Berkeley, West Virginia; Page: *7;* Enumeration District: *0015;* FHL microfilm: *1241755.*
223. R. L. Polk & Co.'s *Martinsburg City Directory 1913-1914, Vol. I,* (Pittsburg, PA: R. L. Polk & Co., Publishers, 1913), 137.
224. United States Federal Census Year: *1930;* Census Place: *Martinsburg, Berkeley, West Virginia;* Page: *5B;* Enumeration District: *0014;* FHL microfilm: *2342260.*
225. United States Federal Census Year: *1930;* Census Place: *Martinsburg, Berkeley, West Virginia;* Page: *4B;* Enumeration District: *0013;* FHL microfilm: *2342260.*
226. NRHP Inventory Nomination Form, "The Baltimore and Ohio and Related Industries Historic District," 7.
227. John McVey, West Virginia Brownfields Assistance Center, "Report: Matthews Foundry Not Contaminated," http://wvbrownfields.org/tag/matthew-foundry/.
228. Main Street Martinsburg, West Virginia, "About Us," http://www.mainstreetmartinsburg.com/about-us/.
229. Matthew Umstead, *Herald-Mail Media,* "Owners Want to bring pre-Civil War foundry back to life in Martinsburg," https://www.heraldmailmedia.com/story/news/local/2018/04/28/owners-want-to-bring-pre-civil-war-foundry-back-to-life-in-martinsburg/44513571/.
230. Matthew Umstead, *Herald-Mail Media,* "Design ideas to help spur redevelopment of Matthews Foundry in Martinsburg," https://www.heraldmailmedia.com/news/tri_state/west_virginia/design-ideas-to-help-spur-redevelopment-of-matthews-foundry-in-martinsburg/article_a57ef7f6-4e55-11e3-9bcc-001a4bcf6878.html?redir=0.
231. National Register of Historic Places (NRHP) Inventory Nomination Form, "Darkesville Historic District," Continuation Sheet 8, 3.
232. Karen Trenary, owner of Union Bryarly Mill, in discussion with author, June 2021.

233. Theodore R. Hazen, "The History of Flour Milling in Early America," https://www.angelfire.com/journal/millrestoration/history.html
234. Polk, *West Virginia Gazetteer and business directory for 1882-83*, 132.
235. Polk, *West Virginia Gazetteer and business directory for 1891-92*, 145.
236. Ancestry, *U.S., Selected Federal Census Non-Population Schedules, 1850-1880*. Provo, UT, USA: Ancestry.com Operations, Inc., 2010.
237. Jefferson County Landmark Nomination Report, "Beeler's Mill Water Wheel," 1.
238. West Virginia Historic Property Form, "Beeler's/Clipp's Mill Property," 5.
239. Jefferson County Landmark, "Beeler's Mill Water Wheel," 1
240. Jefferson County Landmark, "Beeler's Mill Water Wheel," 9.
241. Polk, *West Virginia Gazetteer and business directory for 1904-1905*, 192.
242. Polk, *West Virginia Gazetteer and business directory for 1904-1905*, 5.
243. Jefferson County Landmark Commission, "History of Jefferson County, West Virginia," http://jeffersoncountyhlc.org/index.php/history-of-jefferson-county/.
244. National Register of Historic Places (NRHP) Inventory Nomination Form, "Feagans' Mill Complex," Section 7, 1.
245. NRHP Form, "Feagans' Mill Complex," Section 8, 15.
246. NRHP Form, "Feagans' Mill Complex," Section 7, 3.
247. Kenneth E. Koons and Warren R. Hofstra, *After the Backcountry: Rural Life in the Great Valley of Virginia, 1800-1900*, (Knoxville: University of Tennessee Press, 2000), xvii-xxix.
248. West Virginia Historic Property Inventory, "Haines/Feagans Mill," 3.
249. Ancestry, "Will of Abraham Haines Jr.," https://www.ancestry.com/mediaui-viewer/tree/4009818/person/-1617758254/media/d99013e6-f359-45e5-bd3b-977edfdbec51?_phsrc=bMR4348&_phstart=successSource.

250. West Virginia Historic Property Inventory, "Haines Mill/Feagans Mill," 4.
251. *Mutual Assurance Society, Declaration for Assurance Book.* Richmond, VA: Library of Virginia Archives Microfilm, Reel 3:27:2320.
252. NRHP Form, "Feagans' Mill Complex," Section 8, 8.
253. Ancestry, *U.S. Southern Claims Commission Master Index, 1871-1880* [database on-line]. Provo, UT, USA: Ancestry.com Operations Inc, 2007.
254. National Archives, "Southern Claims Commission Case Files," https://www.archives.gov/research/military/civil-war/southern-claims-commission.
255. West Virginia Historic Property Inventory, "Haines Mill/Feagans Mill," 5-6.
256. NRHP Form, "Feagans' Mill Complex," Section 8, 9.
257. Jefferson County, WV Deed Book O, 223.
258. Polk, *West Virginia Gazetteer and business directory for 1904-1905, Vol. II,* 804.
259. NRHP Form, "Feagans' Mill Complex," 10.
260. NRHP Form, "Feagans' Mill Complex," Section 8, 17.
261. NRHP Form, "Feagans' Mill Complex," Section 8, 11.
262. NRHP Form, "Feagans' Mill Complex," Section 8, 11.
263. National Archives at St. Louis; St. Louis, Missouri; *WWII Draft Registration Cards for West Virginia, 10/16/1940-03/31/1947;* Record Group: *Records of the Selective Service System, 147;* Box: *151.*
264. West Virginia Historic Property Inventory, "Haines Mill/Feagans Mill," 5.
265. West Virginia Historic Property Inventory, "Haines Mill/Feagans Mill," 5-6.
266. Wikipedia, "Chesapeake & Ohio Canal," https://en.wikipedia.org/wiki/Chesapeake_and_Ohio_Canal.
267. *Shepherdstown Cement Mill* brochure published by the Jefferson County, West Virginia Historic Landmarks Commission.
268. Jefferson County Historic Landmarks Commission Nomination Report: "Potomac Mills/Boteler's Cement Mill," 3.

269. Jefferson County Historic Landmarks, "Potomac Mills/Boteler's Cement Mill," 4.
270. Jefferson County Historic Landmarks, 4.
271. Jefferson County Historic Landmarks, 3.
272. *Shepherdstown Cement Mill* brochure.
273. Polk, *West Virginia Gazetteer and business directory for 1882-1883*, 354.
274. Jefferson County Historic Landmarks, 5.
275. Jefferson County Historic Landmarks, 6.
276. Historic Architectural and Engineering Record (HAER) No. WV-5, "Thomas Shepherd's Grist Mill," 2.
277. Fleming Family History, "Thomas Shepherd," https://sites.rootsweb.com/~barbpretz/ps05/ps05_053.htm. p. 4.
278. HAER Record No. WV-5
279. "Shepherd's Mill Wheel Turns 100," *The Shepherdstown Chronicle*, July 29, 1994, 1.
280. "Shepherd's Mill Wheel Turns 100," 6.
281. First Known Thomas Shepherd Family, "Descendants of Thomas Shepherd in Ireland and New Jersey," http://www.geocities.ws/NapaValley/Vineyard/4904/shep_wil.html.
282. First Known Thomas Shepherd Family, "Descendants of Thomas Shepherd."
283. Gertrude E. Gray, *Virginia Northern Neck Land Grants, 1742-1775.*, Vol. II, (Baltimore, MD: Genealogical Publishing Co., 1997), 50.
284. Shepherdstown, WV, "Brief History of the Survey Area." http://www.shepherdstown.us/wp-content/uploads/2014/06/PK-Shptwn-History.pdf.
285. Find A Grave, "Capt. Thomas C. Shepherd Sr. (1705-1776)," https://www.findagrave.com/memorial/6827652/thomas-c.-shepherd.
286. First Known Thomas Shepherd Family, "Descendants of Thomas Shepherd."
287. The West Virginia Encyclopedia, "Bee Line March," http://www.wvencyclopedia.org/articles/425.

288. RSF Trip Reporter online, "West Virginia: Following the Footsteps of George Washington—in an Aston Martin," https://rsftripreporter.net/west-virginia-following-the-footsteps-of-george-washington-in-an-aston-martin/.
289. HAER Record No. WV-5, 2.
290. Fleming Family History, "Thomas Shepherd," 2.
291. Kerns, "Historic Mills of Old Frederick County, Va."
292. Shepherdstown, WV, "Brief History of the Survey Area."
293. Theis, "Group Wowed by Shepherd's Mill Tour."
294. Polk, *West Virginia Gazetteer and business directory for 1882-1883*, 353-355.
295. United States Federal Census Year: *1870*; Census Place: *Bolivar, Jefferson, West Virginia*; Roll: *M593_1689*; Page: *481B*.
296. United States Federal Census Year: *1880*; Census Place: *Shepherdstown, Jefferson, West Virginia*; Roll: *1404*; Page: *46B*; Enumeration District: *003*.
297. Polk, *West Virginia Gazetteer and business directory for 1891-92*, 343.
298. National Register of Historic Places Nomination Form, "Shepherd's Mill," 6.
299. "Shepherd's Mill Wheel Turns 100," 6.
300. United States Federal Census Year: *1910*; Census Place: *Shepherdstown, Jefferson, West Virginia*; Roll: *T624_1682*; Page: *11A*; Enumeration District: *0058*; FHL microfilm: *1375695*.
301. United States Federal Census Year: *1930*; Census Place: *Shepherdstown, Jefferson, West Virginia*; Page: *8B*; Enumeration District: *0009*; FHL microfilm: *2342270*.
302. Kelch, "Early 18th Century Grist Mill Filled with Storied Artifacts."
303. NRHP Inventory Nomination Form, "Shepherd's Mill," 3.
304. Cox, "Shepherd's Mill curiosity continues."
305. Kelch, "Early 18th Century Grist Mill Filled with Storied Artifacts."
306. "Shepherd's Mill Wheel Turns 100," 1.
307. "Shepherd's Mill Wheel Turns 100," 6.

Chapter 2 - Potomac Highlands

308. The West Virginia Encyclopedia, "Eastern Panhandle."
309. Berkeley County Historical Society, "History of Berkeley County, WV."
310. West Virginia Encyclopedia, "Eastern Panhandle."
311. Linda Allmond Fralish, ed., *Historic Mills of America*. (Ft. Worth, TX: Landmark Publishing, 2000), 315.
312. Map of Hardy County Virginia, Surveyed and Drawn under the direction of John Wood, 1822.
313. Charles Morrison, West Virginia History, "Early Land Grants and Settlers Along Patterson Creek," http://www.wvculture.org/hiStory/journal_wvh/wvh40-2.html.
314. Fralish, *Historic Mills of America*, 315.
315. United States Federal Census Year: *1850*; Census Place: *District 23, Hardy, Virginia*; Roll: *950*; Page: *90a*.
316. United States Federal Census Year: *1870*; Census Place: *Union, Grant, West Virginia*; Roll: *M593_1686*; Page: *286B*.
317. Find A Grave, "David L. Cassady," https://www.findagrave.com/memorial/172008631/david-l-cassady.
318. Ancestry, "West Virginia, U.S., Wills and Probate Records, 1724-1985, for D. L. Cassady," https://www.ancestry.com/imageviewer/collections/9087/images/007616678_00202?usePUB=true&_phsrc=bMR3859&_phstart=successSource&usePUBJs=true&pId=115601.
319. *Grant County Press*, http://www.oocities.org/gchgs/GrantCountyPress1976.html.
320. Yolanda J. Spicer, *Grant County Press Valley Dollar Saver*, September 18, 1985, "Williamsport Grist Mill is Heritage Weekend Feature."
321. "Caudy's Castle Part One," https://www.youtube.com/watch?v=JAiWBO_z7X8.
322. "Caudy's Castle Part Two," https://www.youtube.com/watch?v=eXwHYBNtCsI.

323. Darlene DeMott, ed. "History of Hampshire County and the Crossings at the Great Cacapon," https://www.thecrossingspoa.com/p/Crossings-History.
324. *Hampshire Review*, "Furnace cast a century of prosperity: 250 years ago, Bloomery's fortune began with a stack of stones," https://www.hampshirereview.com/living/article_264c6624-a017-11ea-8955-23c27e6ed9b2.htm.
325. Jim King, *Hampshire Review*, "A Man of History," https://www.hampshirereview.com/news/article_5f12c756-63a3-11ea-8dcd-e71841337710.html.
326. Maxwell, Hu and H L Swisher, *History of Hampshire County West Virginia From its Earliest Settlement to the Present*, (Morgantown WV: A. Brown Broughner Printer, 1897), 533-536.
327. DeMott, "History of Hampshire County and The Crossings at Great Cacapon."
328. United States Federal Census Year: *1880*; Census Place: *Bloomery, Hampshire, West Virginia*; Roll: *1403*; Page: *423B*; Enumeration District: *023*.
329. DeMott, "History of Hampshire County and The Crossings at Great Cacapon."
330. Historic Hampshire, "Bloomery Presbyterian Church," http://www.historichampshire.org/churches/BloomeryPresbyCh.htm.
331. DeMott, "History of Hampshire County and The Crossings at Great Cacapon."
332. DeMott, "History of Hampshire County and The Crossings at Great Cacapon."
333. DeMott, "History of Hampshire County and The Crossings at Great Cacapon."
334. Polk, *West Virginia Gazetteer and business directory for 1891-1892*, 67.
335. National Register of Historic Places (NRHP) Inventory Nomination Form, "Augusta Milling Company," Section 7, 1.
336. NRHP Form, "Augusta Milling Company," Section 8, 5.
337. NRHP Form, "Augusta Milling Company," Section 8, 5.

338. Munske and Kerns, eds. *Hampshire County West Virginia 1754-2004*, 52.
339. NRHP Form, "Augusta Milling Company," Section 8, p. 6.
340. Historic Hampshire, "Sites Suffering from Neglect or Vandalism," http://historichampshire.org/preserve/disappear.htm.
341. Ancestry, "Caudy George Davis," https://www.ancestry.com/family-tree/person/tree/38048478/person/29806229858/facts.
342. Hampshire County, WV Deed Book 194, 151-153.
343. Hampshire County, WV Deed Book 96, 20-21.
344. Hampshire County, WV Deed Book 96, 22.
345. Hampshire County, WV Deed Book 92, 232-233.
346. United States Federal Census Year: *1940*; Census Place: *Capon, Hampshire, West Virginia*; Roll: *m-t0627-04405*; Page: *2A*; Enumeration District: *14-4*.
347. United States Federal Census Year: *1920*; Census Place: *Capon, Hampshire, West Virginia*; Roll: *T625_1952*; Page: *3A*; Enumeration District: *45*.
348. United States Federal Census Year: *1910*; Census Place: *Black Creek, Frederick, Virginia*; Roll: *T624_1629*; Page: *2B*; Enumeration District: *0030*; FHL microfilm: *1375642*.
349. Polk, *West Virginia Gazetteer and business directory for 1904-1905*, Vol. 1, 364.
350. Polk, *West Virginia Gazetteer and business directory for 1900-1901*, 245.
351. United States Federal Census Year: *1900*; Census Place: *Capon, Hampshire, West Virginia*; Page: *1*; Enumeration District: *0026*; FHL microfilm: *1241759*.
352. Ancestry, Virginia Department of Health Death Records 1912-2014, https://www.ancestry.com/imageviewer/collections/9278/images/43004_172028008151_0055-00303?pId=677216.
353. United States Federal Census Year: *1870*; Census Place: *Capon, Hampshire, West Virginia*; Roll: *M593_1687*; Page: *479B*.
354. Abraham Thomson Seacrest, *Spaid Genealogy From the First of the Name in This Country to the Present Time with a Number of Allied*

Families and Historical Facts, (Columbus, OH: Nitschke Bros. Printed for the Compiler, 1922), 21-23.
355. Seacrest, *Spaid Genealogy*, 17.
356. Rob Wolford, historian, in discussion with author, June 2020.
357. Seacrest, *Spaid Genealogy*, 125-126.
358. United States Federal Census Year: *1860;* Census Place: *Southern, Hampshire, Virginia;* Archive Collection Number: *T1132;* Roll: *8;* Page: *153;* Line: *1;* Schedule Type: *Industry.*
359. Seacrest, *Spaid Genealogy*, 90.
360. Ancestry, "John Jacob Kline," accessed on September 14, 2021; https://www.ancestry.com/family-tree/person/tree/4616373/person/6948690067/facts.
361. Ancestry online, "Elizabeth Spaid," accessed on September 14, 2021; https://www.ancestry.com/family-tree/person/tree/4616373/person/6949897758/facts.
362. *Administrator Bonds, 1866-1868*; Author: *West Virginia. Circuit Court (Hampshire County)*: Probate Place: *Hampshire, West Virginia.*
363. Hampshire County, WV Deed Book 49, 406-407.
364. United States Federal Census Year: *1850*; Census Place: *District 16, Frederick, Virginia*; Roll: *945*; Page: *259a.*
365. Gary Mason, *Beyond the Great North Mountain: A History and Guide*, (Gore, VA: 2ZensQUILL Press, 2016), 167.
366. Mason, *Beyond the Great North Mountain*, 167.
367. "National Register of Historic Places (NRHP) Inventory Nomination Form, "Yellow Spring Mill," Continuation Sheet 8, 4.
368. Mason, *Beyond the Great North Mountain*, 167.
369. "NRHP Form, "Yellow Spring Mill," Continuation Sheet 8, 5.
370. "NRHP Inventory Nomination Form, "Yellow Spring Mill," Continuation Sheet 8, 6.
371. Wilmer P. Kerns, Ph.D., *Historical Records of Old Frederick and Hampshire Counties, Virginia (Revised)* (Bowie, MD: Heritage Books, Inc., 1992), 38.
372. Kerns, *Historical Records of Old Frederick and Hampshire Counties,* 175-6.

373. Historic Hampshire, "Historic Hampshire County, West Virginia, West Virginia's Oldest County: Settlement and Early Growth, http://www.historichampshire.org/histwvgs.htm.
374. Munske and Kerns, eds., *Hampshire County, West Virginia*, 50.
375. United States Federal Census Year: *1920*; Census Place: *Capon, Hampshire, West Virginia*; Roll: *T625_1952*; Page: *1B*; Enumeration District: *44*.
376. Mason, *Beyond the Great North Mountain*, 167.
377. NRHP Form, "Yellow Spring Mill," Continuation Sheet 8, 6.
378. Samuel Gordon Smyth, *A genealogy of the Duke-Shepherd-Van Metre family: from civil, military, church, and family records and documents*, (Lancaster, PA.: New Era Print Co., 1909), 57.
379. Wikipedia, "Military Career of George Washington," https://en.wikipedia.org/wiki/Military_career_of_George_Washington.
380. Wikipedia, "Fort Pleasant."
381. Find A Grave, "Isaac Vanmeter, (1757-1837)," https://www.findagrave.com/memorial/35175688/isaac-vanmeter.
382. Ancestry, "Colonel Jacob VanMeter," https://www.ancestry.com/mediaui-viewer/collection/1030/tree/111349866/person/120085990374/media/e9771ce7-4f93-449a-b87c-dc06b2dad97b?_phsrc=bMR5386&usePUBJs=true.
383. Ancestry, "Colonel Jacob VanMeter."
384. Kerns, "Historic Mills of Old Frederick County, Va."
385. Map of Hardy County Drawn under the direction of John Wood, 1822.
386. Kerns, "Historic Mills of Old Frederick County, Va."
387. Kelly Williams, author and historian, in discussion with author, August 2021.
388. Kerns, "Historic Mills of Old Frederick County, Va."
389. Wikipedia, "Willow Wall," https://en.wikipedia.org/wiki/Willow_Wall.
390. Newspapers, "Obituary for Isaac Van Meter (aged 70)," https://www.newspapers.com/image/372971205/?article=c6bc30ac-28ae-44a0-ab2e-145d6b0d24b1&focus=0.49743173,0.49024037,0.6171668,0

.5366521&xid=3355&_ga=2.79478420.1852109248.1628351559-114782035.1526934498.
391. Kelly Williams, in discussion with author, August 2021.
392. Hardy County, WV Deed Book 38, 94.
393. Ancestry, "Daniel Renick McNeill," achttps://www.ancestry.com/family-tree/person/tree/14324175/person/211211123/facts?_phsrc=bMR5693&_phstart=successSource.
394. United States Federal Census Year: *1900;* Census Place: *Moorefield, Hardy, West Virginia;* Page: *12;* Enumeration District: *0037;* FHL microfilm: *1241759.*
395. Hardy County, WV Deed Book 53, 310-311.
396. Hardy County, WV Deed Book 55, 292-295.
397. *Moorefieled Examiner,* "The Old Water Wheel..." March 8, 2000.
398. Hardy County, WV Deed Book 63, 453-454.
399. Hardy County, WV Deed Book 67, 117-118.
400. United States Federal Census Year: *1930;* Census Place: *Moorefield, Hardy, West Virginia;* Page: *4A;* Enumeration District: *0006;* FHL microfilm: *2342269.*
401. Hardy County, WV Deed Book 70, 283.
402. Hardy County, WV Deed Book 72, 101.
403. Hardy County, WV Deed Book 72, 155-156.
404. Hardy County, WV Deed Book 75, 601-602.
405. Hardy County, WV Deed Book 76, 25-26.
406. Nancy Nolen, in Facebook chat conversation with author, August 6, 2021.
407. Hardy County, WV Deed Book 119, 608.
408. Hardy County, WV Deed Book 204, 729.
409. Wikipedia, "Irregular Military," https://en.wikipedia.org/wiki/Irregular_military.
410. Wikipedia, "John Hanson McNeill," https://en.wikipedia.org/wiki/John_Hanson_McNeill.
411. Ancestry, "Strother McNeill," https://www.ancestry.com/family-tree/person/tree/117811843/person/172084460559/facts.
412. Wikipedia, "McNeill's Rangers," https://en.wikipedia.org/wiki/McNeill%27s_Rangers.

413. Wikipedia, "Willow Wall."
414. Sidney Williams Gooding, George M. Williams, Ph.D., and Kelly Sloan Williams, editors, *Old Fields in Peace and War: Rebecca Van Meter's Diary 1855-1865*, (Parson, WV: McClain Printing Company, 2012), 240.
415. Polk, *West Virginia Gazetteer and business directory for 1882-1883*, 197.
416. Polk, *West Virginia Gazetteer and business directory for 1891-1892*, 251.
417. Polk, *West Virginia Gazetteer and business directory for 1900-1901*, 321.
418. Polk, *West Virginia Gazetteer and business directory for 1904-1905*, 488.
419. Seymour Whipp, Keyser *News-Tribune*, "The Passage of the Old Mill Wheel," April 2, 1953.
420. Pearl Berg, "Antioch Grist Mill," [unpublished manuscript].
421. Pearl Berg, "Antioch Grist Mill."
422. Whipp, "The Passing of the Old Mill Wheel."
423. Whipp, "The Passing of the Old Mill Wheel."
424. William C. Blizzard, *Mountain Trader*, "Antique at Antioch," September 1964.
425. Blizzard, "Antique at Antioch."
426. *Keyser News-Tribune*, "Antioch Woolen Mill Equipment Purchased for Display at Museum," July 24, 1968.
427. Betty Dzubba, letter to the author postmarked July 14, 2020.
428. Whipp, "The Passing of the Old Mill Wheel."
429. WV Genweb, "Laurel Dale, West Virginia," https://www.wvgenweb.org/mineral/Laurelt.htm.
430. Mineral County, WV Deed Book 3, 429-431.
431. United States Federal Census Year: *1860*; Census Place: *District 2, Hardy, Virginia*; Page: *724*.
432. United States Federal Census Year: *1870*; Census Place: *Union, Grant, West Virginia*; Roll: *M593_1686*; Page: *286A*.
433. Ancestry.com. *U.S., Register of Civil, Military, and Naval Service, 1863-1959* [database on-line]. Provo, UT, USA:

Ancestry.com Operations, Inc., https://www.ancestry.com/imageviewer/collections/1932/images/30439_065525-00099?treeid=&personid=&hintid=&usePUB=true&usePUBJs=true&_ga=2.232547551.1928840341.1631061005-114782035.1526934498&pId=601150.

434. United States Federal Census Year: *1880*; Census Place: *New Creek, Mineral, West Virginia*; Roll: *1408*; Page: *141A*; Enumeration District: *033*.
435. Polk, *West Virginia Gazetteer and business directory for 1882-1883*, 502.
436. Mineral County, WV Deed Book 10, 572.
437. Ancestry.com. West Virginia, U.S., Marriages Index, 1785-1971 [database online]. Provo, UT, USA: Ancestry.com Operations, Inc., 2011.
438. WV Genweb, "Laurel Dale, West Virginia."
439. Ancestry, "Jacob Hilkey," https://www.ancestry.com/family-tree/person/tree/2314478/person/402022059247/facts?_phsrc=bMR4918&_phstart=successSource.
440. Ancestry, "Jacob Hilkey."
441. Mineral County, WV Deed Book 18, 601.
442. United States Federal Census Year: *1900*; Census Place: *New Creek, Mineral, West Virginia*; Page: *1*; Enumeration District: *0071*; FHL microfilm: *1241766*.
443. WV Genweb online, "Laurel Dale, West Virginia."
444. Mineral County, WV Will Book 3, 543-544.
445. Mineral County, WV Deed Book 98, 113-114.
446. National Register of Historic Places (NRHP) Inventory Nomination Form, "Boggs Mill," Section 8, 2.
447. NRHP Form, "Boggs Mill," Section 7, 1.
448. NRHP Form, "Boggs Mill," Section 8, 4.
449. NRHP Form, "Boggs Mill," Section 7, 1.
450. Ancestry, "Capt. John Boggs," https://www.ancestry.com/mediaui-viewer/tree/76012044/person/220106245405/media/e8ad3b1e-48dd-4d07-8ef5-0d4c0bc05802?_phsrc=bMR4311&_phstart=successSource.

451. Ancestry, "John Boggs," https://www.ancestry.com/mediaui-viewer/tree/104098419/person/172221993025/media/ddba6390-5539-472c-a5cb-1326199fb51c?_phsrc=bMR4312&_phstart=successSource.
452. The National Archives at Washington, D.C.; Washington, D.C.; *Special Schedules of the Eleventh Census (1890) Enumerating Union Veterans and Widows of Union Veterans of the Civil War*; Series Number: *M123*; Record Group Title: *Records of the Department of Veterans Affairs*; Record Group Number: *15*; Census Year: *1890*.
453. United States Federal Census Year: *1870*; Census Place: *Union, Pendleton, West Virginia*; Roll: *M593_1697*; Page: *444A*, Year: *1880*; Census Place: *Union, Pendleton, West Virginia*; Roll: *1411*; Page: *62C*; Enumeration District: *047*.
454. United States Federal Census Year: *1920*; Census Place: *Union, Pendleton, West Virginia*; Roll: *T625_1968*; Page: *9A*; Enumeration District: *127*.
455. NRHP Form, "Boggs Mill," Section 8, 3.
456. United States Federal Census Year: *1940*; Census Place: *Union, Pendleton, West Virginia*; Roll: *m-t0627-04438*; Page: *6A*; Enumeration District: *36-7B*.
457. Charlotte Lambert Feagans, daughter of the owner, Facebook comment dated July 28, 2021.
458. Wikipedia, "Circleville, West Virginia," https://en.wikipedia.org/wiki/Circleville,_West_Virginia.
459. Oren Frederic Morton, *A History of Pendleton County, West Virginia*. (Franklin, WV: Published by the Author, 1910), 135.
460. Pendleton County, WV Deed Book 18, 617.
461. Wikipedia, "Bergton, Virginia," https://en.wikipedia.org/wiki/Bergton,_Virginia.
462. Lewis H. Yankey, Lonzo Dove, and Patricia T. Ritchie, "Family of Absalom Dove and Catherine Feathers," https://www.ancestry.com/mediaui-viewer/tree/57183684/person/38351371606/media/9c8f9ba5-1009-4fee-9f2b-a1423dc16e84?_phsrc=bMR5490&_phstart=successSource.

463. Ancestry, Historical Data Systems, comp. *U.S., Civil War Soldier Records and Profiles, 1861-1865* [database on-line]. Provo, UT, USA: Ancestry.com Operations Inc, 2009.
464. United States Federal Census United States Federal Census Year: *1850;* Census Place: *South Branch and North Fork, Pendleton, Virginia;* Archive Collection Number: *T1132;* Roll: *4;* Page: *110;* Line: *1;* Schedule Type: *Industry.*
465. Polk, *West Virginia state gazetteer and business directory for 1882-1883,* 263.
466. Polk, *West Virginia state gazetteer and business directory for 1891-1892,* 128-129.
467. Polk, *West Virginia state gazetteer and business directory for 1900-1901,* 144.
468. Polk, *West Virginia State Gazetteer and business directory for 1904-05,* 195.
469. United States Federal Census Year: *1900;* Census Place: *Circleville, Pendleton, West Virginia;* Page: *6;* Enumeration District: *0094;* FHL microfilm: *1241769.*
470. United States Federal Census Year: *1850;* Census Place: *Dry Run, Pendleton, Virginia;* Roll: *968;* Page: *46b.*
471. Ancestry, "John B. Bennett," https://www.ancestry.com/family-tree/person/tree/111178056/person/380083640487/facts?_phsrc=bMR5472&_phstart=successSource.
472. United States Federal Census Year: 1910; Census Place: Circleville, Pendleton, West Virginia; Roll: T624_1693; Page: 2A; Enumeration District: 0092; FHL microfilm: 1375706.
473. United States Federal Census Year: 1920; Census Place: Circleville, Pendleton, West Virginia; Roll: T625_1968; Page: 5B; Enumeration District: 122; Image: 39.
474. United States Federal Census Year: *1930;* Census Place: *Circleville, Pendleton, West Virginia;* Page: *15A;* Enumeration District: *0002;* FHL microfilm: *2342285.*
475. Pendleton County, WV Will Book 6, 15-16.
476. Pendleton County, WV Deed Book 49, 167-171.
477. Pendleton County, WV Deed Book 84, 121-122.

478. Morton, *A History of Pendleton County, West Virginia*, 232.
479. Augusta County, VA Deed Book 24, 104.
480. Pendleton County, WV Deed Book 10, 507.
481. Ancestry, "Mary 'Polly' Probst," https://www.ancestry.com/family-tree/person/tree/82579146/person/242092610342/facts.
482. Pendleton County, WV Deed Book 11, page 429.
483. Ancestry, "William Kiser," https://www.ancestry.com/family-tree/person/tree/82579146/person/242091594547/facts.
484. Ancestry, "William Kiser."
485. Morton, *A History of Pendleton County, West Virginia*, 366.
486. United States Federal Census Year: *1850*; Census Place: *South Fork and District 50, Pendleton, Virginia*; Archive Collection Number: *T1132*; Roll: *4*; Page: *111*; Line: *1*; Schedule Type: *Industry*.
487. Ancestry, "Mary Jane Kiser," https://www.ancestry.com/family-tree/person/tree/82579146/person/242092610343/facts.
488. Ancestry, "Sylvester Mitchell," https://www.ancestry.com/family-tree/person/tree/82579146/person/242093206772/facts.
489. Ancestry, "Leafy A. Mitchell," https://www.ancestry.com/family-tree/person/tree/82579146/person/242093206781/facts.
490. Hannah Byrd DuPoy, in email to the author, December 2020.
491. Ibid.
492. Veterans of Foreign Wars, "Past VFW National Commander Homan Dies at 87," https://www.vfw.org/media-and-events/latest-releases/archives/2010/6/past-vfw-national-commander-homan-dies-at-87.
493. Veterans of Foreign Wars, "Past VFW National Commander Homan Dies at 87."
494. Veterans of Foreign Wars, "Past VFW National Commander Homan Dies at 87."
495. Veterans of Foreign Wars, "Past VFW National Commander Homan Dies at 87."
496. Visit to Homan Mill, June 16, 2021.
497. Eston Teter interview, "Water-Powered Mills of Pendleton County West Virginia: The South Branch of the Potomac,"

directed by Gerald Milnes. Augusta Heritage Center, Davis & Elkins College. A Project of the Fort Seybert Heritage Educational Association, 2008.
498. Morton, *History of Pendleton County, West Virginia*, 261.
499. United States Federal Census Year: *1850*; Census Place: *South Fork, Pendleton, Virginia*; Roll: *968*; Page: *1b*.
500. United States Federal Census Year: *1860*; Census Place: *Pendleton, Virginia*; Page: *14*.
501. United States Federal Census Year: *1870*; Census Place: *Bethel, Pendleton, West Virginia*; Roll: *M593_1697*; Page: *372B*.
502. Morton, *History of Pendleton County, West Virginia*, 261.
503. United States Federal Census Year: *1850*; Census Place: *South Fork, Pendleton, Virginia*; Roll: *968*; Page: *2*
504. United States Federal Census Year: *1850;* Census Place: *South Branch and North Fork, Pendleton, Virginia;* Archive Collection Number: *T1132;* Roll: *4;* Page: *110;* Line: *1;* Schedule Type: *Industry*.
505. United States Federal Census Year: *1850*.
506. Morton, *History of Pendleton County, West Virginia*, 134.
507. Michael J. Buseman, "Vending Vice: The Rise and Fall of West Virginia State Prohibition 1852—1934," [master's thesis, 2012] (2012), 26, https://researchrepository.wvu.edu/etd/324.
508. Buseman, "Vending Vice," 167.
509. Buseman, "Vending Vice," 26.
510. David E. Kyvig, *Repealing National Prohibition* (Chicago: University of Chicago Press, 1979), 6.
511. *West Virginia Freeman*, July 6, 1881.
512. Buseman, "Vending Vice," 128.
513. Buseman, "Vending Vice," 127.
514. Pendleton County, WV Record Book 1890-1897.
515. Surety Bonds, "License and Permit Bonds," https://www.suretybonds.com/license-permit-bonds.html
516. Buseman, "Vending Vice," 129.
517. Buseman, "Vending Vice," 129.

518. Joseph Connor, "The Mann Act: How a Law Meant to Help Women was Misused," https://www.historynet.com/online-exclusive-mann-oh-mann-how-a-law-can-be-misused.htm.
519. Food and Drug Administration, "Part One: The 1906 Food and Drug Act and its Enforcement," https://www.fda.gov/about-fda/changes-science-law-and-regulatory-authorities/part-i-1906-food-and-drugs-act-and-its-enforcement.
520. *Highland Recorder*, March 13, 1908.
521. West Virginia Department of the Arts, Culture, and History, "The Revenooers Enforcing Prohibition in West Virginia," http://www.wvculture.org/goldenseal/winter17/Prohibition.html.
522. Wikipedia, "The Eighteenth Amendment to the United States Constitution," achttps://en.wikipedia.org/wiki/Eighteenth_Amendment_to_the_United_States_Constitution.
523. *Annual Report from State Commissioner of Prohibition for Fiscal Years 1922-1923*, 9, E.F. Morgan Papers, Box 29, West Virginia Regional History Collection, Morgantown, WV, West Virginia University.
524. Joan Ashley, *Goldenseal Magazine*, "The View from Brandywine: Looking Back with Lester Hoover," Vol. 18, No. 4, Winter 1992, 26.
525. Interview with Olin Hoover July 2021.
526. Ashley, "The View from Brandywine," 26.
527. Ashley, "The View from Brandywine," 27.
528. Pendleton County Deed Book 7, 509-510.
529. Olin Hoover.
530. Olin Hoover.
531. Olin Hoover.
532. West Virginia Encyclopedia, "McCoy's Mill."
533. West Virginia Encyclopedia, "McCoy's Mill."
534. Morton, *History of Pendleton County, West Virginia*, 393.
535. Oren Frederic Morton, *A History of Highland County, Virginia*. (Monterey, VA: Published by the Author, 1911), 218.
536. West Virginia Encyclopedia, "McCoy's Mill."
537. Daniel Taylor, in discussion with author, May 2021.

538. Geni, "William McCoy, Jr. (1830-c.1861)," https://www.geni.com/people/William-Little-Billy-McCoy-Jr/6000000039945084336?through=6000000101146219823.
539. Morton, *History of Pendleton County*, 258.
540. Morton, *History of Pendleton County*, 421.
541. Find a Grave, "William Harrison Boggs," https://www.findagrave.com/memorial/76705209/william-harrison-boggs.
542. Society for the Preservation of Old Mills, "Mill List with Sites: West Virginia," https://www.spoom.org/content.aspx?page_id=86&club_id=664666&item_id=60416.
543. Dutch Hex Sign, "History," http://dutchhexsign.com/history.htm.
544. Dutch Hex Sign, "History."
545. Dutch Hex Sign, "About the Magik," http://dutchhexsign.com/magik.htm.
546. *Pendleton Times*, August 16, 2001, "History of Sugar Grove," https://sites.rootsweb.com/~wvpendle/sugargrove.htm.
547. *Pendleton Times*, "History of Sugar Grove."
548. Brandon, Paula, and Tom Mitchell, in discussion with author, June 2021.
549. George Washington's Mount Vernon, "Surveying," https://www.mountvernon.org/library/digitalhistory/digital-encyclopedia/article/surveying/.
550. Ancestry, "Jacob Mitchell," https://www.ancestry.com/family-tree/person/tree/21219857/person/46576485274/facts.
551. Brandon, Paula, and Tom Mitchell, in discussion with author, June 2021.
552. United States Federal Census Year: 1900; Census Place: Sugar Grove, Pendleton, West Virginia; Roll: 1769; Page: 2B; Enumeration District: 0097; FHL microfilm: 1241769.
553. United States Federal Census Year: *1910*; Census Place: *Magisterial District, Pendleton, West Virginia*; Roll: *T624_1693*; Page: *4B*; Enumeration District: *0095*; FHL microfilm: *1375706*.
554. United States Federal Census Year: *1920*; Census Place: *Sugar Grove, Pendleton, West Virginia*; Roll: *T625_1968*; Page: *5A*; Enumeration District: *125*.

555. United States Federal Census Year: *1930*; Census Place: *Sugar Grove, Pendleton, West Virginia*; Page: *6B*; Enumeration District: *0006*; FHL microfilm: *2342285*.
556. Brandon, Paula, and Tom Mitchell, in discussion with author, June 2021.
557. United States Federal Census Year: *1930*; Census Place: *Sugar Grove, Pendleton, West Virginia*; Page: *6B*; Enumeration District: *0006*; FHL microfilm: *2342285*.
558. Brandon, Paula, and Tom Mitchell, in discussion with author, June 2021.
559. Fitz Steel Overshoot Water Wheels Bulletin 78, (Hanover, PA December 1928), https://www.angelfire.com/journal/pondlilymill/fitz.html.
560. "History of Mitchell Mill," [unpublished manuscript].
561. Brandon, Paula, and Tom Mitchell, in discussion with author, June 2021.
562. Brandon, Paula, and Tom Mitchell, in discussion with author, June 2021.
563. Wikipedia online, "Onego, West Virginia," https://en.wikipedia.org/wiki/Onego,_West_Virginia.
564. Polk, *West Virginia Gazetteer and business directory for 1882-1883*, 267.
565. Polk, *West Virginia Gazetteer and business directory for 1882-1883*, 267.
566. United States Federal Census US Federal Census Year: *1880;* Census Place: *Union, Pendleton, West Virginia;* Roll: *1411;* Page: *64C;* Enumeration District: *047*.
567. Find a Grave, "Andrew Dolly," https://www.findagrave.com/memorial/82700856/andrew-dolly.
568. Find a Grave, "Johann 'John' Dahle Dolly," https://www.findagrave.com/memorial/200328952/johann_%22john%22-dahle_dolly.
569. Find a Grave, "Andrew Dolly."
570. Morton, *A History of Pendleton County*, 199.

571. United States Federal Census Year: *1860;* Census Place: *Pendleton, Virginia;* Page: *110.*
572. The National Archives at Washington, D.C.; Washington, D.C.; *Special Schedules of the Eleventh Census (1890) Enumerating Union Veterans and Widows of Union Veterans of the Civil War;* Series Number: *M123;* Record Group Title: *Records of the Department of Veterans Affairs;* Record Group Number: *15;* Census Year: *1890.*
573. Polk, *West Virginia Gazetteer and business directory for 1891-1892,* 266.
574. Polk, *West Virginia Gazetteer and business directory for 1900-1901,* 365.
575. Polk, *West Virginia Gazetteer and business directory for 1904-1905,* 559.
576. United States Federal Census Year: *1900;* Census Place: *Union, Pendleton, West Virginia;* Page: *15;* Enumeration District: *0098;* FHL microfilm: *1241769.*
577. United States Federal Census Year: *1910;* Census Place: *Union, Pendleton, West Virginia;* Roll: *T624_1693;* Page: *6B;* Enumeration District: *0096;* FHL microfilm: *1375706.*
578. United States Federal Census Year: *1920;* Census Place: *Union, Pendleton, West Virginia;* Roll: *T625_1968;* Page: *10A;* Enumeration District: *126.*
579. United States Federal Census Year: *1930;* Census Place: *Union, Pendleton, West Virginia;* Page: *14A;* Enumeration District: *0007;* FHL microfilm: *2342285.*
580. United States Federal Census Year: *1860;* Census Place: *Franklin, Pendleton, Virginia;* Page: *152.*
581. Wikipedia, "Journeyman," https://en.wikipedia.org/wiki/Journeyman.
582. Historical Data Systems, comp. "U.S., Civil War Soldier Records and Profiles, 1861-1865," [database on-line]. Provo, UT, USA: Ancestry.com Operations Inc., 2009.
583. Historical Data Systems, comp. "U.S., Civil War Soldier Records and Profiles, 1861-1865."

584. National Register of Historic Place (NRHP) Inventory Nomination Form, "Priest Mill," Section 8, 1.
585. Tom and Teresa Calhoon, in discussion with author, June 2021.
586. United States Federal Census Year: *1910*; Census Place: *Franklin, Pendleton, West Virginia*; Roll: *T624_1693*; Page: *3A*; Enumeration District: *0093*; FHL microfilm: *1375706*.
587. NRHP Form, "Priest Mill," Section 8, 1.
588. Wikipedia, "Governor (device)," https://en.wikipedia.org/wiki/Governor_(device).
589. NRHP Form, "Priest Mill," Section 7, 1.
590. Smithsonian Magazine, "Edison vs. Westinghouse: A Shocking Rivalry," https://www.smithsonianmag.com/history/edison-vs-westinghouse-a-shocking-rivalry-102146036/.
591. Smithsonian Magazine, "Edison vs. Westinghouse."
592. Smithsonian Magazine, "Edison vs. Westinghouse."
593. Tom and Teresa Calhoon, in discussion with author, June 2021.
594. NRHP Inventory Nomination Form, "Priest Mill," Section 8, 1.
595. Find A Grave, "Robert Peal Priest," https://www.findagrave.com/memorial/140719872/robert-peal-priest.
596. United States Federal Census Year: *1930*; Census Place: *Franklin, Pendleton, West Virginia*; Page: *7A*; Enumeration District: *0004*; FHL microfilm: *2342285*.
597. United States Federal Census Year: *1940*; Census Place: *Franklin, Pendleton, West Virginia*; Roll: *m-t0627-04438*; Page: *16A*; Enumeration District: *36-4A*.
598. Ancestry, "Paul Russell Priest," https://www.ancestry.com/family-tree/person/tree/83349972/person/362159752508/facts.
599. Ancestry, "Paul Russell Priest."
600. Republican American Obituaries online, "Vincent John Budris," https://obits.rep-am.com/2012/03/10/vincent-j-budris/.
601. Email from Robert Hiller dated December 5, 2020.
602. Pendleton County, WV Deed Book 18, 41-43.
603. Pendleton County, WV Deed Book 19, 87.

604. United States Federal Census Year: *1910*; Census Place: *Magisterial District, Pendleton, West Virginia*; Roll: *T624_1693*; Page: *5A*; Enumeration District: *0095*; FHL microfilm: *1375706*.
605. Ancestry online. *U.S., World War I Draft Registration Cards, 1917-1918* [database on-line]. Provo, UT, USA: Ancestry.com Operations Inc, 2005. Original data: United States, Selective Service System. World War I Selective Service System Draft Registration Cards, 1917-1918. Washington, D.C.: National Archives and Records Administration. M1509, 4,582 rolls. Imaged from Family History Library microfilm.
606. West Virginia Vital Research Records online, George Waggy Death Certificate.
607. United States Federal Census Year: *1920*; Census Place: *Sugar Grove, Pendleton, West Virginia*; Roll: *T625_1968*; Page: *8A*; Enumeration District: *125*.
608. United States Federal Census Year 1920.
609. Brenna Mitchell, *Pendleton's Boys of '17*, (Sugar Grove, WV: Published by the Author, 2019), 313.
610. Ancestry, "George Waggy," https://www.ancestry.com/family-tree/person/tree/103919777/person/110038675768/facts.
611. *Wills;* Author: *West Virginia.* County Court (Pendleton County); Probate Place: *Pendleton, West Virginia, 156-157.*
612. Email from Brenna Mitchell dated February 16, 2021
613. Traveling 219, "The Seneca Trail," http://www.traveling219.com/stories/elkins-marlinton/the-seneca-trail-history/.
614. Traveling 219, "The Seneca Trail."
615. John H. Gwathmey, ed. Historical register Of Virginians in the Revolution, soldiers, sailors and marines, 1775-1783. (Richmond, VA: 1938), 120.
616. National Register of Historic Places (NRHP) Inventory Nomination Form, "McNeel Mill," Section 8, 1.
617. NRHP Inventory Nomination Form, "McNeel Mill," Section 8, 1.
618. Alcock, "What Genealogists should know about 18th Century Virginia Law."

619. Find A Grave, "Valentine Cackley, Sr.," https://www.findagrave.com/memorial/219181454/valentine-cackley
620. NRHP Inventory Nomination Form, "McNeel Mill," Section 8, 2.
621. United States Federal Census Year: *1850;* Census Place: *District 47, Pocahontas, Virginia;* Roll: *969;* Page 261a.
622. Ancestry.com. *U.S., Sons of the American Revolution Membership Applications, 1889-1970* [database on-line]. Provo, UT, USA: Ancestry.com Operations, Inc., 2011. Original data: Sons of the American Revolution Membership Applications, 1889-1970. Louisville, Kentucky: National Society of the Sons of the American Revolution. Microfilm, 508 rolls.
623. Pocahontas County, WV Deed Book 8, 247.
624. Images by Mark Summerfield online, "McNeel Mill," http://msummerfieldimages.com/mcneel-mill.
625. Ancestry.com. *U.S., Register of Civil, Military, and Naval Service, 1863-1959* [database on-line]. Provo, UT, USA: Ancestry.com Operations, Inc., 2014.
Original data: Department of Commerce and Labor, Bureau of the Census. Official Register of the United States, Containing a List of the Officers and Employees in the Civil, Military, and Naval Service. Digitized books (77 volumes). Oregon State Library, Salem, Oregon.
626. Polk, *West Virginia Gazetteer and business directory for 1904-1905*, 496.
627. NRHP Form, "McNeel Mill," Section 7.
628. Pocahontas County, WV Will Book 14, 357.
629. Pocahontas County, WV Will Book 24, 447.
630. Pocahontas County, WV Deed Book 181, 665.
631. Pocahontas County Historical Society, "Society Milestones," http://www.pocahontashistorical.org/pchsdates.htm.
632. National Register of Historic Places (NRHP) Inventory Nomination Form, "Elkins Milling Company," Section 8, 4.
633. NRHP Form, "Elkins Milling Company," Section 7, 1.
634. NRHP Inventory Nomination Form, "Elkins Milling Company," Section 7, 1.

635. William H Rice, Citizens for Historical Opportunity, Preservation, and Education, "Historical Notes on the Elkins Milling Company and the Darden Mill," http://www.c-hopewv.org/millhistory.htm.
636. Friends of Blackwater, "Henry Gassaway Davis," achttps://saveblackwater.org/henry-gassaway-davis/.
637. Friends of Blackwater, "Henry Gassaway Davis."
638. Elkins-Randolph County Tourism, "Elkins, West Virginia," https://elkinsrandolphwv.com/place/elkins-west-virginia/.
639. Rice, "Historical Notes on the Elkins Milling Company and the Darden Mill."
640. Gluesem, "Darden Mill," https://www.gluseum.com/US/Elkins/134996249860681/Darden-Mill.
641. West Virginia Rail Museum, "Oral History Project," https://wvrailmuseum.com/.
642. Michael Snyder, *Show Time Magazine, Charleston Gazette-Mail*, "The Old Mill at Harman," August 10, 1980.
643. Randolph County, WV Deed Book X, 38-39.
644. Randolph County, WV Deed Book 62, 22-24.
645. Find a Grave Index, "Gertrude Cunningham," https://www.findagrave.com/memorial/85761012/gertrude-cunningham.
646. Find a Grave Index, "Solomon Cunningham," https://www.findagrave.com/memorial/85761604/solomon-cunningham.
647. The National Archives at Washington, D.C.; Washington, D.C.; NAI Title: *U.S., Civil War Pension Index: General Index to Pension Files, 1861-1934*; NAI Number: *T288*; Record Group Title: *Records of the Department of Veterans Affairs, 1773-2007*; Record Group Number: *15*; Series Title: *U.S., Civil War Pension Index: General Index to Pension Files, 1861-1934*; Series Number: *T288*; Roll: *115*
648. Find a Grave Index, "Aaron H. Day," https://www.findagrave.com/memorial/106916206/aaron-h.-day.
649. United States Federal Census Year: *1920*; Census Place: *Dry Fork, Randolph, West Virginia*; Roll: *T625_1971*; Page: *9A*; Enumeration District: *149*.

650. United States Federal Census Year: *1930*; Census Place: *Dry Fork, Randolph, West Virginia*; Page: *6A*; Enumeration District: *0007*; FHL microfilm: *2342288*.
651. Randolph County, WV Deed Book 138, 36-37.
652. United States Federal Census Year: *1940*; Census Place: *Dry Fork, Randolph, West Virginia*; Roll: *m-t0627-04444*; Page: *7B*; Enumeration District: *42-6*.
653. Randolph County, WV Deed Book 196, 480-481.
654. Bucher Fund, "Bucher Family Fund," https://www.tuckerfoundation.net/endowed-funds/grants/bucher-family-fund/.
655. Bucher Fund, "Bucher Family Fund."
656. NRHP Inventory Nomination Form, "Day-Vandevander Mill," Section 11.
657. Bucher Fund, "Bucher Family Fund."

Chapter 3 - Over the Mountains

658. Wikipedia, "Highland County, Virginia," https://en.wikipedia.org/wiki/Highland_County,_Virginia.
659. Wikipedia, "Highland County, Virginia."
660. West Virginia Encyclopedia, "Pendleton County, West Virginia," http://www.wvencyclopedia.org/articles/1832.
661. Oren Frederic Morton, *A History of Highland County, Virginia*. (Monterey, VA: Published by the Author, 1911), 400.
662. Morton, *A History of Highland County, Virginia*, 391.
663. Ancestry, *Virginia, U.S., Land, Marriage, and Probate Records, 1639-1850* [database on-line]. Provo, UT, USA: Ancestry.com Operations, Inc., 2004.
664. Find A Grave, "Jared Simmons," https://www.findagrave.com/memorial/125833258/jared-simmons.
665. Biggs, "Water-Powered Mills of the Cowpasture River Valley," op. cit.

666. Virginia Heritage, "A Guide to the Grain and Flour Bags Collection, 19th – 20th Century," https://ead.lib.virginia.edu/vivaxtf/view?docId=fcpl/vif00057.xml.
667. United States Federal Census Year: *1850*; Census Place: *Rockingham, Virginia*; Roll: *974*; Page: *31b*.
668. United States Federal Census Year: *1860*; Census Place: *Pendleton, Virginia*; Page: *32*.
669. Ancestry, "Marietta E. Puffenbarger," accessed on September 2, 2021; https://www.ancestry.com/family-tree/person/tree/104612788/person/340039815548/facts?_phsrc=bMR5410&_phstart=successSource.
670. United States Federal Census Year: *1870*; Census Place: *Sugar Grove, Pendleton, West Virginia*; Roll: *M593_1697*; Page: *431B*.
671. United States Federal Census Year: *1870*; Census Place: *Weston, Lewis, West Virginia*; Roll: *M593_1691*; Page: *384B*.
672. Virginia Heritage, "A Guide to the Grain and Flour Bags Collection."
673. United States Federal Census Year: *1880;* Census Place: *Stonewall, Highland, Virginia;* Archive Collection Number: *T1132;* Roll: *31;* Line: *1;* Schedule Type: *Industry*.
674. United States Federal Census 1880.
675. United States Federal Census 1880.
676. Highland County Virginia, "History," http://www.highlandcova.org/Compplan/History.htm.
677. Find A Grave, "James H. Simmons," https://www.findagrave.com/memorial/123132052/james-h-simmons.
678. Find A Grave, "James H. Simmons."
679. Virginia Heritage, "A Guide to the Grain and Flour Bags Collection."
680. Nelson Simmons, in discussion with author, November 2020.
681. Lorraine White, "The New Hampden Mill (Blue Grass, Virginia): A Case Study," 2006, 9-10.
682. White, "The New Hampden Mill," 7.
683. White, "The New Hampden Mill," 8.
684. White, "The New Hampden Mill," 9.

685. Kathy Hanks, *The Hutchinson News*, "Bill Rexroad was a man of many talents," https://www.hutchnews.com/article/20140506/News/305069885.
686. Wikitree, "Johann Zacharias 'Johannes' (Rexrode) Rexroth (abt. 1724-1799)," https://www.wikitree.com/wiki/Rexrode-33.
687. Wikitree, "Johann Zacharias 'Johannes' (Rexrode) Rexroth."
688. Wikitree, "John Rexrode," https://www.wikitree.com/wiki/Rexroad-49.
689. Wm. D. Rexroad, *The Rexrode Mill at New Hampden, Virginia: A History* (Hutchinson, KS: Dolphin Publications, 2008), 11.
690. Rexroad, *The Rexrode Mill at New Hampden, Virginia*, 11.
691. White, "The New Hampden Mill," 6.
692. Rexroad, *The Rexrode Mill at New Hampden, Virginia*, 31.
693. White, "The New Hampden Mill," 6.
694. Rexroad, *The Rexrode Mill at New Hampden, Virginia*, 11.
695. Rexroad, *The Rexrode Mill at New Hampden, Virginia*, 23.
696. Rexroad, *The Rexrode Mill at New Hampden, Virginia*, 12.
697. Ancestry, *U.S., World War I Draft Registration Cards, 1917-1918* [database on-line]. Provo, UT, USA: Ancestry.com Operations Inc, 2005, https://www.ancestry.com/imageviewer/collections/6482/images/005153809_02273?treeid=.
698. Rexroad, *The Rexrode Mill at New Hampden, Virginia*, 18.
699. Ancestry, "Daniel Webster "Dan" Kiser Jr.," https://www.ancestry.com/family-tree/person/tree/10258652/person/122261521843/facts.
700. Rexroad, *The Rexrode Mill at New Hampden, Virginia*, 12.
701. Rexroad, *The Rexrode Mill at New Hampden, Virginia*, 28.
702. Rexroad, *The Rexrode Mill at New Hampden, Virginia*, 19.
703. Rexroad, *The Rexrode Mill at New Hampden, Virginia*, 19.
704. White, "The New Hampden Mill," 9.
705. Rexroad, *The Rexrode Mill at New Hampden, Virginia*, 31.
706. "New Hampden Mill DHR Appeal," https://www.youtube.com/watch?v=USQKT0VcvDU&t=187s.
707. "New Hampden Mill DHR Appeal."

708. DHR Virginia Department of Historic Resources, "Rehabilitation Tax Credits Frequently Asked Questions," https://www.dhr.virginia.gov/tax-credits/rehabilitation-tax-credits-frequently-asked-questions/#A.
709. Preservation Alliance of West Virginia, "Historic Rehabilitation Tax Credit in West Virginia," https://www.pawv.org/historic-rehabilitation-tax-credits.html.

Chapter 4 - New River / Greenbrier Valley

710. *West Virginia Explorer Magazine*, "New River Gorge Region."
711. National Park Service, "Geology of New River Gorge."
712. *West Virginia Explorer Magazine*, "Greenbrier Valley Region," https://wvexplorer.com/communities/regions/greenbrier-valley-region/.
713. Three Railroads, "National Coal Heritage Area and Coal Heritage Trail," https://coalheritage.wv.gov/coal_history/Pages/Three-Railroads.aspx.
714. Three Railroads, "National Coal Heritage Area and Coal Heritage Trail."
715. Wikipedia, "Chesapeake and Ohio Railway," https://en.wikipedia.org/wiki/Chesapeake_and_Ohio_Railway.
716. Wikipedia, "Chesapeake and Ohio Railway."
717. Three Railroads, "Quinnimont," http://newriversub.8m.net/pages/Quinnimont.html.
718. Coal Campus USA, "Layland, WV, and Laurel Creek Mines," http://www.coalcampusa.com/sowv/river/layland/layland.htm.
719. Three Railroads, "Quinnimont."
720. Shunpiking to Heaven Backroads Blog, "The Cotton Hill Mill of West Virginia," https://shunpikingtoheaven.blogspot.com/2010/09/cotton-hill-mill-of-west-virginia.html.
721. David Ball, in discussion with author, May 2021.
722. Wikipedia, "Francis turbine," https://en.wikipedia.org/wiki/Francis_turbine.

723. Vintage Machinery, "Isaac Straub & Co.," http://www.vintagemachinery.org/mfgindex/detail.aspx?id=2161.
724. Smokestak Antique Engine Community, "Queen of the South," https://www.smokstak.com/forum/threads/queen-of-the-south-grist-mill.77372/.
725. Jullie Hattier, in discussion with author, January 2021.
726. West Virginia Public Broadcasting, "New River Gorge to be designated as a National Park," https://www.wvpublic.org/government/2020-12-22/new-river-gorge-to-be-designated-as-a-national-park#:~.
727. West Virginia Tourism, "Glade Creek Grist Mill: Babcock's World Class Attraction," https://wvstateparks.com/glade-creek-grist-mill-babcock/.
728. *Glade Creek Grist Mill* pamphlet published by Babcock State Park.
729. *Glade Creek Grist Mill* pamphlet.
730. Hazen, "A History of the Fitz Water Wheel Company."
731. Hazen, "A History of the Fitz Water Wheel Company."
732. Cook's Old Mill at Greenville, West Virginia, "Cook's Old Mill," http://www.cooksoldmill.com.
733. Oren Frederic Morton, *A History of Monroe County, West Virginia*, (Staunton, VA: The McClure Company, Publishers, 1916), 285.
734. Fred Ziegler, email to the author dated July 25, 2021.
735. Fred Ziegler email.
736. Fred Ziegler, *The Settlement of The Greater Greenbrier Valley, West Virginia*. (Charleston, WV: 35th Star Publishing, 2019), 104.
737. Ziegler, *The Settlement of the Greater Greenbrier Valley*, 104.
738. Wikipedia, "Cornstalk," https://en.wikipedia.org/wiki/Cornstalk.
739. Ancestry, "Sons of the American Revolution Membership Application of James Bolton McBurney," Ancestry.com. *U.S., Sons of the American Revolution Membership Applications, 1889-1970* [database on-line]. Provo, UT, USA: Ancestry.com Operations, Inc., 2011.
740. Legget/Smith Family Papers, "Valentine Cook, Captain," https://gregliggett.com/tng/showmedia.php?mediaID=442&medialinkID=697.

741. Ibid.
742. Shawn W. Cockerell, Kristen K. de Graauw, Alfred M. Ziegler, and Amy E. Hessl, "Precision dating of Cook's Mill, a Civil War era structure in West Virginia," *Dendrochronologia*, Vol. 43, April 2017, 20-26.
743. Cook's Old Mill at Greenville, West Virginia, "Ownership—1797 to 2008," http://cooksoldmill.com/text/enthus-ownership-record.html.
744. Cook's Old Mill at Greenville, West Virginia, "Ownership—1797 to 2008."
745. Polk, *West Virginia Gazetteer and business directory for 1891-1892*, 188.
746. Cook's Old Mill at Greenville, West Virginia, "Ownership—1797 to 2008."
747. Cook's Old Mill at Greenville, West Virginia, "Ownership—1797 to 2008."
748. Cook's Old Mill at Greenville, West Virginia online, "Mill Area and History," http://www.cooksoldmill.com/text/general.html.
749. Wikipedia, "Allegheny Front," https://en.wikipedia.org/wiki/Allegheny_Front.
750. Mustain and Gioulis, "Comprehensive Historic Resource Survey of Second Creek," 8.
751. Mustain and Gioulis, "Comprehensive Historic Resource Survey of Second Creek," 9.
752. Vernessa Pontius, email to author dated November 9, 2020.
753. Mustain and Gioulis, "Comprehensive Historic Resource Survey of Second Creek," 25.
754. Morton, *A History of Monroe County, West Virginia*, 303.
755. Morton, *A History of Monroe County, West Virginia*, 302-303.
756. Morton, *A History of Monroe County, West Virginia*, 302-303.
757. Morton, *A History of Monroe County, West Virginia*, 87.
758. Alcock, "What Genealogists should know about 18th Century Virginia Law."
759. Larry Mustain, in discussion with author, September 2021.

760. Mustain and Gioulis, "Comprehensive Historic Resource Survey of Second Creek," 15.
761. Pontius email.
762. Joe Nickell, "The History of the Nickell Family with supplementary information by Milton Cox Nickell." (Hazel Green, KY: 1952), 4.
763. Nickell, "The History of the Nickell Family," 5-6.
764. Nickell, "The History of the Nickell Family," 5.
765. Pontius email.
766. National Register of Historic Places (NRHP) Inventory Nomination Form, "Nickell Homestead and Mill," Section 8, 1.
767. Pontius email.
768. NRHP Form, "Nickell Homestead and Mill," Section 8, 1.
769. Pontius email.
770. NRHP Form, "Nickell Homestead and Mill," Section 8, 1.
771. Pontius email.
772. Polk, *West Virginia Gazetteer and business directory for 1904-1905*, 551.
773. United States Federal Census Year: *1850*; Census Place: *District 39, Monroe, Virginia*; Roll: *961*; Page: *466b*.
774. United States Federal Census Year: *1860*; Census Place: *Monroe, Virginia*; Page: *997*.
775. United States Federal Census Year: *1870*; Census Place: *Second Creek, Monroe, West Virginia*; Roll: *M593_1695*; Page: *13B*.
776. Monroe County, WV Will Book 5, 386-387.
777. United States Federal Census Year: *1880*; Census Place: *Second Creek, Monroe, West Virginia*; Roll: *1409*; Page: *381C*; Enumeration District: *086*.
778. J. R. Cole, *History of Greenbrier County, Illustrated*, (Lewisburg, WV: Published by the Author, 1917), 93.
779. Pontius email.
780. United States Federal Census Year: *1920*; Census Place: *Irish Corner, Greenbrier, West Virginia*; Roll: *T625_1953*; Page: *7A*; Enumeration District: *54*.

781. United States Federal Census Year: *1930*; Census Place: *Irish Corner, Greenbrier, West Virginia*; Page: *17B*; Enumeration District: *0013*; FHL microfilm: *2342266*.
782. United States Federal Census Year: *1940*; Census Place: *Irish Corner, Greenbrier, West Virginia*; Roll: *m-t0627-04404*; Page: *21A*; Enumeration District: *13-15*.
783. Pontius email.
784. Mustain, July 2021.
785. *Driving Back Roads*, "Zenith: A Hidden West Virginia Treasure," http://drivingbackroads.com/2020/05/11/zenith-a-hidden-west-virginia-treasure/.
786. Pontius email.
787. Pontius email.
788. Pontius email.
789. Mike Jackson, *The Journal of the American Institute of Architects*, "Block by Block: The History of CMUs, a Construction Staple," https://www.architectmagazine.com/technology/block-by-block-the-history-of-cmus-a-construction-staple_o.
790. United States Federal Census Year: *1870*; Census Place: *Sweet Springs, Monroe, West Virginia*; Roll: *M593_1695*; Page: *49B*.
791. Find A Grave, "Augustus Ballantyne Beamer," https://www.findagrave.com/memorial/6228730/augustus-ballantyne-beamer.
792. Ancestry.com. *U.S., College Student Lists, 1763-1924* [database online]. Provo, UT, USA: Ancestry.com Operations, Inc., 2012.
793. *The Centennial History of the Associate Reformed Presbyterian Church, 1803-1903, Prepared and Published by order of the Synod.* (Charleston, SC: Walker, Evans & Cogwell Co., 1905), 173.
794. United States Federal Census Year: *1860*; Census Place: *Monroe, Virginia*; Page: *1017*.
795. United States Federal Census Year: *1870*; Census Place: *Second Creek, Monroe, West Virginia*; Roll: *M593_1695*; Page: *17A*.
796. National Archives and Records Administration, Washington, D.C.; *Record of Appointment of Postmasters, 1832-Sept. 30, 1971*; Roll #: *140*; Archive Publication #: *M841*.

797. United States Federal Census Year: *1900*; Census Place: *Sweet Springs, Monroe, West Virginia*; Page: *11*; Enumeration District: *0098*; FHL microfilm: *1241767*.
798. *Find A Grave Index, 1600s-Current* [database on-line]. Provo, UT, USA: Ancestry.com Operations, Inc., 2012.
799. Polk, *West Virginia Gazetteer and business directory for 1891-1892*, 418.
800. United States Federal Census Year: *1870*; Census Place: *Sweet Springs, Monroe, West Virginia*; Roll: *M593_1695*; Page: *49B*.
801. United States Federal Census Year: *1900*; Census Place: *Sweet Springs, Monroe, West Virginia*; Page: *11*; Enumeration District: *0098*; FHL microfilm: *1241767*.
802. Polk, *West Virginia Gazetteer and business directory for 1900-1901*, 592.
803. Polk, *West Virginia Gazetteer and business directory for 1904-1905*, 897.
804. Polk, *West Virginia Gazetteer and business directory for 1904-1905*, 897.
805. United States Federal Census Year: *1910*; Census Place: *Sweet Springs, Monroe, West Virginia*; Roll: *T624_1690*; Page: *14B*; Enumeration District: *0102*; FHL microfilm: *1375703*.
806. Monroe County, WV Deed Book 57, 391.
807. Dr. Greg Ware, email to author dated September 8, 2021.
808. United States Federal Census Year: 1940; Census Place: Sweet Springs, Monroe, West Virginia; Roll: T627_4434; Page: 15A; Enumeration District: 32-8.
809. United States Federal Census Year: *1940*; Census Place: *Sweet Springs, Monroe, West Virginia*; Roll: *m-t0627-04434*; Page: *1A*; Enumeration District: *32-7*.
810. Find a Grave, "Clarence Napoleon Shires," https://www.findagrave.com/memorial/5359737/clarence-napoleon-shires.
811. Monroe County, WV Deed Book 121, 87-90.
812. Monroe County, WV Deed Book 261, 427.
813. Funeral, "Georgia Obituaries: Mary Ware," https://georgia.funeral.com/2014/04/24/mary-ware/.

814. Driving Back Roads, "Zenith a Hidden West Virginia Treasure."
815. West Virginia Department of Environmental Protection, "Second Creek Watershed Based Plan," https://dep.wv.gov/WWE/Programs/nonptsource/WBP/Pages/WBP.aspx.
816. West Virginia Department of Environmental Protection, "Second Creek Watershed Based Plan."
817. National Register of Historic Places Inventory Nomination Form, "Reed's Mill," Section 8, 3.
818. Morton, *A History of Monroe County, West Virginia*, 427.
819. Monroe County, WV Will Book 1-2, 232-233.
820. Morton, *A History of Monroe County, West Virginia*, 396.
821. NRHP Inventory Nomination Form, "Reed's Mill," op. cit., Section 8, 2.
822. My Farm Life, "The Best Varieties of Heirloom Corn," https://findanyanswer.com/goto/530010.
823. Roxy Todd, *Charleston Gazette-Mail*, "Monroe farm still mills Bloody Butcher corn," https://www.wvgazettemail.com/life/monroe-farm-still-mills-bloody-butcher-corn/article_02ef433e-a67a-57c9-b83d-086e9be693be.html.
824. Driving Back Roads, "Reed's Mill Second Creek, WV," http://drivingbackroads.com/2021/06/01/reeds-mill-second-creek-wv/.
825. Driving Back Roads, "Reed's Mill Second Creek."
826. Preservation Alliance of West Virginia, "Endangered Properties List: Reed's Mill," https://pawv.org/endanger/reeds-mill.
827. NRHP Inventory Nomination Form, "Reed's Mill," Section 8, 2.
828. Todd, "Monroe farm still mills Bloody Butcher corn."
829. Jessica Farrish, *Beckley Register-Herald*, "Beckley's old mill still offers hope for economic development," https://www.register-herald.com/news/beckley-s-old-mill-still-offers-hope-for-economic-development/article_623f0d16-3cca-57a3-81d1-62ddbfdecba9.html.
830. Rick Steelhammer, *Charleston Gazette-Mail*, "Beckley group seeks National Register status for 1838 mill operated by town's founder," https://www.wvgazettemail.com/news/beckley-group-

seeks-national-register-status-for-1838-mill-operated-by-town-s-founder/article_e44264bf-1fd3-535f-85e0-4a21394ec359.html.
831. Farrish, "Beckley's old mill still offers hope for economic development."
832. Wiki 2, Wikipedia Republished, "National Register of Historic Places in Raleigh County, West Virginia," https://wiki2.org/en/National_Register_of_Historic_Places_listings_in_Raleigh_County,_West_Virginia.
833. Farrish, "Beckley's old mill still offers hope for economic development."
834. Steelhammer, "Beckley group seeks National Register status for 1838 mill operated by town's founder."
835. West Virginia Explorer Magazine, "Alfred Beckley Mill," https://wvexplorer.com/attractions/historic-landmarks/alfred-beckley-mill//.
836. *Friends of Cooper's Mill* pamphlet, published by Friends of Cooper's Mill, Inc.
837. *Friends of Cooper's Mill* pamphlet, published by Friends of Cooper's Mill, Inc.
838. *Friends of Cooper's Mill* pamphlet.
839. National Register of Historic Places Inventory Nomination Form, "Cooper's Mill," Section 7, 1.
840. *Friends of Cooper's Mill* pamphlet.
841. NRHP Inventory Nomination Form, "Cooper's Mill," Section 7, 1.
842. NRHP Inventory Nomination Form, "Cooper's Mill," Section 7, 1.

Chapter 5 - Mountain Lakes

843. West Virginia Department of Arts, Culture, and History, "Mountain Lakes," http://www.wvculture.org/arts/ethnic/mountainlake.html.

844. West Virginia Encyclopedia, "Nicholas County," http://www.wvencyclopedia.org/articles/1670.
845. West Virginia Tourism, "Lakes and Lighthouses Galore in the Heart of West Virginia," https://wvtourism.com/lakes-lighthouses-road-trip/.
846. Ruth Woods Dayton, *Greenbrier Pioneers and Their Homes*, (Baltimore, MD: Clearfield Co, Inc./Genealogical Publishing Company, 2009), 293.
847. Rootsweb, "Grinding at Blaker's Mill," http://sites.rootsweb.com/~hcpd/Tour/blaker.htm.
848. United States Federal Census Year: *1850;* Census Place: *District 18, Greenbrier, Virginia;* Roll: *947;* Page: *255a.*
849. United States Federal Census Year: *1860;* Census Place: *District 2, Greenbrier, Virginia;* Page: *400.*
850. United States Federal Census Year: *1870;* Census Place: *Blue Sulphur, Greenbrier, West Virginia;* Roll: *M593_1687;* Page: *333A.*
851. United States Federal Census Year: *1880;* Census Place: *Blue Sulphur, Greenbrier, West Virginia;* Roll: *1402;* Page: *279D;* Enumeration District: *032.*
852. Wikipedia, "Blaker's Mill," https://en.wikipedia.org/wiki/Blaker_Mills,_West_Virginia#/media/File:Blakers_Mill.jpg.
853. Rootsweb, "Grinding at Blaker's Mill."
854. Wikipedia, "Blaker's Mill."
855. Conversation with Dean Harden June 28, 2020.
856. West Virginia University, "Jackson's Mill," https://jacksonsmill.wvu.edu/heritage-education.
857. West Virginia University, "Jackson's Mill."
858. Wikipedia, "Randolph County, West Virginia," https://en.wikipedia.org/wiki/Randolph_County,_West_Virginia.
859. Geni, "Col. Edward Jackson (1759-1828)," https://www.geni.com/people/Col-Edward-Jackson/6000000001445695907.
860. National Register of Historic Places (NRHP) Inventory Nomination Form, "Jackson's Mill," Section 7, 1.
861. Wikipedia, "Jackson's Mill," https://en.wikipedia.org/wiki/Jackson%27s_Mill.

862. Jackson Brigade, http://www.jacksonbrigade.com/genealogy-of-john-jackson/col-edward-jackson/.
863. West Virginia University, "Jackson's Mill."
864. West Virginia University, "Jackson's Mill."
865. Encyclopedia Virginia, "Jackson, Thomas J. 'Stonewall,' (1824-1863)" https://encyclopediavirginia.org/entries/jackson-thomas-j-stonewall-1824-1863/.
866. West Virginia Encyclopedia, "Jackson's Mill," https://www.geni.com/people/Col-Edward-Jackson/6000000001445695907.
867. Find A Grave, "James Madison Jackson, https://www.findagrave.com/memorial/100444997/james-madison-jackson.
868. Polk, *West Virginia Gazetteer and business directory for 1882-1883*, 206.
869. Polk, *West Virginia Gazetteer and business directory for 1891-1892*, 219.
870. Polk, *West Virginia Gazetteer and business directory for 1900-1901*, 270.
871. Polk, *West Virginia Gazetteer and business directory for 1904-1905*, 409.
872. Polk, *West Virginia Gazetteer and business directory for 1904-1905*, 409.
873. NRHP Form, "Jackson's Mill," Section 7, 1.
874. NRHP Form, "Beaver Mill," Section 8, 4.
875. NRHP Form, "Beaver Mill," Section 7, 4.
876. NRHP Form, "Beaver Mill," Section 8, 3.
877. Living Places, https://www.livingplaces.com/WV/Wood_County/Parkersburg_City.html.
878. WikiTree, "William McClung (1738-1833)," https://www.wikitree.com/wiki/McClung-5.
879. NRHP Form, "Beaver Mill," Section 8, 5.
880. NRHP Form, "Beaver Mill," Section 8, 3.
881. Find A Grave, "Col. George Alderson (1789-1871)," https://www.findagrave.com/memorial/199915514/george-alderson.
882. National Register of Historic Places (NRHP) Inventory Nomination Form, "Fidler's Mill," Section 7, 2.

883. NRHP Form, "Fidler's Mill," Section 7, 2.
884. United States Federal Census Year: *1870*; Census Place: *Banks, Upshur, West Virginia*; Roll: *M593_1700*; Page: *350A*.
885. United States Federal Census Year: *1900*; Census Place: *Salt Lick, Braxton, West Virginia*; Page: *12*; Enumeration District: *0009*; FHL microfilm: *1241756*.
886. United States Federal Census Year: *1920*; Census Place: *Banks, Upshur, West Virginia*; Roll: *T625_1968*; Page: *9B*; Enumeration District: *130*.
887. NRHP Form, "Fidler's Mill," Section 8, 2.
888. Marie Mollohan, *By the Banks of the Holly*: *Notes and Letters from the Desk of Bernard Mollohan*, (Lincoln, NE: iUniverse Publishing, 2005), 389.
889. National Register of Historic Places (NRHP) Inventory Nomination Form, "Mollohan Mill," Section 8, 1.
890. Ancestry, "Original Land Grant George Mollohan," https://www.ancestry.com/mediaui-viewer/tree/30809420/person/27351501943/media/2b66966b-2b85-41af-abf2-2e89364e5d75?_phsrc=bMR4338&_phstart=successSource.
891. Lucullus Virgil McWhorter, William Elsey Connelley, and John Patterson McLean, *The Border Settlers of Northwestern Virginia from 1768 to 1795*, (BiblioBazaar, 2016), 189.
892. Ancestry, "James Mollohan Will & Family Story," https://www.ancestry.com/mediaui-viewer/tree/5683901/person/-1267944486/media/43c47953-ae64-459e-a99e-fb93ad731065?_phsrc=bMR4344&_phstart=successSource.
893. Mollohan, *By the Banks of the Holly*, 464-466.
894. Mollohan, *By the Banks of the Holly*, 407.
895. Mollohan, *By the Banks of the Holly*, 198.
896. Mollohan, *By the Banks of the Holly*, 432.
897. Mollohan, *By the Banks of the Holly*, 387.
898. Mollohan, *By the Banks of the Holly*, 418.
899. Mollohan, *By the Banks of the Holly*, 408.
900. Mollohan, *By the Banks of the Holly*, 418.
901. Mollohan, *By the Banks of the Holly*, 417.

902. Mollohan, *By the Banks of the Holly*, 439.

Chapter 6 - Mountaineer Country

903. West Virginia Encyclopedia, "Monongalia County," http://www.wvencyclopedia.org/articles/2022.
904. Monongalia Historical Society, "Grist Mill," http://www.monongaliahistoricalsociety.org/grist-mill.html.
905. Norma Jean Venable, *Easton Roller Mill, Morgantown, West Virginia*. (Morgantown, WV: Published by the Monongalia Historical Society, 1994), 12.
906. United States Federal Census Year: *1880*; Census Place: *Bethel, Clark, Ohio*; Roll: *998*; Page: *4D*; Enumeration District: *034*.
907. United States Federal Census Year: *1900*; Census Place: *Bethel, Clark, Ohio*; Page: *6*; Enumeration District: *0002*; FHL microfilm: *1241245*.
908. United States Federal Census Year: *1910*; Census Place: *Bethel, Clark, Ohio*; Roll: *T624_1158*; Page: *6B*; Enumeration District: *0003*; FHL microfilm: *1375171*.
909. Danielle L. Hogan, *Easton: The Rise and Fall of a Community* (Morgantown, WV: Published by the Monongalia Historical Society, 1999), 4.
910. Hogan, *Easton: The Rise and Fall of a Community*, 6.
911. Hogan, *Easton: The Rise and Fall of a Community*, 6.
912. United States Federal Census Year: *1880*; Census Place: *Union, Monongalia, West Virginia*; Roll: *1409*; Page: *245C*; Enumeration District: *097*.
913. Venable, *Easton Roller Mill*, 12.
914. Polk, *West Virginia Gazeteer and business directory for 1882-83*, 137.
915. Venable, *Easton Roller Mill*, 12.
916. National Register of Historic Places (NRHP) Inventory Nomination Form, "Easton Roller Mill," Section 8, 3.
917. Venable, *Easton Roller Mill*, 12.
918. Venable, *Easton Roller Mill*, 13.
919. NRHP Form, "Easton Roller Mill," Section 8, 3.
920. Venable, *Easton Roller Mill*, 13.

921. United States Federal Census Year: *1920*; Census Place: *Morgan, Monongalia, West Virginia*; Roll: *T625_1964*; Page: *12B*; Enumeration District: *101*.

922. United States Federal Census Year: *1930;* Census Place: *Morgan, Monongalia, West Virginia;* Page: *17B;* Enumeration District: *0032;* FHL microfilm: *2342282*.

923. Venable, *Easton Roller Mill,* 13.

924. United States Federal Census Year: *1930;* Census Place: *Morgantown, Monongalia, West Virginia;* Page: *15A;* Enumeration District: *0021;* FHL microfilm: *2342282*.

925. Venable, *Easton Roller Mill,* 13.

926. United States Federal Census Year: *1940*; Census Place: *Morgan, Monongalia, West Virginia*; Roll: *m-t0627-04433*; Page: *11B*; Enumeration District: *31-34B*.

927. NRHP Form, "Easton Roller Mill," 2.

928. Venable, *Easton Roller Mill,* 23.

929. "Now...and Long Ago," Preston County Historical Society Newsletter, Fall 2012, 1.

930. Ancestry, "1801 Monongalia County Petition for a Mill Road," https://www.ancestry.com/mediaui-viewer/tree/1507597/person/-1789991534/media/79e2348c-60f7-48b2-b2a8-3d681c66a084?_phsrc=bMR4419&_phstart=successSource.

931. Janice Cole Sisler, "Hazlett Memories," [unpublished manuscript], 2-3.

932. Sisler, "Hazlett Memories," 3.

933. Polk, *West Virginia Gazetteer and business directory for 1891-1892*, 196.

934. United States Federal Census Year: *1900;* Census Place: *Grant, Preston, West Virginia;* Page: *4;* Enumeration District: *0100;* FHL microfilm: *1241770*.

935. Polk, *West Virginia Gazetteer and business directory for 1904 Vol. I,* 358.

936. United States Federal Census Year: 1930; Census Place: Portland, Preston, West Virginia; Roll: 2552; Page: 16A; Enumeration District: 0015; Image: 71.0; FHL microfilm: 2342286.

937. Carl. E. Feather, West Virginia Culture, "The Buckwheat Stops Here: Preston County's Hazelton Mill," http://www.wvculture.org/goldenseal/Fall13/buckwheat.html.
938. Preston County Buckwheat Festival, "History of the Preston County Buckwheat Festival," https://kvfdwv.wixsite.com/buckwheatfest/history.
939. Visit Mountaineer Country, "Preston County Buckwheat Festival."
940. Feather, "The Buckwheat Stops Here: Preston County's Hazelton Mill,"
941. Theresa Marthey, *Exponent Telegram*, "Buckwheat Festival is a 78-year tradition in Preston County," *https://www.wvnews.com/theet/news/buckwheat-festival-is-a-78-year-tradition-in-preston-county/article_6fe68b3d-78bd-599e-bb0d-699ad74742dc.html.*
942. Ellen Ficklen, *The Washington Post*, "Milling Around," https://www.washingtonpost.com/archive/lifestyle/1991/07/26/milling-around/d39a03c4-1fe8-4c9e-98a3-4cb56f17d9e2/.

Chapter 7 - Northern Panhandle

943. West Virginia Encyclopedia, "Northern Panhandle."
944. National Register of Historic Places (NRHP) Inventory Nomination Form, "Reed's Mill," Section 8, 2.
945. NRHP Form, "Shepherd's Mill," Section 8.
946. Ancestry, "Wills, 1777-1947; Index to Wills, 1777-1971," West Virginia County Court (Ohio County); Probate Place: Ohio, West Virginia.
947. US Federal Census Year: *1880*; Census Place: *Liberty, Ohio, West Virginia*; Roll: *1411*; Page: *500C*; Enumeration District: *213*.
948. United States Federal Census Year: *1900*; Census Place: *Cambridge Ward 2, Guernsey, Ohio*; Page: *2*; Enumeration District: *0005*; FHL microfilm: *1241273*.

949. United States Federal Census Year: *1910*; Census Place: Zanesville Ward 2, Muskingum, Ohio; Roll: *T624_1221*; Page: *6B*; Enumeration District: *0093*; FHL microfilm: *1375234*.
950. United States Federal Census Year: *1920*; Census Place: *Columbus Ward 5, Franklin, Ohio*; Roll: *T625_1381*; Page: *2B*; Enumeration District: *105*.
951. *The Roller Mill*, E.L. Burdick & Co. 1897, Vol. 16, 640, https://books.google.com/books?id=OBMVAQAAMAAJ&pg=PA623&source=gbs_toc_r&cad=4#v=onepage&q&f=false
952. *The Roller Mill*, 640.

Conclusion

953. William A. Breyfogle, *Wagon Wheels: A Story of the National Road* (New York: Aladdin Books, 1956), p. 149.

Index

A

Adamson, G. W. 262
Adamson, John R. 262
Adamson, Joseph 262
Adamson, William 274
Aiken, Leonidas 189
Ailes, Helen W. 81
Ailes, Stephen 81
Ailes, Walter 80
Alderson, Col. George 395
Alderson, George Henry Clay 395
Alt, Squire H. A. 161, 162
A. M. SNIDER MILL 201
Anderson, Colbert 84
Anderson, Colbert III 84
Anderson, Colbert Jr. 84
Anderson, Thomas 84
Anderson, Tom 417
Anderson, William 417
Anderson, William B. 239
ANTIOCH MILL 205
Ardinger, Joseph Thornton Van Lear 97
Ardinger, Thomas 97
Arehart, W. H. 160

Arthur, William D. 425
Augusta Milling Company 179
Auxer, Jim 149
Aylor, Ava Leatherman 198

B

Baldwin, Homer P. 198
Baldwin, William Henry 198
Ballard, John 354
Ball, David 327, 328, 329
Ball, Emma Fry 327, 328, 329
Ball, Oscar Preston (O. P.) 327, 328, 329
Ball, Sally 328
Ball, T. J. 329
Barnwood Builders 350
Baughman, Jacob 341
Baughman, Margarita Schwizler 341
Beamer, Rev. Augustus Ballantyne 354, 355, 359
Beamer, Romanza Miller (Mrs. R. S.) 355
Beamer, Romanza Silstine Miller (Mrs. R. S.) 354, 355
Bean's Mill 197
BEAVER MILL 393
Beckley, Alfred 368
Beckley, John 369
Beckley, John James 368
BECKLEY MILL RUINS 367
Bedinger, Capt. Henry 78
Bedinger, Henry 84, 145
Bedinger, Maj. Henry 79, 80
BEDINGER MILL 77
Bedinger, Sarah 80
Bedington 84
Beeler, Benjamin 126
Beeler, Christopher 126
BEELER'S MILL 125
Beeson, Edward 96, 119
Beeson, Richard Sr. 96
Bender, Americus 102
Bender, Henry 101, 102
Bender, Peter 102

Bender, Rebecca 102
Bender, Rebecca Doyle 101, 102
Bennett, Elijah 225
Bennett, Elizabeth 225
Bennett, Moses 225
Berg, Pearl 211
Berkel, Kandise 206
Berkel, Larry 206
Billmeyer, D. W. 207
Billmeyer, James 207
Birnbach, Sheila 127
Blaker, Elizabeth Susan Lewis 382
Blaker, Ida Florence 382
Blaker, James 382
Blaker, John A. 382
Blaker Jr., Robert Hockman 382
Blaker, Mamie Frances 382
BLAKER'S MILL 381
Blaker, Susie Alice 382
Bloomery Mill 110
BLOOMERY MILL 169
Blunt, Major Harry 140, 141
Bodkin (Botkin), John 306
Boggs, Aaron 218, 262
Boggs, Aaron Carr 222, 262
Boggs, Captain John 200
Boggs, Charles 218
Boggs, Edward W. 247
Boggs, Elizabeth Carr 218, 222
Boggs, Frank 222
Boggs, Gen. James 218, 247
Boggs Jr., John 218, 221
Boggs, Jr., John 219
Boggs, Margaret 218
BOGGS MILL 217
Boggs, Mrs. Mason 270
Boggs, Ona 222
Boggs Sr., John 218
Boggs, Sr., John 218
Boggs, William Harrison 247
Bonar, Charles 162
Boreman, Governor Arthur 238
Boteler, Alexander 140

Boteler, Dr. Henry 139, 140
Botkin, Capt. John 306
Botkin II, John 306
Botkin, John A. 307
Botkin, Joseph 306
BOTKIN-SIMMONS MILL 305
Bowers, Bill 253
Bowers, Erma Hoover 243
Bowers, Louise 222
Bowers, Roy 237, 238
Boyd, Gen. Elisha 84
Boyd, John E. 84
Braddock, Gen. Edward 173
Braddock's Trail 156
Bright, Kyle 395
Brown, Laura 213
Bryan, Morgan 73, 78
Bryarly, Henry Payne 119
Bryarly, Mrs. Mary P. 119
Bryarly, Richard 119
Bryarly, Richard Henry 119
Bryarly, Robert P. 119
Bucher, Dr. Samuel 300, 301
Bucher, Margaret 300, 301
Buckles, James 119
Buckles, Robert 119
Budris, Shirley 270
Budris, Vincent 270
Buffenbarger, Ester 228
BUNKER HILL MILL 83
Bushfield, William 434
Bushfield, William Blair 434
Bussey, John 206
Byrd, Agnes Jane Humphreys 349
Byrd, James William 229, 349
Byrd, Luther 349

C

Cackley, John 284
Cackley, Valentine 284
Calhoon, Teresa 270
Calhoon, Tom 270
Campbell, Mrs. Roy L. 270

INDEX 513

Canterbury, Aaron V. 342
Capito, Jemima 417
Capper, Meredith 185, 186
Carr Sr., Jacob 218
Carr, Sr., Jacob 218
Cassady, David 161, 162
Cassady, Elizabeth Lyon 161
Cassady, Lois Lyon 163
Cassady, William 161
Caudy, Henry "James" 173
Caudy, Henry \"James\" 171, 190
Caudy, James 171, 190
Caudy, James IV 190
Centreville Mills 342
Charlotte of Mecklenburg 144
CIRCLEVILLE MILL 223
Clarke, Eric 329
Clay, Henry 395
Cline and Chapman Roller Mill 87
Cline, Asa 185, 189
Cline, Elizabeth Spaid 185
Cline, Samuel S. 87
Clipp, T. Wilmer 127
Cofer, William 395
Combs, Alice 199
Combs, Lemuel 199
Conrad, Benjamin 408, 409
Conrad Jr., Ulrich 246
Conrad Sr., Ulrich 246
Cook, Effie Wimer 226
Cook, Isaac 226
Cook, Jacob A. 342
Cook, Riley 342
COOK'S OLD MILL 339
Cook Sr., Valentine 340, 341, 342
Cook, Susannah Baughman 341
Cooper, Elisha B. 375
Cooper, Josiah 375
COOPER'S MILL 373
Cooper, Thomas Moody 375
Cornstalk 341
COTTON HILL MILL 325
Crosier, Will 354

Croucher family 179
Croucher, J. D. 178
Croucher, Victoria 178
Cunningham, Gertie 299
Cunningham II, Mary 299
Cunningham, James 299
Cunningham, James S. 299
Cunningham, J. B. 85
Cunningham, Mary 299
Cunningham, S. B. 85
Cunningham, Solomon 299
Cushwa, Barnet 96
Cushwa, H. T. 114
Cushwa, John 96
Custer, Eric 87
Cutlip, J. K. 395

D

Dahle (Dolly), Andrew 263
Dahle, Johann "Cornyackle/Barleycorn" 262, 263
Dally, J. K. 263
Daniels, David 96
Daniel's Mill 197
DARDEN-ELKINS MILL 291
Darden, Ralph 293
Dare, Lydia 101
Darke, General William 119
Davenport, Elizabeth 80
DaVinci, Leonardo 49
Davis, Ada Spaid 190
Davis, Carson 182, 190, 191
Davis, Caudy 182, 190, 191
Davis, Charles Jr. 191
Davis, Charles Sr. 191
Davis, Guy 191
Davis, Hannah Caroline Spaid 190
Davis, Henry Gassaway 293, 294
Davis, Jesse 211
Davis, Margaret Harrison 206
Davis, Phoebe 263
Davis, Samuel B. 206
Davis, Samuel Barker 206

Davis, Thomas Beall 293
Davis, William E. 182
Day, Aaron 299
Day, David Miles 299
Day, John 160, 161
Day, Mary 299
DAY-VANDEVENDER MILL 297
Decker, Tobias 412
DeHaven family 87
Dickson, Lucille 356
Dolly, Amby 263
Dolly, Amby Harper 262, 263
Dolly, George Washington 263
Dolly, J. R. 263
Dove, Abel 224
Dove, Abraham Lincoln 224
Dove, Absalom 224
Dove, Americus 224
Dove, Jacob 224, 225
Dove, Nimrod 224, 225
Dove, William 225
Drury, Percy 133
Duke, John H. 147
Duncan, Matthew 96
Dunn, E. L. 342
DuPoy, Hannah Byrd 230
Duvall, Joseph 107
Dye, Mary Evelyn 207
Dyer, Allen 274
Dzubba, Betty 211

E

Eagle Roller Mills 161
EASTON ROLLER MILL 415
Eaton, Hattie 183
Eaton, Joseph Edward 183
Ebert, Sr., Mrs. G. H. 160
Edison, Thomas 267, 269
Eisenhower, President Dwight D. 361, 362
Elkins, Stephen 293, 294
Equality Mills 110, 113
Evans, John Daniel 425

Evans, John G. 425
Evans, Joseph Dayton 425
Evans, Oliver 33, 49, 189, 237, 327, 394
Eye, Christian 228
Eye, Robert L. 279

F

Farrell, Robert 356
Feagans, Cecil 132, 133
FEAGANS MILL 129
Feagans, Silas H. 131, 132
Feagans, Wilder Clayton 132
Feagan, Wilder Clayton 132
Ferrell, Kathleen McClung 356
Fidler, Hudson 401
Fidler, Hudson V. 400
Fidler, Russell 400
FIDLER'S MILL 399
Fidler, Valerius 400
Fidler, William 400
Fidler, William Martin 400
Fike, Harrison 425
Fike, Peter 425
Fisher, John G. 96
Fitz, John 111, 113
Fitz, John Samuel 114
Fitz, Samuel 111, 113, 114
Flesher, F. B. 388
Flesher, V. B. 388
Floory, James 259
Foltz, Samuel 173, 174
Fourneyron, Benoit 49
Fout, Mag 212, 213
Frank, Ashby 190
French, Charles 179
French, Marshall 179
FRENCH'S MILL 177
Fry, Philip 327
Fuerst, David 369

G

Gard, Samuel 190

INDEX

Gard, Sarah Caudy 190
Garvin, Cephus Newton (C. N.) 183, 184, 185
Garvin, Courtney 184
Garvin, David John 183, 184, 185
Garvin, George 184
Garvin, Margaret Spaid 184, 185
Garvin, Sarah Jane 185
Gattrel, Shepherd 147
George III, King 144
Germino, Joe 81
Giles, Janita 87
Giles, Paul 87
Girard, Minnie 295
Girard, Samuel D. 295
Glackens, Ira 149
Glackens, Nancy 149
Glackens, William 149
GLADE CREEK MILL 331
Grant, General Ulysses S. 131
Green, Robert 228
Greenville Roller Mills 342
Griffith, D. W. 190
Griscom, Walter 435
Gromer (Cromer), Frederick 347, 348, 350, 359
GROMER-NICKELL'S UPPER-RODGERS MILL 345
Gup, Ted 362

H

Hagerman's Mill 425
Haines, Abraham 130
Haines, E. B. 132
Haines, Edward B. 131
Haines, Joshua 130
Haines, Nathan 130
Hall, Charles 171
Hall's Mill 441
Hammond, Dr. Allen C. 106, 107
Hannum, Joseph 182
Hanover Foundry 111
Harden, Dean 383, 388

Harold, J. T. 239
Hartsook, Cathi 179
Hartsook, Dan 179
Hassett, Ben 274
Hattier, Julie 329
Havener, B. S. 239
Hawse, Kenneth 202
Hayes, Rutherford B. 369
HAZELTON MILL 423
Hazlett, Samuel 424, 425
Head Spring Mill 132
Hedges, Nancy Mullenax 315
Hibbard, Aaron 101
Hibbard, Mary Ann 101
Hilkey, Betty 213
Hilkey, Jacob 161, 212, 213
Hilkey, Nancy 161
Hilkey, Sarah Elmira Lyon 161
Hilkey, William 161
Hilkey, William "Billy" 212
Hiller, Robert 273, 274
Hiner Mill 257
Hite, Jost 73
Hockman, Jacob 382
Hockman, Mary Niswander 382
Hofecker, Glen 247
Hofecker, Iris 247
Hogsett, Everett 361
Hollywood Woolen Mill 360
Homan, Leafy Mitchell 229, 230
HOMAN MILL 227
Homan, Richard 230, 231, 232
Homan Sr., Virgil 229, 230
Hook, Eleanor McVicar 185
Hook, Thomas 185, 186
Hoover, Elizabeth 242
Hoover, George 242, 243
Hoover, Greg 238
Hoover/Huber, Sebastian/Bastian/Boston 228
Hoover, Jacob 228, 229, 242
Hoover Jr., William 243
Hoover, Lester 241, 242, 243

Hoover, Mary Jane Rexrode 242, 243
Hoover Mill 237
HOOVER MILL 235
Hoover, Olin 238
Hoover, Peter 228, 242
Hoover, Raymond 243
Hoover, Sebastian 242
Hoover Sr., William 242
Hoover, Virgil 243
Hoover, William 237, 239, 240, 242, 243
Hoover, William J. 242, 243
Hoover, William Jr. 243
Hoover, William W. 243
Howell, Aleatha 441
Howell, Aleathea 447
Howell, Ardell 441
Howell, Benny 441
Howell, Dan 441
Howell, Mary 93
HOWELL'S MILL 439
Howell, Winfield 441
Howell, Winfred 441
Huffman, Robyn 356
Humphreys, J. 349
Humphreys, James 342, 349
Humphreys, James W. 349
Humphreys, Mary Susan Byrd 349
Hunter, Col. David 79
Hunter, General David 131
Huntington, Collis P. 326

I

Independent Roller Mill Company 97
Ingersoll, Barbara 126, 127
Ingersoll, Tom 126, 127
Isler, Abraham 126
Isler, Sarah Beeler 126

J

Jackson, B. 387
Jackson, Col. Edward Blake 386, 387
Jackson, Cummins 386, 387
Jackson, Edward 387
Jackson, Elizabeth 386
Jackson, Gen. Thomas Jonathan "Stonewall" 107, 386, 387
Jackson, J. G. 387
Jackson, Julia Ann 386
Jackson, J. W. 387
Jackson, Laura 387
Jackson, President Andrew 246
Jackson's Mill 383
JACKSON'S MILL 385
James, Martha 133
Janney, Abel 101
Janney, Aquilla 92, 101
Janney, G. Campbell 93
Janney, George C. 93
Janney, Israel 92
Janney, John Jonas 101
Janney, John Tabb 92
Janney, Lydia Mendenhall 101
Janney, Mary Howell 93
Janney, Mary Tabb 92
JANNEY MILL 91
Janney, R. 93
Janney, Ruth 92
Jefferson, Thomas 306
Jobe, J.J. 132
John Henry 326
Johnson, Bob 396
Johnson, George 174
Johnson, Ken 174, 175
Johnson, Kenneth Glenwood 171, 173, 174
Johnson, Lee 183, 184
Johnson, William S. 184
Jourdan, Katherine M. 434

K

Kelch, Patrinka 149
Keller, Charles R. 133
Keller, Jacob 133
Kennedy, John 81

INDEX 517

Kerns, Wilmer 186
Kilburn, Jack 356
Kile, J. T. 239
Kilmer family 97
Kisamore, Adam 263
Kisamore, Margaret Dolly 263
Kiser, Barbra Wise 228
Kiser, Daniel 253
Kiser, Daniel W. 314
Kiser, David 228
Kiser, Harrison 229
Kiser, Harvey 229
Kiser, Jacob 228
Kiser, James Pleasant (Pleas) 229
Kiser Jr., John 228
Kiser, Polly Probst 228, 229
Kiser Sr., John 228, 229
Kiser, William 228, 229, 314
Kline, Mary Elizabeth 185
Koch, Felty 340
Koontz, Henry 416, 417
Kuh, John 213
Kuh, Lewis 213
Kuh, Margie 213
Kuh, Mary 213
Kyvig, David 238

L

LaBelle, Dave 342
LaBelle, Ernie 342
Laderer, Delores 435
Laderer III, William 435
Lambert, Alva 299
Lambert, Idelta Sponaugle 224, 226
Lambert, Nora 299
Lambert, Roy Keith 226
Landis, Susan 369
Lauck, Isaac 106
LAUREL DALE MILL 209
Lawrence, Rachel B. 299
Layton, Rhonda 213
Leatherman, George T. 198
Lee, Gen. Robert E. 387

Leffel, James 113
Legge, John F. 147
Legg, George T. 85, 87
Leith, Jefferson Davis 174
Lemke, Tom 369
Levi Neeley Mill 375
Lewis, George 382
Lewis, Harvey 382
Lewis, Susan Hockman 382
Ley, William C. 418, 419
Liggett, B. C. 199
Liggett, Ethel 199
Light, Peter 78, 79
Light, Susannah 78
Lilly, Robert "Miller Bob" 375
Lind, Lester 300
Lind, Mary Beth Bucher 300
Lutz, Danny 130, 133, 447
Lutz, Karen 133
Lyon, Arnold S. 162
Lyon, Cora 199
Lyon, David C. 162, 199
Lyon, Hiram 161, 162
Lyon, Margaret Cassady 161
Lyon, Sarah Elmira 161
Lyon's Mill 34
LYON'S MILL 159

M

Mack, Henry 416
Malcolm, Harrison 308
Mann, James R. 240
Manson, Dana 182
Manson, Henry 182, 186
Markwood Woolen Mill 207
Marshall, Chief Justice John 196
Martin, Upton S. 147
Mason, James 133
Mathias & Jenkins 202
Mathias, J. T. 202
Mathias, Samuel 202
Mathias & Snider 202
Matthews, Josiah 150

Matthews, Josiah David 114
Matthews, Sampson Lockhart 284
Matthews, Samuel 85
Matthews, Thomas Edward 114, 150
Maxwell, John 78
May, Z. Taylor 382
McCay, Joseph 96
McCloskey, Deidre 21
McClung, Abigail 395
McClung, Elizabeth 395
McClung, Herman Omer 355, 356
McClung, John 394, 395
McClung, Joseph 395
McClung Mill 190
MCCLUNG MILL 353
McClung, Omer 356
McClung, Sadie Anna Miller 356
McClung, William 394, 395
McClure, Col. John 269
McCoy, Benjamin 246
McCoy, Caroline 246
McCoy, Gen. William 246
McCoy, Gen. William 246
McCoy II, Caroline 247
McCoy III, Capt. William 246, 247
McCoy III, Capt. William 247
McCoy II, William 246, 247
McCoy IV, William 247
McCoy, John 247
McCoy, John Wright 247
McCoy Mill 229
McCoy's Mill, 313
MCCOY'S MILL 245
McCoy V, William 247
McCoy, William 222
McDonald, John 160, 161
McDowell, Archibald 359, 360
McDowell, Catharine 359, 360
McElroy, J. B. 126
McFeely, Thomas 435
McNeel, Bill 285
McNeel, Dr. H. W. 285
McNeel, Harvey Winters 285, 286

McNeel, Isaac 285
McNeel, John 284
McNeel, John Lanty 286
McNeel, Joseph Wilson 286
McNeel, Lanty 286
McNeel, Martha 286
MCNEEL MILL 283
McNeel, Nora 286
McNeel, Richard 284
McNeer, Anderson 342
McNeer, Richard T. 342
McNeer's Flour Mill 342
McNeill, Ada 199
McNeill, Capt. John Hanson 200
McNeill, Charles 212, 213
McNeill, Daniel Renick 197, 198, 200
McNeill, George 198
McNeill, George William 198
McNeill, John William 199
McNeill, Margie Helen 213
McNeill, Mary Jane Hilkey 212, 213
McNeill, Mary Jane McClung 197
McNeill, Mitch 199
McNeill, Rhonda 199
McNeill, Sarah "Sadie" Van Meter 198
McNeill's Rangers 200
Mendenhall, James 96, 101
Middle Creek Mill 120
Miley, G. R. 199
Miller, Archibald 355
Miller, Geo. W. 198
Miller, James E. 355
Miller, John (older) 237
Miller, John (soldier) 237
Miller, John (younger) 237
Miller, Martyn 355
Miller, Mont P. 198
Miller, Sadie Anna 355
Miller, Thomas Jefferson (T. J.) 354, 355
Mitchell, Benjamin 229, 255, 257, 278
Mitchell, Benjamin Hurl 278, 279
Mitchell, Brenna 278, 279

INDEX 519

Mitchell, Cara Homan 231, 232, 259
Mitchell, Dr. Brandon 231, 259
Mitchell, George Washington 229
Mitchell, Hannah Swadley 257
Mitchell, Hattie Eye 278
Mitchell, Hugh 257, 258
Mitchell, Jacob 255
Mitchell, Mary Jane Kiser 229
Mitchell Mill 278
MITCHELL MILL 251
Mitchell, Paula 237, 243, 259
Mitchell, Samuel 257
Mitchell, Sylvester 229
Mitchell, Tom 259
Mollohan, Bernard 408, 409
Mollohan, Charles 409
Mollohan, Elmer A. 409, 410
Mollohan, George Bernard 409
Mollohan, George D. 408
Mollohan, Harrison 409
Mollohan, James 407, 408, 409
Mollohan, Marie "Beth" 409, 410
Mollohan, Martha \ 407, 408
Mollohan, Mary Strong 408
MOLLOHAN MILL 405
Mollohan Sr., George 407
Mollohan, Winnie 409, 410
Monroe, James 346
Moore, Gen. Andrew 395
Moore, Margene Mitchell 257, 258
Morris, Isaac 418
Morris, Laura 183
Morris, N. L. 183
Morton, Owen Frederic 359
Moulden, Dave 179
Mullenax, James 315
Mustain, Larry 360, 361, 362
Myers, Henry 78, 79

N

Napier, Elmer 2, 182, 350, 374
Natufians 9
Neely, Charles 314

Neely, Lou Ann 314
Nickell, Barbara 348
Nickell, Barbara McCombe 348
Nickell, Charles Coray (C. C.) 348, 349
Nickell, Isaac 348
Nickell, James Albert 348
Nickell, James Madison 348, 349, 350
Nickell Jr., John 348
Nickell Sr., John 348
Nickell, Thomas 347, 348
Nicola, J. B. 425
Nolen, Nancy 199

O

Oates, A. C. 183
Oates family 108
Oates, Max 108
Oates, Minnie 183
OLD FIELDS MILL 195
ONEGO MILL 261
O'Neill, Sonny 222

P

Padgett, George R. 160, 163
Parker, Tyler 213
Patterson, David 96
Patterson, Elizabeth Christie 96
Patterson, Hugh 97
Patterson, Hugh Vance 96
PATTERSON MILL 95
Patterson, Samuel 96
PATTERSON'S NEW GRISTMILL 99
Patterson's New Mill 96
Patterson, William 96, 100
Patterson, William Jr. 96, 101
Patterson, William (son of Hugh) 96
Patton, Robert 347
Paxton, Mark 315
Peck, Daniel 400
Pfeifer, Laura J. 434
Pickenpaugh, Estella Ley 418, 419

Pickenpaugh, Fred 418, 419
Pickford, Edward 213
Pickford, Sherree 213
Pitts, John 199
Pitts, Mary 199
Pizzoni, Dan 369
Plowman, William 96
Pollack, John 382
Porterfield, Wendell S. 81
Potomac Mills 144
POTOMAC MILLS/THE SHEPHERDSTOWN CEMENT MILL RUINS 137
Prendergast, Lt. Richard G. 107
Priest, Mary 267
PRIEST MILL 265
Priest, Paul 266, 269, 270
Priest, Robert 266, 269
Priest, Sadie 267
Priest, Samuel 266, 267, 269, 270
Priest, S. Elliot 270
Priest, Thomas 266
Prince, Clarkson 368
Prince, William 368
Probst, Daniel 228
Puffenbarger, Albert 314
Puffenbarger, Christian 255, 307
Puffenbarger, Elizabeth 278
Puffenbarger, Gertrude 257
Puffenbarger, Harry 314
Puffenbarger III, Georg 253, 255
Puffenbarger, Lillian 314
Puffenbarger, Marietta 307
Puffenbarger, Mary 307
Puffenbarger, Mary Mitchell 255, 307
Pugh, Emmett 369

R

Raina, David 199
Raina, Rebecca 199
Raines, Stewart 225
Rankin, Andrew J. 313
Reed, Andrew E. 360

Reed, Aubrey 360, 362
Reed, Carson 435
Reed, Irene 435
Reed, Isaac 360
Reed, Joe 360
Reed, Margaret Ann McDowell 360
Reed, Robert 434, 435
REED'S MILL (Monroe County) 357
REED'S MILL (Ohio County) 433
Reed, Will 360
Rexroad, Bill 313
Rexroad, William D. 312
Rexrode, Augustus 228
Rexrode, Bob 314
Rexrode, Elizabeth Kiser 228
Rexrode, George 313
Rexrode, Henry 228
Rexrode, John 313
Rexrode, Joseph 228
Rexrode, Margaret 313
Rexrode, Mary Ann Kiser 228
Rexrode Mill 306
REXRODE MILL 311
Rexrode, Ray 314
Rexrode, Sarah Kiser 228
Rexrode, Solomon 313
Rexrode, William C. 313, 314
Rexroth, Johann Zacharias 313
Reynolds, A. S. 147
Reynolds, George 139, 140
Rice, Bill 97
Rice, Karen 97
Rice, Lacy I., Jr. 97
Rice, Lacy I. Sr. 97
Ridgeway, Frances 103
Roaring Creek Mill 332
Roberts, A. P. 207
Roberts, William 434
Rodgers, Bertha Byrd 349
Rodgers, Catherine 349
Rodgers, Daniel 349
Rodgers, Homer D. 349
Rodgers, James Madison 349

INDEX 521

Rodgers, Michael 349
Rodgers Mill 359
Rogers, Brashear 207
Rogers, Henry 45
Rogers, Isaac 207
Ross, Alexander 73
Ross, Alfred 84
Rotruck, Lacey 207, 208
Rotruck, Scott 207, 208
Rubenstein, Alex 419
Rubenstein, Keri Lawson 2, 419

S

Secrist, Abraham 189
Secrist, Catherine 189
Secrist, Frederick 189
Secrist, Morgan 189
Seldon, Fred 183
Seldon, Goldie Eaton 182, 183
Seldon, Henry 182, 183
Seldon, Kenneth 191
Shaw, Hank 449
Shepherd, Abraham 78, 79, 145
Shepherd, Capt. Thomas 78, 144, 145, 434
Shepherd, Daniel 434
Shepherd, Elizabeth Van Meter 144, 145, 196
Shepherd Jr., Thomas 145
Shepherd's Mill 78, 190
SHEPHERD'S MILL 143
Shepherd, Thomas 196
Sherrard, Col. Robert 173, 174
Sherrard, Robert B. 174
Shipman, Benjamin 119
Shires, A. V. 355
Shires, Clarence 355
Shires, Herbert 355
Shreve, Ira Parker 207
Sibray, David 368, 369
Simmons, Ike 230
Simmons, James Howard 307, 308
Simmons, Jared 308

Simmons, Jonathan 185, 186
Simmons, Maggie Botkin 307
Simmons, Martha 279
Simmons, Nancy Hook 185
Simmons, Nelson 308
Sisler, Janice Cole 424
Skavenski, Vickie 222
Smith, Jeff 369
Smith, Logan 293
Snider, Albert Moze "A. M." 202
Snider, A. M. 202
Snider, Arthur 202
Snider & Bright 202
Snider, Clarice 202
Snider, Eliza Catherine Mathias 202
Snider, Gussie 202
Sopher, Teresa 369
Sopher, Tom 368, 369
Souder, E. B. 202
Spaid, Angeline 190
SPAID-EATON MILL 181
Spaid, Frederick 184
Spaid, Hannah 185
Spaid, Hiram 190
Spaid, Jemima 190
Spaid, John 185
Spaid, Margaret 183
Spaid, Margaret McVicar 184
Spaid, Mary Elizabeth Kline 185
Spaid, Michael 182, 184, 185, 186, 190
Spaid, Nicholas 190
Spicer, James 163
Sponaugle, Harman 226
Spottswood, Alexander 359
Spring Run Grist Mill 332
Staley, John D. 147
Starry, Silas 149
Stephen, Adam (prob. son of Robert) 106
Stephen, Alexander 106
STEPHEN-HAMMOND-OLD SPRING MILL 105
Stephen, Maj. Gen. Adam 106

Stephen, Robert 106
Stephens, Adam 96
Stephenson, Capt. Hugh 78
Stevenson, Capt. Hugh 145
Stiles, Mrs. 270
Stoney Creek Grist Mill 332
Stover, RJ 103
Stover, Sarah 100, 101, 102, 103
Strode, Samuel 96
Stuart, John 359
Stultz, D. Edgar 127
Swamp Dragons 200, 219

T

Talbott, George 355
Talbott, Malinda Elizabeth Miller (M. E.) 355
Talbott, M. E. 354
Tate, Matt 286, 287
Taylor, Daniel 246, 247, 248
Taylor, Julie 262
Taylor, William 284
Tesla, Nicola 267
Teter, Eston 237
Teter, Philip 224
Thomas, Adam 144, 149, 150
Thomas, George 382
Thomas, J. T. 213
Thomas, Mary 211
Thomas, Sarah 212
Thomas, Shannon Purvis 144, 149, 150
Thomas, William Warner 211, 212, 213
Thompson and Carter Mill 149
Thompson Jr., Luther 149
Todd, Addison 306, 307
Todd, John H. 307
Todd Jr., John 306, 307
Todd Sr., John 306
Trenary, John 120
Trenary, Karen Bryarly 119, 120
Trumbo, Levi 274
TRUMBO MILL 273
Tuscarora Iron Works 126

TUSCARORA IRON WORKS 109

U

UNION BRYARLY MILL 117

V

Vance, Annabelle 202
Vandevender Frank 300
Vandevender, Russell 300
Van Meter, Abraham 84, 160, 197, 199
Van Meter, Ann 197
Van Meter, Ann Markee Sibley 196
Van Meter, Col. Jacob 196, 197, 198
Van Meter, Garrett 196
Van Meter, Isaac 73, 196, 197
Van Meter, Isaac II 197, 198
Van Meter, Isabel 84
Van Meter, Jacob 198
Van Meter, Jacob Inskeep 197
Van Meter, James 198
Van Meter, John 73, 144, 196
Van Meter, Nancy 84
Van Meter, Rebecca 196, 197, 200
Van Meter, Susan 197
Van Meter, Tabitha Inskeep 196, 197

W

Waggy, Edward 228, 278, 279
Waggy, George 228, 278, 279
Waggy, John Marshall 279
Waggy Jr., William 228
Waggy, Mina 279
WAGGY-MITCHELL MILL 277
Waggy, Susannah (Susan) Kiser 228
Waggy, William 278, 279
Waggy, William Lewis 228, 278
Walker, Jane 131
Walker, Nathan 131
Walls, Frank 419
Walters, Richard 419
Ware, Dr. Greg 355, 356
Ware, Kenneth 356

INDEX 523

Ware, Mary Ann McClung 356
Warner family 327
Warner, Fred 299
Warner, Retta 299
Washington, Bushrod 253, 255
Washington, George 33, 78, 92, 130, 145, 156, 173, 196, 253, 255, 263
Weaver, Eldridge 417, 418
Weirick, William F. 126
Welch, Alexander 395
Weller, John 126
Wells, Jim 342
Wells, M. P. 418
Wells, Nan 342
Westinghouse, George 267, 269
Whipp, Seymour 211
White, Catherine Jackson 387
White, Lorraine 315
Willet, John 424
Willet, Samuel 424
Williams, George M. 286
Williams, Henry 237
Williams, Kelly 198
Wills, Jack 374
Wills, Owen 375
Wilson, E. G. 400
Wilson, George 306
Wilson's Mill 197
Wimer, George 225
Wimer, Henry 225
Wimer, Isaac C. 225, 226
Wimer, Jacob C. 226
Wimer, Jacob L. 225, 226
Wolf, Harry 224
Wolford, Charles 102
Wolford, Frank 103
Wolford, Rob 173, 174, 184
Wood, John 197
Woods, William H. 395
Worley, Scott 369
Wymer, Henry 224

Y

YELLOW SPRING MILL 187
Yontz Mill 97
Yontz, William T. 96, 97
Young, Darla 270
Young, Jake 270
Young, William 33

Z

Ziegler, Barbara 343
Ziegler, Fred 343
Zollickoffer, Henry 85
Zyrkle, John 224

About the Author

Tracy Lawson grew up reading mystery stories—and now she approaches historical research with unbridled enthusiasm and a detective's eye. *Historic Mills of West Virginia* is her fourth nonfiction book. She is also the author of six novels, including *Answering Liberty's Call: Anna Stone's Daring Ride to Valley Forge*, the first in the Ladies of the Revolution Series.

She and her husband, economist Robert Lawson, live near Dallas, Texas. They have one grown daughter.

35th Star Publishing
Charleston, West Virginia
www.35thstar.com